TUNNEL OF LOVE

MARTIN HARDY

TUNNEL OF LOVE

MARTIN HARDY

First published as a hardback by deCoubertin Books Ltd in 2016.

First Softback Edition.

deCoubertin Books, Studio I, Baltic Creative Campus, Liverpool, L1 OAH.

www.decoubertin.co.uk

ISBN: 978-1-909245-56-3

Copyright © Martin Hardy, 2016, 2017.

A CIP catalogue record for this book is available from the British Library.

All images copyright © Newcastle United FC unless otherwise stated.

Cover design and typeset by Leslie Priestley.

Printed and bound by Nørhaven.

FOR MATTHEW

CONTENTS

MARTIN HARDY –
TUNNEL OF LOVE

EVERYWHERE YOU LOOK THERE IS BLACK AND WHITE.

Everywhere you look there are hearts on people's sleeves.

They're coming out of the tunnel.

The fans are shouting from the pit of their stomach.

It's boiling hot. It's London. It's Wembley.

The roar, the 24-year wait of a roar.

The black and white stripes are walking out at Wembley. Slowly, meticulously, carrying the shirt, the shirt you love, with such pride. Three hundred miles from home, in the capital, and we're here, we're all here, and there's just a noise, this incredible noise, from the support of your team, from people you know, from people you've known most of your life.

From people you love.

There's chaos amongst those supporters at the tunnel end of Wembley Stadium, from where Newcastle United have just emerged. They're expressing the pride you feel. The whole region is on the march. The noise is everywhere. The excitement is visible.

You want to run down the steps from the press box and jump amongst them.

It's the first FA Cup final of your life since you were one. You drip with emotion.

It matters. It matters more than you've admitted to anyone.

I'll be professional. I'll keep it together.

Really? You?

And you're in bits, and people knew you would be.

You can't speak. You just watch.

You watch your team walk out at Wembley and you watch the fans of your team at Wembley

1

make a roar that wakes every corner of your soul.

It blows you away.

You've waited so long.

And when the men in black and white stripes have lined up, to the side of the halfway line, and the 30,000 people of your region have managed to calm themselves, and the first line, 'Abide with me; fast falls the eventide' has rolled over every emotion of your body, and the tears have filled your eyes, you have to somehow go to work.

ALAN SHEARER – ONE LOVE

THE FARMHOUSE IN RURAL CHESHIRE WAS OWNED BY THE PARENTS of David Platt. In the kitchen sat Douglas Hall, Freddie Fletcher, Freddy Shepherd and Kevin Keegan.

The football agent Tony Stevens walked into the room. Behind him was Alan Shearer.

'I'm not going to say this and that,' said Shearer. 'The only thing I want to know is, can I have the number nine shirt? That's all I want to know, the rest I'll leave to Tony.'

Keegan stood up. 'You've got it,' he said.

Shearer walked out and left.

Shearer was 25. He was the captain of England. He had finished top scorer in the summer's European Championships. He had already won the Premier League title with Blackburn Rovers, with whom he had scored 30 league goals or more in the previous three seasons. There had been contact with Inter Milan. Manchester United, who had just won their third Premier League title, had already made their move.

He was the most coveted player in Europe in the summer of 1996.

Newcastle had just three things in their corner; burning ambition, Kevin Keegan and Shearer's place of birth, Gosforth, about three miles from St James' Park.

That would prove to be enough.

'Alan had been to see Alex Ferguson the day before,' Keegan said. 'I met him in Huddersfield in a terraced house that nobody knew about.

'Jack Walker always said he'd let him go for £15 million.

'He promised Alan that, so everybody knew, it was a buyout clause for a better word. He'd talked to Sir Alex and I went to David Platt's mam and dad's place in Cheshire with Douglas, Freddy and Freddie Fletcher. Freddie was very influential in what we did at Newcastle, we called him the Jockweiller,' Keegan said in Sky's Sporting Heroes.

'You'd like him in the trenches with you. We'd spoken about how we would do it and what it would be like.

'Alan asked for the number nine shirt. That's how easy Alan was.

'We sat with Tony. The deal was done within about 10 or 15 minutes, honestly. That's my recollection of it. Douglas wanted him, Sir John wanted him and Freddie wanted him. He wanted to come.

'It was an easy deal to say but then the next part was the difficult part.

'Tony went to talk to Alan about what had been agreed for him, in a different room.

'Douglas phoned up Jack Walker (the owner of Blackburn Rovers). We were on a speakerphone. Douglas said, "Jack, we've just talked with Alan Shearer, we've agreed terms with him, we're ready to sign him. We believe the fee is £15 million."

'Jack said, "That's correct, but it's one hit."

'We said, "What?"

'He said, "I want the £15 million plus the levy (which is about 11 per cent). It's £17 million, one hit, you pay it today and he's your player."

'You usually pay over four years. We put the phone down, looked at each other, and went, "Phew, you can't do that."

'Douglas said, "We can," and we did it. That's what happened with Alan. He was the easiest player to sign, he wanted to come, he wanted to wear the number nine shirt.

'Everybody wanted to wear it; there's not many who can carry it. Not like Alan Shearer.'

Ferguson was enraged by the U-turn.

'We got Shearer there with his agent and we took the bank manager with us,' added Freddy Shepherd, the former Newcastle chairman. 'We put him in a different room. I think David Platt was a friend of the agent we were using at the time.

'We could trust him. He wouldn't tell anybody. We got there and I had made a promise to Martin Edwards [the Manchester United chief executive] that we wouldn't compete against each other. We said we wouldn't go to more than £10 million for him.

'I got outside the back door and I phoned Martin up and he lived beside me in Majorca. I said, "Martin, we agreed to tell each other – I knew he'd already broke it and offered more – but I still said, "We will offer more than the ten for Shearer."

'He went, "Aah, ok, fine." He was a real gentleman Martin. He said, "I appreciate you telling me." He didn't say anything back to me!

'I walked back through the door and I thought, "I've kept my word". Shearer was there. Keegan was there. We all went through the whole thing and Shearer said, "I've got to speak to Jack".

'I heard him say, "Jack, I've done what I promised for you. We got the title. You always promised I could go."

'He said, "Yeah, hang on he wants to speak to you."

'I got the phone and Jack went, "Freddy, I'm telling you something now, you can have him for what's agreed, but if it was Manchester United, it would be £20 million for him!"

'He said, "I'm doing you a favour. You can have him for £15 million."

'We went to the bank manager in the kitchen, "He wants the money up front." Usually it's paid in two or three tranches. The bank manger said, "Okay then." He was a Newcastle fan. We did the deal upfront so Jack got all his money.'

Keegan was the first to leave, to meet up with the players he had left on the runway at Heathrow Airport.

'Kevin left early,' added Shepherd. 'We had to sort Shearer's wages out. We were going to Osaka in Japan so he went off.

'We got the next plane over. Keegan was on the first plane. We got the second plane, me and Douglas, and then we went to the training ground. That's how it was done. Man U really made an effort to get him. They really, really made an effort, but we won.'

Martin Edwards, by contrast, could not hide his disappointment. The Manchester United chairman and chief executive, along with Ferguson, had failed once more to persuade Shearer to move to Old Trafford.

'There was no way Blackburn were prepared to let him come to us,' said Edwards. 'The club made that clear by rejecting our offer.'

Keegan had first to tell Les Ferdinand he would not be wearing Newcastle's iconic number nine shirt.

'It's not about the shirt for you Les, it's not that important,' Keegan told him. 'It's a number and it was part of the deal to get Alan here. You'll be a great partnership. I don't want you to worry about losing the number nine shirt. It's not that significant.'

Ferdinand looked at Keegan and pointed at the gold pendant that hung from his chain.

'How come you still wear the number seven then boss?' Ferdinand asked.

Keegan confirmed to his players what [Terry] McDermott had said as the flight to the Far East had took off, that they were indeed signing Alan Shearer. Then he spoke publicly for the first time of what Newcastle had just done.

'This signing is for the people of Newcastle,' he said. 'It just shows you the ambition of Newcastle United. We are the biggest thinking team in Europe now.

'We're not the biggest, most successful team, but we're the biggest thinking club and we have tremendous support from above which allows me to buy players.'

'I was particularly impressed with Alex Ferguson,' said Shearer. 'But Kevin Keegan also has great qualities and it was the challenge of coming home and wearing the famous black and white shirt which made up my mind for me.'

The £15 million fee was the first time an English club had broken the world transfer record since 1951. It eclipsed the £13.3 million Barcelona had paid for Ronaldo. It was a truly staggering moment. It called for something special.

On 6 August, a week later, Tyneside came to a halt, as did much of the country's media. Sky News went live to St James' Park, where the Leazes End was full of supporters, whilst more than 10,000 waited in the car park.

Nine men in suits sat at a makeshift top table to officially announce the signing.

'Welcome Home to the One and Only Alan Shearer,' was written in large letters on a blue sign behind the main stage that had been erected. There were seven huge Newcastle Brown Ale beer mats around the lettering and two pictures of the club crest. There was one empty seat in the middle and then Sir John Hall, the Newcastle chairman and majority shareholder, started speaking.

'Probably I wouldn't have come here if I didn't realise how much we were spending!' he said.

'In four years we've come a long, long way. We've come a tremendous way. Look at the tremendous stadium we've built behind us and now we've learned it's too small. We're going to have to build a bigger stadium and plans are under way.

'We will invest huge sums in our academy. We will be at the forefront of sports science.

'We have built, under Kevin, an excellent squad of players. It's very difficult to improve on that squad, but I'm sure we'd all agree, that today we've found that player.

'More specially, he's a Geordie. I feel a great pride in bringing him back to the North East. It's a great region. It's a hotbed of soccer. This club is going places. Alan Shearer, together with all the other players, is an investment in the future of this football club.'

And then came the rallying call.

'I am delighted, absolutely thrilled and delighted, to Kevin and the board, thank you for bringing Alan here, it's my great pleasure to welcome Alan Shearer to Newcastle United Football Club.'

Shearer ran up steps from within the Leazes End.

He looked to the back of the stand, to see where the rows of people ended. He shook Sir John Hall's hand and then Kevin Keegan, the most significant figure in the modern history of that football club, pulled out a seat for him.

'Obviously thanks for the tremendous welcome that you gave us all today,' said Keegan. 'It's a great privilege for me.

'It's more days than I care to remember that I went to a Blue Star Soccer Day, sponsored by the brewery, and Alan was there.

'It's your money, it's the money you've spent. It's the money you've spent on your replica shirts, home and away.

'It's the money you've spent on your season tickets and your bonds, and your platinum clubs, and the programmes, and the black and white magazines and I see it as my job, and it's a privilege to have the job, of reinvesting that money.

'You put it in and I put it into the team, so that when you come to watch the product on the park here it's the very, very best that we feel we can provide, because that's what you deserve.

'It's his day. It's your day. It's lovely to see a Geordie come back home. We've sold them off time and time again up here and we've built stands with the money. We've tried to buy other players to replace them.

'That's gone at this club now. He's come here because he knows he's got a great chance of winning something,

'We've bought him because we know even with the great players we've got he's going to improve them. He's yours. It's your days.'

There was applause right throughout the stand.

Finally, Shearer spoke.

'Can I just say has anyone got any spare tickets for Sunday?' he joked.

'Personally I'd just like to thank the welcome that has been given to me and my family. Nothing should surprise me with the fans of Newcastle but the reception certainly has done. If any supporters deserve success it is the fans of this club. I will try with the rest of the players to bring it to them.

'As anyone knows I've always wanted to play for this club. I've never hidden that fact. It's a dream come true.

'To play in front of my mam and dad at Newcastle is something else. I wanted to come here with my best years in front of me. I'm very excited. I just want the games to come along so I can get playing and training. The players have made me extremely welcome.'

ITN then asked if there was additional pressure from being the most expensive player in the world.

'The price tag has nothing at all to do with me,' said Shearer. 'All I do is try to do my best.'

Sky News asked if this would be his last move. 'I hope it is,' he replied. 'I hope I can spend the rest of my career here.'

He was asked about the time he played in goal, briefly, during a trial at Newcastle when he was young.

'The story is out of all proportion,' he said. 'I came for a trial along with loads of other Geordie lads. It was about numbers. We had a game and everyone had to take their turn in goal and I was no different to everyone else. I was in goal for 15 minutes and I've never heard the last of it.

'To say I spent all week in goal is not true.'

GMTV then spoke of the added pressure on trying to end Newcastle's barren run of silverware.

'I don't believe it's pressure,' said Shearer. 'If it is, give me more of it. I can only do my best.'

In the car park at the back of the Leazes End of St James' Park that day were more than 10,000 Newcastle fans. It was raining, everyone missed that. It should have been a warning.

'Ladies and gentleman, Newcastle United presents Alan Shearer!' shouted Alan Robson, a local disc jockey, perched on a makeshift gantry.

There was a huge roar.

Shearer ran up the stairs. He had a short-sleeved Newcastle shirt on and he was wearing black Adidas tracksuit bottoms. He punched the air with both fists and he waved.

There were arms in the air wherever you looked. Most of them were in short sleeved Newcastle shirts. It looked like a goal had been scored at a game.

He smiled wider and he waved his fists more.

He turned to show the number on the back of his shirt.

He had the number nine.

There was another roar.

The cry went up. 'Shearer, Shearer.'

He turned back round and waved his arms, as if conducting an orchestra.

He was given a microphone.

'At the end of the day I'm one of yous!' he said. There were more cheers. 'If anyone deserves success it's you lot, thanks very much.'

Thousands of arms were raised in celebration once more.

Mothers danced with their babies. Children were everywhere.

A song started.

'He's coming home, he's coming home, Shearer's coming home.'

It was a party in the rain.

The *Sunderland Echo's* front page read, 'Oh no, look who the Mags have signed now!'

Newcastle had Alan Shearer.

They were bound to win something.

His first game was at Wembley. Perfect. The Charity Shield, against Manchester United. An early chance for revenge.

Newcastle lost 4–0, and when the game finished, the heavens opened once more.

STEPHEN FAIRS –
BE THERE

AWAY FROM THE SMILES, AND THE THOUSANDS OF FANS, AND THE Tyneside sports shops running out of the letters S, H, E, A and R was doubt.

Away from the dramatic decision to break the world transfer record, Kevin Keegan was faltering.

On Saturday, 18 January 1992, a crowd of 15,663 had watched Newcastle lose 4–3 to Charlton, having led three-nil after 34 minutes. The entire team that finished the game that day cost £850,000.

The transformation to four and a half years later was staggering. Newcastle United still wore black and white stripes and still played at St James' Park, but after that it was hard to find similarities to the club which Keegan had walked into on 5 February 1992.

Nobody knew where Newcastle were going that day.

Everybody in world football knew who they were after breaking the world transfer record.

It was a club that was becoming increasingly difficult to keep the shackles on – on the cusp of being out of control even – a one city club with the relentless demand that went with it.

Keegan had been at its centre, from the day he disbelievingly found a training ground that had not been touched since he had left as a player in 1984. Keegan changed everything, physically he led, but the change went to the heart of the mentality of the supporters and to those who sat with him around the Newcastle boardroom and plotted and fought and sometimes railed against his tenacity.

There had been threats to walk out before: following a victory against Swindon, shortly after he had taken over when promises about finance for players had not been upheld; and again in the cooling embers of the summer of 1996, after which Newcastle awoke to find they had not, after a monumental campaign, become champions of England.

It was hoped that Keegan was recharging, but those close to him knew he was tired, and scarred from the campaign.

'At the time I had a big ten-year contract all signed and sealed which gave me a big loyalty payment at the end, when I would be 53,' he wrote in his autobiography.

'The problem was that I felt I might be dead by then the way things were going. I put it to the board that if they were to sack me if we had a bad start to the season it would cost them a fortune.

'Sir John favoured the long-term plan and to be honest I was enjoying it all so much [when that contract was signed], I was my own boss, no one argued with me and no one tried to interfere in team selection.

'The upshot was that we sat down [in the summer of 1996], discussed and agreed to a two-year contract which would give me £1 million a year, with £1 million to be paid three months after the actual flotation of the company on the stock market.'

All of that was kept private.

The public face of the club, and indeed Keegan, belied this discord.

Newcastle signed Shearer and the wind could not have been much more forcibly blasted into the club's sails. The Charity Shield scoreline had caught the eye – Newcastle's players would subsequently say they were exhausted from a three week trip to the Far East – but Keegan was losing his single-minded mentality. He dropped Peter Beardsley, then picked him and then regretted it.

Newcastle were awful. It was their first time at Wembley in meaningful competition since the League Cup final of 1976 and they did not play. Eric Cantona and Nicky Butt scored in the first half, David Beckham added a fine third and with three minutes remaining Roy Keane completed a rout. The day was not supposed to end like that. Then the heavens opened. Soaking wet, defeated and inside the stadium Keegan was left to rue his decision.

'The fans were clapping the team all the way back to the dressing room and that made the thrashing even worse,' said Keegan.

Newcastle lost the first league game of the season as well, at Everton. Again, they did not score. A midweek home game with Wimbledon saw Alan Shearer get his first goal for the club, a curling free-kick from 20 yards. The celebration was a reminder of the pressure that a £15 million price tag had weighed upon him. He looked genuinely delighted and Newcastle won 2–0, but again, the performance was not great.

Shearer scored in the next game as well, at home to Sheffield Wednesday, but then Peter Atherton and Guy Whittingham scored. Newcastle had lost two of their first three games. It had been December before that happened in the previous campaign, and we were still in August.

Newcastle were 13th, having signed the most expensive player in the world. There was also a problem with David Ginola, who had been refused a move to Barcelona, something the player struggled to accept.

'I went to the board again and said that if they weren't happy with the way things were going and wanted to make changes it was fine by me,' Keegan added. 'But there was no resignation offered, or asked for, no row, or fall out.'

Next up was Sunderland at Roker Park, the first derby there in four years.

Northumbria Police, and the two clubs, in an act of extreme folly, banned away supporters from both fixtures. Fans from Newcastle and Sunderland united to try and overturn the decision. There were marches and pressure was applied but no one budged, not in time anyway. No one really thought about the fans.

It was a night game at Roker Park, on 4 September, and the atmosphere was vitriolic. It was not a place to be for anyone with connections to Newcastle United, a witch hunt went on throughout the ground to find any hidden supporters from Tyneside. There was a fight during the first half in the Roker End, and some Newcastle fans were removed. By then Sunderland were winning, following a Martin Scott penalty, after Robbie Elliott had tripped Steve Agnew. It was a lonely place to be when Scott scored.

At half-time it was still 1–0.

If Newcastle had lost they would have gone third bottom. Sunderland would have gone third top.

Instead, the new team finally clicked. Sunderland were blown away in the second half.

In the 52nd minute Alan Shearer saw off two players to find Les Ferdinand to his right, he went past Richard Ord and Scott and floated a cross that Peter Beardsley met with his head.

It was a superb, angled header, redirecting the pace of the cross and squeezing in at the far post in front of the Fulwell End. There was another search around the ground for celebration. It was confined in the main to the pitch and the Newcastle dugout. There was relief in there. Then just past the hour Shearer chased down Ord near his own goal and won a corner. David Ginola hoisted it over and Ferdinand was unstoppable, powering a downward header past Tony Coton.

Dal Singh was there with his friend Steve Fairs, also a lifelong Newcastle fan.

Dal was blind, a telephonist with Barclays on the central exchange. Steve was his eyes for the night.

'He was able to get two tickets for the blind and partially sighted area of Roker Park,' said Steve.

'He needed a chaperone and it was in the main stand, to the left of the tunnel.

'It was an aggressive night. There were some nasty chants going on.

'When Newcastle equalised there was an incident going on above us because we could hear lots of banging.

'Across in the Clock Stand and in the paddock there was an incident. Then in one of these corporate hospitality boxes near us, something was kicking off.

'We were up celebrating Beardsley's header. This bloke next to me goes, "Listen, you're out of order, you shouldn't be doing that."

'I said, "I'm supporting my team".

'I was even more conscious of what was going on around us after that. I realised it was a tense atmosphere and Dal had been jumping around when the goal went in. I said to him, "We need to be a bit careful here. We can't celebrate like that again."

'He went, "okay" and by that point we were hiding our colours.

'Dal was plugged in to hospital radio listening to the match via the seats.

'When Newcastle got the corner, Dal knew, but as it came across, he accidentally pulled his earphones out of the socket.

'Ferdinand rose like a salmon and buried it. I was so excited but I just tensed my body and held the emotion in.

'Dal went, "What's happened? What's happened?"

'I whispered to him, "Ferdinand's just scored!"

'He leapt into the air and went, "Get in you bastards!"

'I grabbed him. "Sit down, sit down man, you're going to get us killed!"'

Keegan did that. He made blind Newcastle fans fearless in Roker Park.

Meanwhile, back in Tyneside, there was chaos in the Newcastle Arena, on the banks of the river Tyne, which had staged a beam back from the game. 7,000 supporters, denied the opportunity of going to the game, packed in to watch a giant screen of the game. When the first feed came through from Roker there

13

was a celebration. One person said it was like watching footage from the moon.

By the time Ferdinand had scored and Steve had dragged the delirious Dal back to his seat, celebrating supporters were toppling over chairs in delirium.

Newcastle won 2–1. It was the fourth derby win a in a row for Newcastle but nobody made much of that.

More, it was the shot in the arm the new team needed.

Newcastle won the next five Premiership games on the bounce, Shearer's goal at Derby on 12 October, his sixth in his ninth league game, took Newcastle top of the league. This was how it was supposed to be in the brochure. They were through to the next round in the UEFA Cup as well, and on 20 October, Manchester United were back in town.

PHILIPPE ALBERT – BE HERE NOW

'ON A DAY WHEN NEWCASTLE WOULD HAVE TAKEN ONE, HERE THEY are, looking for number five ... with Philippe Albert! ...'

The importance of commentary can never be understated, get it wrong, talk too much, miss the mood, do it from a studio for goodness sake, and it punishes the memory. You can't watch it again if it's wrong, but when it's right, when it's so right that it becomes part of the history, it adds poetry to the occasion.

Martin Tyler nailed the moment Philippe Albert chipped and bewildered Peter Schmeichel so precisely that it was like an assist on the goal. 'Absolutely glorious,' he shouted.

Perfect.

That it was the fifth, the icing so delicately and beautifully placed by an elegant defender, that at times epitomised what Keegan's team was all about, made it feel like it was meant to happen. Albert scored the fifth and slid on his knees in front of the dugouts at St James' Park. He was joined by teammates. Everyone looked so happy. You forget that sometimes, sometimes, when it all works, it's about enjoyment, and having the time of your life.

'It was one of those moments when he almost saw something was going to happen,' said Tyler. 'A fifth goal was around the corner but to do it like that was the most extraordinary moment of an extraordinary day.

'It summed up all the entertaining potential Newcastle had around those years. They were tremendous to watch. When they all hit it off on the same day they were unplayable, and that was one of those days.

'When St James' Park is bouncing like that it's a ground you want to be at. The old gantry wasn't particularly accessible but it was a great position. In commentary you learn to trust your love of the game.

'I felt there was another goal there. It happened more or less on cue, but for him to do something I presume he'd never done in any point in his career, was very impressive. If it had been Paul Gascoigne or Glenn Hoddle you still would have went wow. But for it to be a centre-half just rubber stamped it. It was a blessing to be there that day.

'I'm not sure at what point I knew it was going in because the ball is in the air and it enters the net slowly.

'Every time we see each other we talk about it. He's very modest about it and I always thank him profoundly for allowing me to find the words for his goal!'

Albert, the elegant Belgian defender, admitted there was more on the goal, and indeed the game, because of the way Manchester United's players had acted at Wembley.

'Every year I talk to Martin Tyler at the semi-final of the FA Cup and every year he talks about that chip,' said Albert.

'We had played Man United at Wembley coming back from the Far East and we were tired. We shouldn't have played the Charity Shield. Man United won 4–0 and at the end some of their players were taking the piss out of us.

'So we wanted our revenge and that 5–0 was our revenge. It's 4–0 at Wembley, you get hammered and they come to Newcastle and you score five. That's a revenge, a fantastic revenge.'

Four goals came before the moment of magic from Albert. Darren Peacock scored with a header, David Ginola smashed one into the top corner, again as Newcastle shot towards the Gallowgate End in the first half, as they had on the fateful night where nothing would go for the them, seven months earlier, a night where a 1-0 win for the visitors saw them seize the initiative in the race for the 1995/96 Premier League title.

This time everything went right, Les Ferdinand scored the third with a header and then Shearer, of course, scored the fourth and danced in joy in front of the Manchester United supporters, tucked away in a corner of the stadium between the Leazes End and the East Stand.

Then Albert swept forward with the ball and scored a goal that Schmeichel could not have saved even if he'd been stood on a ladder.

'The game before he used to come very quick off his line to reduce the angle,' added Albert.

'He was very good at it. I knew if I was in that situation he would come straight away. I had only one idea, I didn't want to kick the ball as hard as I can.

'My only idea was, "I am going to chip him." I didn't see him coming off his line but I knew he was there.

'You have one chance to make the chip and the ball goes in the net. A fantastic memory. Honestly, it's great. Chipped goals are the best goals, especially if it's against Man U!

'When I go back to Newcastle during one day I maybe have to explain 200 times or 300 times about the goal. In Belgium nobody talks about it.

'I used to work on the Champions League. I used to go to Chelsea and even the Chelsea fans, they recognise me and say what a chip against Schmeichel, we hate Man U, we hate Man U!

'Everywhere I go in England I have to talk about that goal. I'm not doing the first step to say to the people, "I'm Albert, remember the chip."

'They come to me and if they come to me they want to talk about it, I will do it with a lot of pleasure.

'I have to live with it. It is fantastic. When you have a central defender who scores a goal like this, against the best goalkeeper in the world, the goal has been watched all round the world. That is something special. I am quite proud of it.'

Pride: there was a fair bit of that washing over Tyneside on 20 October, 1996. As soon as the game finished, all over the city, the celebration started. There is a pub for every occasion in Newcastle. They were all full on that Sunday evening. Nothing could spoil a sublime day.

That moment you walked into the Hotspur, opposite the bus station, along the street from the Ladbrokes where a 50p bet on John Cornwell to score Newcastle's first goal against Charlton in 1987 had won you twenty quid, dripping with joy, and hugged your friends, smiling and laughing, will never go.

No need for words. No pontificating or procrastinating. Just joy, pure joy; the disbelief of the delighted. You drank and you smiled and then you talked and you sang. The glory of a supporter. The endless miles of pain for a brief, as it would turn out, snapshot of another land. Stuffing Man United, on telly.

Piers Morgan watched the game in his front room. He was editor of the *Daily Mirror* then.

'A dull old Sunday so I sat in front of the box watching Newcastle, incredibly, thrash Manchester United 5–0,' he recounted in his book, *The Insider*.

'It was stunning to watch, and when I called in to the office it was all they were talking about. "Let's splash it," I said. "Erm, we can't do that, it's just a football match," was the universal response. "Yes, but it's news, we're all amazed, so the public will be amazed too."

'Most people thought I'd taken leave of my senses but we did it anyway, under the headline "5–0."

'Sales of the *Mirror* rose by 50,000 copies. A quarter of the increase was in Liverpool alone, where apparently it became a collector's item. There were also heavy extra sales in places like Newcastle (obviously), North London and Leeds.'

'Absolutely glorious,' said Tyler, and he was so, so right.

Keegan should have left St James' Park that night and never come back.

Everything he stood for happened that day.

His legacy should have been that extraordinary game, not what would follow.

KEVIN KEEGAN –
THE END

'THEY WILL STILL BE CELEBRATING HERE WHEN WE WIN THE TITLE,' said Alex Ferguson as he left St James' Park. Sir John Hall said to Martin Tyler, 'You've just seen the future Premiership champions.'

Newcastle's next game after beating Manchester United was against Oldham Athletic in the Coca Cola Cup. Newcastle won one-nil.

In the next three UEFA Cup ties, against Ferencvaros, and then twice against Metz, Newcastle won twice and drew once to progress to the quarter-final of the competition.

A lot had gone on away from the football team.

Sir John Hall had led a charge through the region to round up the most popular sports – rugby, basketball and ice hockey – and run them under the umbrella of the Newcastle United Sporting Club. It was an idea he had seen at Barcelona and in Portugal.

Newcastle United bought the Falcons rugby side, the Durham Wasps ice hockey team, and the Newcastle Eagles basketball club. The notion of finance being filtered through the football club, away from the football team, drew an immediately hostile reaction from the club's support.

There was what would prove a futile push to move Newcastle to a new stadium in Leazes Park, to a 55,000 all-seater stadium (with the potential to extend to 75,000) that was being bitterly, and ultimately successfully opposed by locals, led by Dolly Potter. (Part of the plan included shrinking St James' Park so it became the St James' Centre, a home for the basketball and ice hockey teams).

Newcastle's move to a PLC structure, something that Sir John Hall believed was essential to the club's continued growth in the Premiership, was on its way.

For the first time since Keegan had made his dramatic return to the club, in 1992, the eye was no longer on the football team. The key ingredient for a truly momentous period in the club's history was being neglected and overlooked.

'It was the success of Newcastle United Football Club that had brought about the plans for the new stadium,' wrote Keegan in his autobiography, published in October 1997.

'Everything had worked because we were a football-led club in a football-daft city and we had always prioritised what happened on the pitch, as we did with the expensive signing of Alan Shearer.

'For that reason I objected strongly to the encroachment into football's domain of the other sports the board was embracing. The demands placed on the St James' Park pitch had led to our withdrawal from the reserve league and the resultant problems were coming home to roost, not least of which was that fringe players were short of fitness.

'I was fielding all the criticism over this decision but the board minutes of 17 May 1996 at a meeting at the Gosforth Park Hotel show that the matter was raised by Russell Cushing [the general manager].

'We took the line then, and I admit that I was at the forefront on this, that if we were not allowed to move our home matches from St James' to Gateshead we did not want to play in the Pontins League.

'We couldn't allow St James' Park to become a cabbage patch, particularly considering the style of play we were trying to develop. The chairman was adamant on this but never said so publicly, which would have relieved a little bit of the pressure on me. It would have helped if he had stated that it was a joint decision but, as usual, the board were happy to let me deal with the flak.'

On 29 January, 1994, Keegan had taken journalists onto the pitch at the end of a fourth round FA Cup tie with Luton. It was a quagmire. Newcastle had drawn 1–1 with Luton and lost the replay. Protecting the pitch, for a team that was all about passing the ball, had been a long-term concern.

Removing the reserves, which was admittedly rash, had reason, but it created problems with the fitness of fringe players.

'Looking back I think it was a mistake, even it was made for all the right reasons,' Keegan would write in his autobiography.

The league form, however, went wrong. There was an unexpected defeat at

Leicester, a comfortable win against Middlesbrough but then two draws, a League Cup exit at the Riverside Stadium, a loss to Arsenal, a goalless draw (unheard of) with Nottingham Forest, a defeat at Coventry, a draw with Liverpool and then a loss to Blackburn ('I felt the spark was no longer there,' Keegan would later say).

'In the dressing room I really ripped into Les Ferdinand,' Keegan added. 'I was also feeling more and more isolated from board members with whom I had worked so closely during the previous four years. I got so fed up I would say, "Go and get on with the float, it's all you're interested in."

'I was in a black mood on the coach back to Newcastle. Perhaps the players were fed up hearing me and were no longer responding to my management style.

'I admitted to Terry McDermott that I didn't think I was motivating the players any more. That was when I decided it was time to go. It had nothing to do with money, contracts or fallings-out. It was a matter of how far we had brought the club.'

*

KEEGAN'S NEXT CONVERSATION WAS WITH FREDDIE FLETCHER. Fletcher by now shared Keegan's belief that he could not take the club to the next level.

Fletcher called a meeting at St James' Park with Shepherd, Douglas Hall and Mark Corbidge, who had joined the board as joint chief executive from NatWest Markets in November to help with the flotation.

Keegan told the quartet what he had told Fletcher, that he would not see out the remaining seven years of the 10-year contract he signed. Keegan went to his office and an hour later Fletcher came to see him. He said that the ideal solution, for the board, the club and the supporters, would be to remain as manager until the end of the season. Keegan was delighted with the plan and said yes. The four met back in the boardroom. There was relief a solution had been found.

'There was no question of me staying after the end of the season,' he said. 'But it gave us four months and something to aim for. I felt that I could roll up my sleeves and get on with the job of trying to win something for the club, either at home or in Europe.'

Tottenham were emphatically put to the sword on 28 December. It was a footballing exhibition once more. Newcastle won 7–1, Shearer and Ferdinand scored two each, Rob Lee scored twice. There was one for Philippe Albert, which was always a good sign. On New Year's Day Newcastle put another three past

Leeds, 3–0. Shearer got another two, Ferdinand added the third. Ten goals in three days. Newcastle were back moving again. They moved to within a point of Manchester United and were five behind leaders Liverpool, with a game in hand. There was a glamorous UEFA Cup quarter-final with Monaco to look forward to and Newcastle had drawn Charlton, who were a struggling Division One side, in the FA Cup.

Nineteen ninety-seven was aready promising much. But then came a leak, through a private conversation from one of the board members, believed to have been Douglas Hall, about Keegan's intentions.

'Someone at that very confidential meeting simply couldn't keep the details to himself,' said Keegan. 'The news leaked out and reached the press. The leak had not come from me. The only person I had told was Jean. I informed the board, making it clear that I was fully aware the source was one of them. I told them if the story was printed I would have difficulty denying it. I was testing them. True to form they did absolutely nothing.

'Often managers hide behind a board. It is rare for a board to hide behind a manager.'

The story came out on Sunday, 5 January, before Newcastle played at Charlton in the Cup. It was a 1–1 draw and Robert Lee scored against his old club. When questions were asked afterwards of Keegan's future, he walked out of the press conference.

In the background to an ever more complicated picture, was the demands of the bank to recoup £6 million from the club. Keegan threatened to sell Les Ferdinand to Everton, and he was told not to do it by the board. Deals were put in place to sell Paul Kitson and Lee Clark instead. Douglas Hall offered reassurances that once the sales went through there would be renewed spending with the bank back on board. There was also the matter the club's board did not want it revealed in a city prospectus that an agreed repayment of £5 million had not been met.

'The people who had built the team were the fans,' said Keegan to Harmison. 'But we were making decisions to suit the float.

'Remember the seats with your names on for 10 years? I sold them and I sold them mainly because the people at the club said the fans trust you, it'll go better if you sell them.

'We sold them on the condition they would have them for 10 years, we were going to be a Sporting Club, we took the ice hockey, the basketball, the rugby. I met these people, they're people, they're human beings, then the float came up and you start to hear things second hand, like we have to get rid of the hockey club, and that we have to buy a catering company because that a will be better in the float.'

'We had a lot going for us but it was fragile,' he added in his autobiography. 'The Shearer deal had taken all our money. We had a first team squad of 21.

'My next conversation at board level was on Tuesday 7 January. They said they needed to see me urgently at the ground. I suggested Sir John's home (who was away). The whole board would be present, as well as the club lawyer.'

*

KEEGAN WAS BEING OUTMANOEUVRED.

Keegan called his wife, who told him to take a lawyer.

Then he called McDermott.

'It's about to end,' he said.

The ride of a lifetime, one that had started with two old friends living in a hotel with no idea of how to save Newcastle from relegation to the third tier of English football, one that had taken them to the very summit of the domestic game, was coming to a stop.

'It was early evening at the house when the directors arrived,' added Keegan.

'Mark Corbidge pressed the fact they were about to go to the city and that I was an integral part of the flotation document, which I had never seen or been consulted about.

'"There was really no choice," he said. Either I had to sign the two-year contract on the table and, despite our agreement of a few days earlier, guarantee that I would stay on for those two years, or I had to leave there and then.

'They had realised they could neither go to the city with the terms they had originally agreed with me, nor lie about it, and they were in a hole.

'I don't know what reaction the board anticipated, but I just looked at them and said, "Right, let's get settled up and finished because there is no way I am going to stay beyond the end of the season. There is no turning back."

'They said they didn't want me to go, that they wished I would stay for the two years and how sad they were but it was apparent to me that they were not the ones making the decisions any more.

'By contrast Mark Corbidge saw me as a part that had to go and he made that very clear. I was asked to forget the handshake with Freddie Fletcher.

'I looked towards Douglas and Freddy and said, "Maybe now you can see why

I don't want to stay at this club."

'Here was a man who had not been with us for five minutes and yet he was the one doing all the talking.

'He certainly wouldn't have left his comfortable office in the city to float Newcastle United in the state it was in when I first arrived.

'"You're not running the club now Douglas," I said, looking at Corbidge. "He is running your club. Where was he when we nearly got relegated?"

'I told them I was ready to settle. They offered me exactly what they were obliged to offer me. My wages were paid only up to that day.

'I was still entitled to the £1 million they had offered me when the club was floated and they promised me I would receive it. All I said was, "Is that what you think my five years with the club is worth?" The directors replied in the affirmative.

'I gave them back by my petrol card and my club credit card. I think that got to Freddie Fletcher. He played a vital role in the development of the club. I couldn't have done it without him, without the Halls' money, without Douglas' brilliance with figures, or Russell Jones' expertise with the stadium, which he built as quickly as we built the team.

'But apparently none of them was making the decisions, and perhaps that was what hurt me the most (Corbidge left shortly after the float).

'My only regret was that I wasn't going to get the opportunity to say my farewells to the players.'

IT HAD BEEN ONE LARGE MAGIC CARPET RIDE, FOR EVERYONE.

You didn't realise you were on it until after it had taken off.

Newcastle became everything and more than you'd ever dreamed of.

There were times it didn't seem real. The city basked in the happiness of it all. Even the strips were unforgettable.

Wins, goals, excitement and pride. You drowned in pride.

No Herefords, just heroes.

And then it stopped. It didn't slowly land, it just stopped.

Everything you expected followed; devastation, confusion, anger and of course, sadness.

It felt like a death.

It would never be like it was with Keegan, and everybody, deep down, knew it.

ROB LEE – HURT

'I'M IN TEARS. A LOT OF THE LADS ARE IN TEARS. TERRY MAC HAS *just told us. Kevin's gone. It's devastating. The reason I signed for Newcastle was Kevin Keegan. That was the only reason. I could have stayed in the Premier League, waited in London for West Ham, but I wanted to play for him. I loved being around him.*

'I loved going to training and training with him. He had that aura about him that you wanted to play well for him.

'He pushed you and he pushed you and he pushed you and because he was your hero you wanted to do well for him. He would always say, "You were great there."

'I signed for Newcastle because of Kevin, a lot of players did. Alan signed and he turned down a lot of clubs for Kevin Keegan.

'It's his hometown club, but if you have another manager in charge he wouldn't have signed, the pull wouldn't have been the same. The pull of his hometown club was huge but his hero was Kevin Keegan. That was the huge pull he had on huge, huge players.

'I knew Newcastle was a big club but I didn't realise how big it was. I'd been there for five years at the time and I learned to love the club.

'We'd heard rumours at the Charlton away game when we drew one-all.

'We heard rumours on the way back, but he'd walked out before. He would put pressure on the board and rightly so. He pushed the club forward and he wanted the club to get better. Throughout his career he'd been successful.

'He was his own man and he knew what he wanted. If people promised him stuff he didn't get he would make a fuss. He wouldn't tolerate it.

'We didn't really hear until Terry McDermott called a meeting.

'It was a massive cloud over the club. If you ask all the players that were there. It was huge for us to lose him at that time. Terry Mac said Kevin had gone and I was in tears.

'We won the Championship easy. We went into the Premier League and Kevin came out with the statement, "We're going to challenge Man United," and from that moment on, we did. Everyone thought he was mad. We went so high so quick.

'When he left we were still in the FA Cup, still going for the league, still in Europe. He didn't leave because he had a bad team, or he was sacked or bad results. We had a great team. A great team, bar one or two tweaks. We'd just signed Alan for £15 million. Him and Les are still the best partnership I've seen.

'They scared the crap out of people. Great service from both wings. We lost the title but everybody, bar no one on that team, thought we wouldn't go back the next season and win the league.

'If Kevin would have stayed we would have won something with him. I genuinely believe that.'

KEVIN KEEGAN – DON'T LOOK BACK IN ANGER

'KEEGAN QUITS,' READ THE EVENING CHRONICLE FRONT PAGE.

It felt like the world was ending. It was the day you had to grow up. Keegan and his magic were no longer a part of Newcastle United, and nothing felt good about that.

The Newcastle board had wanted to announce the departure that same night, but Keegan told them to wait until 11 o'clock, for his family, his wife Jean, and his two daughters Laura, 18 and Sarah 14, to get out of England. Keegan understood the storm that was about to be unleashed, even if the board and Mark Corbidge didn't.

Keegan said a weight had been lifted off his shoulders. At times it is difficult to explain how heavy a club Newcastle United can be. He had not just picked it up, he had made it float.

When reality crashed, when it was announced that Keegan had quit, rather than reveal the detail or that he had been forced to go, all hell broke loose.

It was that big a story. It dominated the news.

The club put together a hasty statement, attributing it to Keegan. In the blur of that night, he did not even check it.

'It was my decision and my decision alone to resign,' it read. 'I offered my resignation at the end of last season but was persuaded by the board to stay.

'I feel that I have taken the club as far as I can and that it would be in the best interests of all concerned if I resigned now. I wish the club and everyone concerned with it the very best for the future.'

There were tributes from the Halls.

'Kevin took over at the helm of a football club destined for relegation to the Second Division and scaled the heights of the Premier League with a style of football never before seen at St James' Park,' said Douglas.

'Kevin leaves the club in a far stronger position than when he arrived and the squad of players he built up is one of the best in Europe. We wish Kevin well in the future.'

His father Sir John appeared rather more surprised by the speed of events.

'It has all happened rather quickly, but the club has to go on and Kevin would want that,' he said.

Keegan was travelling through the Channel Tunnel with his family at that point, desperate to escape.

Terry McDermott and Arthur Cox were handed the reins for Newcastle's next game, against Aston Villa. Keegan had called McDermott to tell him what had happened.

'Obviously I'm saddened and I'm still shocked,' said McDermott. 'But Kevin wanted Arthur and myself to carry on. He said: "Go and give those fans what they deserve, a trophy." If we win one, we'll dedicate it to Kevin Keegan for what he's done for the club and the area.'

There are times when the emotional outpouring has been overdone at St James' Park, when the desire of television cameras mixes badly with the egos of some supporters.

There are times when you watch the goings on outside of the stadium on a non-matchday through your hands.

That day was not one of them. It was genuine sadness. The *Evening Chronicle* called it Black Wednesday, and that was not far wrong.

One of Tyneside's great icons had gone. Of course people were upset. He was part of your childhood, part of your clumsy steps into adulthood. A major factor in people's lives.

Keegan left Newcastle United with nothing. Three months after the share flotation he received the £1 million that had been agreed at Wynyard Hall on the fateful night. The squad he left behind, which had cost net £41 million would go onto be dismantled and bring in around £38 million.

Three million pounds for five years of Keegan? Yes please. It was a steal, an absolute steal.

It was, however, about so much more than money.

He made going to the match as magical as it had been when you were a young child. You can't put a price on that.

BOBBY ROBSON AND KENNY DALGLISH – ONE TO ANOTHER

'YOU'RE WINDING ME UP,' KENNY DALGLISH SAID.

'No,' he replied.

Dalglish still wasn't sure.

'I dialled Terry McDermott's mobile number,' he added. 'Mark Lawrenson answered.'

'Kenny, have you heard the news?' Lawro said.

'Is it true?' Dalglish asked him.

'Yes, Kevin's resigned,' Lawro replied

Kenny Dalglish was driving to a funeral in Scotland on 8 January when he heard.

'As I drove on I thought about Kevin,' he recalled in his autobiography. 'He always came across as a smashing fellow. We were friendly without being close friends.

'When he resigned I didn't feel any sympathy for him. Kevin wouldn't have wanted that. He made the decision to resign because he thought it was for the best. Kevin left Newcastle because he said he had taken the team as far as he could.

'People linked me to the Newcastle job because I had been out of management since being sacked by Blackburn.

'I had taken a couple of holidays, gone skiing, played golf, watched some matches and generally puttered about. I had started working for David Murray [the Rangers chairman] at Carnegie.

'I wanted to become involved again. I don't know who was Newcastle's first choice when they looked round for the right person to replace Kevin.'

Unknown until now, according to Freddy Shepherd, was that there was a secret approach to land Alex Ferguson from Newcastle's biggest rivals.

'We tried to get Alex Ferguson when Keegan left,' said Shepherd. 'Ferguson wanted £1 million off Manchester United.

'Keegan left and Alex Ferguson at the same time wanted more money off Man U. We tried to get Alex. We didn't achieve it. We had telephone calls with his agent. We tried to get him.

'We didn't get to the level of talking figures. We just got approached by his agent. They approached us to see if we'd be interested in taking him.

'We knew he was unlikely to leave, but we played the game. "Of course we'd be interested," we said.

'I think he phoned up because Keegan had left. We didn't approach a manager the next day.

'It never went any further than that, then he did the deal with Manchester United to stay.

'I was sitting on the back of my boat in Majorca and Martin Edwards called. He said, "Have you got anything to tell me?" I nearly fell in the water.

"No," I replied.

'He said, "You've made a move for Alex and you've got no chance of getting him. He won't leave Manchester. You had no chance, they were winding you up."'

Instead, Newcastle's big hitters headed to Barcelona.

'We went to Bobby,' said Sir John Hall. 'He was the right choice and we'd heard he wanted to come back, that Elsie (Robson's wife) wanted to come back. They'd been everywhere.

'A journalist set up a meeting for us in Barcelona. Freddy and Douglas flew out and I flew up from Marbella and met surreptitiously at Bobby's house in Sitges and sat in the garden.

'Bobby said, "Yes, I want to come back." We did a deal with him. He was coming, absolutely great.

'We told him about Louis Van Gaal (replacing him) but Bobby could not believe this would happen at a club like Barcelona.

'When I spoke to Bobby the next day his tone had changed. He told us he was staying at Barcelona. Maybe he thought he could use this (approach) as a way to negotiate a deal with Barcelona. Van Gaal came in, Bobby went upstairs.'

Kenny Dalglish meanwhile, out of management since being sacked at Blackburn in 1995, was waiting for a call.

'They spoke to two or three other people about the job as well as me, including Bobby Robson,' he wrote in *Dalglish, My Autobiography*.

'They first talked to me on the Friday, 10 January, two days after Kevin's resignation, and we arranged to meet on the Monday at the Tickled Trout, a hotel near Preston.

'On that Sunday night I went to Sky's Panasonic awards. I was sat next to Alan Shearer. When I saw him, I thought it was a set up. No one knew I was soon to meet Newcastle.

'Newcastle had approached me. If Newcastle wanted reassurance about anything, they knew the best thing was to talk to me, so we met at the Tickled Trout. Douglas Hall was there with Freddy Shepherd and Freddie Fletcher.

'After we'd talked for an hour and a half, they said they would let me know. I still thought Bobby Robson might be in for it but Freddie Fetcher phoned me at 9.45 the next morning, offering me the job.

'"We'd like to get it done today," Freddie said. So I got in the car and headed for Newcastle.

'When I was driving up there, a journalist rang me and told me Bobby Robson had announced he was staying at Barcelona and that he wouldn't be accepting the Newcastle position.

'That was strange because when Newcastle phoned me they said they had told Robson he was not getting the job.

'Newcastle must have thought I was the best one for the job or the best one available.

'I arrived in Newcastle and the deal was done and dusted in two minutes. I told them what my personal terms were and they said no problem.

'After my meeting with the board, some of the players came up to see me. I had a chat with Alan, Peter Beardsley, Lee Clark, Les Ferdinand and Robert Lee. Then I went to meet the press.'

Dalglish was eventually sat on a small sofa in a small group when the television cameras had been turned off.

He was warm, engaging and funny. It was a side the people of the North East needed to see. There had a been a truly heroic reaction to the tragedy of Hillsborough. Eventually, as manager of Liverpool after attending nearly every funeral, it became too much and he stepped down, having won three league titles. As a decorated player at Anfield he had won six, ironically after following Keegan into the number seven shirt.

He had been a Rangers fan as a boy, but made his name at Celtic, where he had picked up another four titles. After Liverpool he returned to management with Blackburn and, along with Shearer, won the Premier League. It was some haul.

'The fans idolised Kevin,' he said. 'He was a god to them. Kevin was always talking the club up, and he delivered the goods with everything bar a bit of silverware. That's the next stage, for us to take it on a bit further than Kevin did.

'The only promise Newcastle supporters will get from me is that I will do the best I possibly can to get what everybody wants. I want exactly the same as them.'

Once more people waited outside the Milburn Stand for his first bow. Supporters hugged him. He looked happy then, perhaps unaware of the weight that had been passed onto his shoulders.

Newcastle won the first game of his reign, the replay against Charlton. Shearer, reunited with the man who took him to Ewood Park, scored the winning goal in extra-time, but Newcastle were knocked out of the FA Cup in the next round, at home to Nottingham Forest, when Ian Woan scored twice after Les Ferdinand had scored. Tyneside was sick to death of Ian Woan by then.

From there results were erratic. Newcastle scored eight goals at home against Everton and Leicester. The Leicester game was genuinely thrilling, 3–1 down with 13 minutes to go before Alan Shearer scored a dramatic hat-trick. There was delight that night. Ferdinand scored again in the next game at the Riverside Stadium in a 1–0 win.

Newcastle were six points behind league leaders Manchester United with a game in hand. There was a UEFA Cup quarter-final looming with Monaco. Southampton were up first and Matt Le Tissier's goal secured a 1-0 win. Everyone on Tyneside was sick to death of him as well.

The first leg against Monaco, at St James' Park, was lost and then Newcastle went back to Anfield for the first time since the fateful night of 12 months previous. Newcastle had slipped to eight points behind Liverpool, although they had a game in hand.

Newcastle, back at Anfield, under Kenny Dalglish, back at Anfield, were awful and by half-time rightfully trailed 3–0. The world seemed different to 1995. It felt like regression, back to the old days, and then Keith Gillespie scored with 19 minutes to go.

Liverpool lost their nerve. Asprilla scored with three minutes left and within a minute Warren Barton charged through, crashed the ball into the Liverpool net and booted a television sound boom as hard as he could.

The away end went wild, properly wild. Most probably still hadn't lost the numbness of what happened at the same stadium, a year earlier.

That was the thawing. It was a goal that would never have meant as much as a winner, or even an equaliser on the night of the first seven-goaler, but it would have restored a bit of faith in football.

And then in injury time Robbie Fowler scored. Four-three. Again.

You went home and you felt ill.

Just over a week later Newcastle's supporters were walking around the race track at Monaco. 'In your Monaco slums,' was the song of choice.

It was breathless. The emotional highway, you could not get off.

Newcastle lost 3–0, having lost the first 1–0 at St James' Park. It was a strong Monaco side, with Emmanuel Petit, Thierry Henry and Fabien Barthez. Newcastle were never really in it. The defeat, and three successive 1–1 draws with Wimbledon, Sunderland in the return Tyne-Wear derby, again with no visiting supporters and Sheffield Wednesday meant Newcastle were fifth with six games to go.

The season felt finished.

You could not envisage what would follow.

Newcastle beat Chelsea and Derby 3–1 and then at Highbury, Robbie Elliott scored with his head from a Darren Peacock cross and even the dismissal of Keith Gillespie with 11 minutes to go could not derail the late surge. Les Ferdinand ended up playing at centre-half. Eighteen of the players who started the game were English.

There followed two goalless draws. The final day of the season was all about mathematics. Manchester United had successfully defended their title, but the fight for second place, which offered devastation and not consolation 12 months earlier, was a possibility, and with it, the added catch of playing in the Champions League.

On the morning of 11 May, Liverpool were second, with 67 points (+25), Newcastle were third, level on points (65) and goal difference (+28) with Arsenal but ahead of them on goals scored (68 to 59). If Arsenal were to win at Derby, Newcastle had to match their scoreline against Nottingham Forest at St James' Park to finish above them.

Both clubs had to hope that Liverpool did not win at Sheffield Wednesday.

It was a similarly muddled picture at the foot of the table.

If Coventry beat Tottenham at White Hart Lane and Sunderland did not win at Wimbledon and if Middlesbrough did not win at Chelsea, then the two other North East clubs in the top division would be relegated.

It seemed completely implausible that all those results would drop.

In six dazzling minutes midway through the first half at St James', victory was assured. Asprilla scored first and then Les Ferdinand added a quick brace. Before half-time it was four after Shearer, whose season had been disrupted by a groin problem and operation, scored his 28th goal of the season. Ferdinand's double took his tally to 29 in all competitions. The pair had scored 50 Premiership goals between them. Shearer, in his last four Premiership campaigns, had scored 121 goals from 148 games.

By half-time at the Baseball Ground, Arsenal were losing and had been reduced to 10 men after Tony Adams had been sent off. Sheffield Wednesday were holding Liverpool at Hillsborough.

Meanwhile at the bottom, Middlesbrough and Sunderland were both drawing and Coventry, whose game kicked off 15 minutes late because of traffic problems on the M25 and M1, were winning 2–1.

If you were a Newcastle fan, it was turning into quite a day.

Arsenal would come charging back and win 3–1 at Derby, but that was irrelevant after Robbie Elliott added a fifth, his fourth in seven games. The concern was at Sheffield Wednesday, where things weren't looking quite so rosy. Kevin Pressman had gone off with a hamstring injury and within 10 minutes his replacement, Matt Clarke, had been sent off for handling outside his penalty area. The forward Andy Booth went in goal. Jamie Redknapp equalised with the free-kick, which meant it was 1–1 there. Newcastle were still second but there were seven minutes left at Hillsborough.

Middlesbrough had gone behind at Leeds and then equalised through Juninho. Jason Euell scored for Wimbledon.

Everything rested on Sheffield Wednesday. Newcastle completed a 5–0 rout and then confirmation came through that Liverpool had not found a way past Booth. Newcastle had again finished runners-up. The 1997/98 season would see the club in the European Cup for the first time. It all felt like a huge, unexpected bonus.

Results from the bottom of the table filtered through, Middlesbrough had drawn and were relegated, Sunderland had lost at Wimbledon. There was still a wait from Tottenham, and then, 15 minutes after the rest of the season had finished, Coventry's victory and Sunderland's relegation was confirmed.

It was some night.

ALAN SHEARER – RUNAGROUND

'IT'S A BAD ONE JACK.'

Alan Shearer was on his way to hospital when he called Jack Hixon, the scout from Whitley Bay who had discovered him as a 14-year-old boy and took him to Southampton.

The pair remained close.

In the 90th minute of the Umbro Tournament against Chelsea at Goodison Park Shearer took a pass from Philippe Albert, about 15 yards past the half way line. There was a light drizzle and no one near him when he stretched to get the pass. He played the ball with his right foot and then his right foot got stuck in the pitch.

He lay in agony, absolute agony, immediately. There was anguish as he writhed on the field. It was the sight of a hard man in serious pain.

By the time he reached the hospital, after calling Hixon, the severity was still becoming known. Alan Shearer, 26, had broken his fibula and ruptured his ankle ligaments.

It was, as he rightly said to Hixon, 'a bad one'. A really bad one as it turned out.

'There were a couple of physically harrowing moments along the way,' Shearer said. 'The first came within weeks of the original operation when they took the stitches out.

'It was the first time I had seen my ankle since the injury and it looked a right mangled mess. I had to turn my head away, otherwise I think I might have fainted.

'Before I reached this stage, everything had gone more or less according to plan. There were one or two hiccups but nothing I was not able to take in my stride.

'The day after the operation I went through the whole recovery process in my mind. The club specialist Rob Gregory's words were etched in my thoughts. "It isn't going to be an easy one Alan," he told me. "Don't expect any miracle or short cuts. You've got to be patient."

'I owe a huge debt to Derek Wright and Paul Ferris, Newcastle's two physios. They devised a superb plan for me and they deserve a medal for putting up with me.

'They were the ones who had to tolerate my mood swings and occasional petulance but I put a lot of hard work into my recovery.

'We didn't want to push things too hard in the early stages for fear of further damaging the ankle, which was already in a fragile state. I pushed my body to its limits. When I first started to run I could not put my foot down flat on the floor without feeling acute pain. I had to run on my toes because it hurt so much. Gradually the pain disappeared.'

In the final week of July, Freddie Fletcher had spoken to Les Ferdinand. When Newcastle tried to find £6 million to keep the bank happy at the end of Keegan's reign, he had suggested such a move. The board did not want it and instead moves were put in place to sell Paul Kitson.

By the summer of 1997, Ferdinand remained one of the most saleable assets and Newcastle were about to cash in, after accepting a £6 million offer from Tottenham.

There was one problem, Ferdinand, fully settled in the area and with 59 goals in his two seasons at St James', did not want to go.

He met Fletcher, who explained it was not his decision.

'But I don't want to go,' said Ferdinand.

'I'm sorry Les, you don't always get what you want in life.'

The transfer progressed, Ferdinand was told the deal was happening and he moved his stuff from Tyneside to a new property in the south. He had met Gerry Francis and given him his word he would sign.

At teatime of 26 July 1997, Fletcher got in his car and drove down to London to see Ferdinand.

He explained the severity of Shearer's injury, and that the club would now prefer to keep him, rather than sell their other main striker to Spurs.

'I'm sorry Freddie,' said Ferdinand. 'You don't always get what you want in life.'

The new season had not started and Newcastle had just lost 57 goals in a day. After Black Wednesday, when Keegan left six months earlier, came Black Saturday.

Dalglish and Newcastle had once more been busy in the transfer market.

Alessandro Pistone had arrived from Inter Milan for £4.3 million and Nikos Dabizas had already moved from Olympiakos for £2 million. It was a different approach to the transfer market and there were eyebrows raised when first John Barnes (33) and then Stuart Pearce (35) arrived.

In light of the crisis at the front, a lot would fall on a young attacking midfielder from Denmark called Jon Dahl Tomasson, who had scored four goals in pre-season. In the first game of the campaign, at home to Sheffield Wednesday, he went clean through and slipped a shot wide. It immediately felt like a big moment. Asprilla would score twice and Newcastle would win 2–1, as they did in the first leg of the Champions League qualifier with Croatia Zagreb, John Beresford scoring twice. He scored again in the next Premiership game, a 1–0 win against Aston Villa. Newcastle had a 100 per cent record and were sixth.

Then, in Zagreb came a night of drama. Newcastle lost the return leg 2–1 after 90 minutes. Extra-time followed, with the ultimate at stake, a place in the Champions League. With 11 minutes of the 120 minutes remaining, Temuri Ketsbaia scored.

Newcastle drew Barcelona in the group stage of the Champions League.

It didn't get any bigger than that.

KEITH GILLESPIE AND TINO ASPRILLA – ATMOSPHERE

'YOU CAN HARDLY HEAR YOURSELF THINK IN THIS NOISE.'

It was a cacophony, an absolute cacophony.

It was always louder at away games, with a roof and a big following, the effort of travel, real regionalism.

But it filled St James' Park that night.

It was about pride and excitement and a sense of history and it made the ground swell with noise.

It was the ground united as one, blasting out song after song.

'Toon Toon black and white army,' was swirling around the stadium, filling all your senses to bursting point and then a pocket of the Gallowgate End cranked it up to a level that didn't seem possible.

'To see the Blaydon Races' was suddenly scrambling your senses and you were jumping up to your feet, and so was the bloke next to you, and the old fella whose legs used to bounce when it all got a bit much. He was up, and so was the cousin you sat on the barrier with for Keegan's debut. You were punching the air, and you were singing the anthem of Newcastle United and there was no room for thought. Tribalism, Tyneside's heady version of it, was everywhere. It was intoxicating. You were drinking the desire, and the passion, and the pride.

'Oh me lads, you should have seen us ganning.' It was ferocious and it was triumphant.

You loved your club. You wanted the world to know it.

Jesus Christ, we're stuffing Barcelona.

It's never felt better.

Listen to how good it feels.

This is our football club world, what do you reckon?

Brian Moore had covered more than 1,000 games before he climbed into his seat in the gantry at St James' Park that night.

'You can't hear yourself think in this noise,' he shouted.

The nation watched Tyneside.

That night, it was the most important place to be in football.

Keith Gillespie was at its centre. He would say it was the greatest game he ever played. The Spanish left-back, Sergi, could not get near Gillespie. The roar of the ground that night put turbo chargers in his boots.

'Aaah, the noise. It was unbelievable,' he recalled. 'Walking out you hear the Champions League music.

'It was my first big Champions League night.

'The noise, you know what the Geordie fans are like, but it's not every day you play Barcelona.

'You were buzzing as soon as the draw was made and the first game was at home.

'The mighty Barcelona at Newcastle. It made it even more special.

'You're walking down the tunnel and you're excited and nervous.

'Everyone is nervous, I'm sure, even the senior players, like John Barnes and Stuart Pearce, were still nervous. Nerves are part and parcel of the game.

'You sort of took a sneaky look down the line and you see people like Rivaldo, Luis Figo, Ivan de la Pena, the whole line was just great players. You were in awe of them, it was like bloody hell, look what we're up against here, I hope they have an off night!'

Everything was on that night. Jon Dahl Thomasson was generally played out of position because of the Shearer and Ferdinand sale. The best days of his career unquestionably came after he left England.

That night, however, there was the first emergence of the player he would become. He had shot wide even before he slipped a through ball to Faustino Asprilla, with just 23 minutes gone, that was behind the Barcelona defence and enough in front of Ruud Hesp to tempt the goalkeeper into a challenge that he did not complete.

Asprilla lay on the turf in the penalty area at the Gallowgate End and chewed gum whilst he waited for Pierluigi Collina to point to the spot. Collina. Barcelona. At St James' Park. You had to pinch yourself at it all and the celebration at the award was more akin to a goal.

Asprilla scored nine times in the league for Newcastle in 48 appearances. He was the ultimate enigma, but some nights in European football looked made for his talents, and this was one.

He put his hands on his hips and strolled over to the penalty spot, waited for the ball to be placed on the spot and then stroked a right-footed shot into the corner of the goal. He did a forward flip in celebration.

On another night in Europe, against Metz, he took his shirt off and put it on the corner flag at the same part of the stadium and waved it in the air after scoring a goal. You dream of doing that, or sliding on your knees in front of the Gallowgate End having completed your hat-trick.

But you don't score hat-tricks against Barcelona.

The boundaries of reality had been pushed far enough already.

Then, however, Keith Gillespie decided to have the game of his life.

'For the first 20 I never really got a chance to get round the full-back,' he added.

'I've watched the game again. The first time I really got the ball was for the second goal. Steve Watson played a quick free-kick. I dropped the shoulder, I remember Ron Atkinson said it's the first time Gillespie's had a chance to run at Sergi and he's skinned him.

'People said it was a trademark for me that I would cross it and end up on my arse. You see the goal and the leap and how high he got.

'I crossed it and I remember as I've slid across it I can see him jump and head it and then I've got up, I turned round to the crowd and then everyone's come over. It was incredible.

'Some people thought Sergi was one of the best left-backs in the world. The funny thing was I didn't know much about him. We didn't have the same coverage of Spanish football then. Maybe that was a good thing.

'I'd seen him play at the Euros for Spain. If you're a left-back for Barcelona or Real Madrid you usually play for Spain. I knew he was a good player but once I had that confidence where I knew I was quicker than him that was all I needed.'

Gillespie dropped the shoulder in the 30th minute, ran to the by-line and crossed a wonderful right-footed cross, and then Asprilla jumped as if everyone in the Leazes End behind him had blown him into the air.

'What a leap,' shouted Moore when he watched the replay, as Atkinson tried to make sense of what was going on around him.

'The leap?' said Gillespie. 'I've never seen a leap like it. How did he get that far off the ground? It made the goal even better, the height he got.'

Atkinson, like everyone, was now caught in the night. He made reference to a 4–2 victory at St James' Park when he was in charge of Manchester United. The atmosphere then had cut a swirl against the scoreline.

This night it grew ever more ferocious to pay homage to what was happening on the pitch.

There was disbelief in those stands at half-time, and then it got better.

A winger in full flow remains one of football's most glorious sights.

Every time Gillespie got the ball from then on was like an adrenaline shot to the blood stream of Newcastle supporters. It propelled you out of your seat so fast you had to make sure you didn't tumble into the rows in front of you.

He was 35 yards inside his own half and the ball from the outstanding Rob Lee was a backwards one, three minutes into the second half. There was no natural momentum.

Gillespie dropped his shoulder to go outside Sergi and then he scarpered, scampering up the line with the kind of genuine speed that had seen him a youth champion in Northern Ireland. He was uncatchable, and he knew it, picking the spot from which to cross, 10 yards parallel to the edge of the Barcelona penalty area, before he hoisted a ball over that once more ended up with him on the ground.

His job was done and there were two defenders to cope with the danger, but the momentum was unstoppable, Asprilla did not begin his jump until the penalty spot yet within two yards his spring had him soaring through the air, between the helpless Miguel Nadal and Luis Figo, to head in the third of an extraordinary hat-trick.

There was delirium wherever you looked.

'When I got the ball in our half there was this roar,' he added. 'That's the thing with wingers. Everyone likes to see people running with the ball, it gets people on the edge of their seats.

'I sort of jinked one way and then jinked past him. I knocked the ball in front of him. I was at the halfway line and I probably only had two or three more touches because I'd knocked it that far in front.

'He was chasing me back, there was still a lot to do. Tino was in the box and there were three of them. It's one of those where you just hope it goes where you want it to. I was knackered after the run like. The leap again, it was just perfect timing. What more could you ask for?

'What was I thinking at that point? I was fucked!'

Spirit and noise would counter any exhaustion.

Within two minutes the same two men in black and white stripes, by now unplayable, almost created a fourth.

'I knew I was having the game of my life,' he said. 'Two minutes later, same again, charging down the line, cross it over, and their 'keeper made a great save, low to his left, otherwise it was four.

'I just wanted the ball at every opportunity.

'It was the best I ever played football, by a long way. There was just noise. When you look back you go, 'Who do you want your best game to be against?' You're going to pick a Barcelona or a Real Madrid, luckily for me it was Barcelona.'

It was not done.

There would still be time for two late goals from Luis Enrique and Figo. It took an age for Collina to blow that final whistle, an absolute age. Let me keep this memory, don't spoil it with an equaliser, please, come on, just this one, please, I want to keep this one. Finally, amid a cacophony of whistles, it was done.

'It was one of the most important games of my career,' said Asprilla. 'When I was back home I was still celebrating. I wasn't even expecting to play.

'It was so special for me and for the fans of Newcastle. The ones that doubted me that day I showed what I was made of. Whoever doubted me, that made the night really special. That was my best game for Newcastle.

'The noise was so loud. Newcastle fans still to talk to me about that night.

'Barcelona could not stop us. You hear the fans. They gave us belief. It was an incredible night.'

It was so, so much more than that.

SIR JOHN HALL
– SLIDE AWAY

THE INCLINATION OF THE THIN, WINDING ROAD ROSE DRAMATICALLY. As it did, the Range Rover dropped a gear and instinctively met the challenge. There was an increase in revs but the car did not change speed and Sir John Hall did not stop talking and pointing.

'See over there Martin? That will be a major development area. I've always been into horticulture. The hall has a fabulous history. We want to bring it back to its best.'

Over there was well maintained wilderness, acre upon acre of well manicured grass and trees. The hall, the isolated hall, was Wynyard, a beautiful building built in the 1820s with 6,000 acres of land, and for 10 years the home of Sir John and his family.

Another half mile along the track the slow crunch of pebble eased and we were outside of the splendour of Wynyard Hall. It was impossible not to be impressed.

At the boardroom table, Hall leaned over.

'Now, Martin? What is it you want to talk about?'

Thirty-six hours had passed since the dramatic beating of Barcelona. Heads had begun to clear, and as they did came the realisation that Sir John Hall was leaving his post. It felt hugely significant. He had been, he repeatedly said, an unwilling owner, but once in the driving seat, with Keegan, the pair had moved as effortlessly through problems as the black motor that was busy cooling in his path.

The vociferous nights in the working men's clubs of the region, many now gone, was where it had started. Hall, the wealthy son of a miner, was brilliant on those nights. It will sit at uncomfortable political polarity that he could rouse fans like Arthur Scargill could rally miners.

A boardroom war followed, one that cost his family hundreds of thousands of pounds, but Hall won, and nothing at the club was the same after that.

Hall was hard, but he had the allure of a good politician at times.

Singing on the pitch, waiting with his wife as she smoked a cigarette at a filling station, holding court on trains, letting Freddie Fletcher loose on a football club, the Geordie Nation speeches, the price of the signings, the cup finals, Europe, Barcelona; Hall looked like he was having a ball.

Yet less than two days after he ended it, after he had walked out of the spotlight he at times looked made for, he was immovable in his opinion that he would never have got involved in Newcastle United if he knew just what it was going to entail.

'If I knew what was going to happen, I would not have got involved,' he said to me. 'I wouldn't do it. I never wanted the job, I was bitterly disappointed when the fans didn't back us in the share issue.

'I wanted to make a people's club. I got involved at a time when I was supposed to be stepping back from work. It has taken a huge chunk out of my personal life at a time when I wanted to enjoy other things. I have been trapped in the job.'

Hall was sat at the table where the decisions that revolutionised Newcastle United were made. In the sumptuous setting of Wynyard, son Douglas and chairman-in-waiting Shepherd had often joined Hall to discuss their grandiose vision of making the Magpies one of Europe's most feared forces.

'If I was in my 40s then yes, I would do it, it is exciting, despite the pressure,' he added. 'But I was close to my 60s and it just developed and dominated our lives, and you get no thanks.

'I would not do it at my age again. I never wanted to come back but we did because of the money,' he added. 'But then we sat down and drew up a business plan and we have established a superb base for the club.

'You always do have self-doubt but you have to mask it. You must always believe you are going to succeed. We have delivered everything we said we would, except maybe getting the kids into the ground, but we are working on that.

'The new ground is very important. The relevance of Newcastle United to the city and the region was more than proved on Wednesday night. It put us on the world map.

'I think at times we took the risks. In a sense it was all a calculated risk. We're talking about a business. I put money in, took the risks, you cannot have it both ways. Wynyard Hall became a guarantor for Newcastle United. When we wanted to borrow I had to put this up as collateral. We'd paid for this, so this was used to guarantee Newcastle United. I took money out of the club but that's the name of the game, capitalism.

'Let's go back, I did what I set out to do and I got the club to put shares on the marketplace – a million pounds worth of shares. I've got the leaflet here, remember that deal?

'Go and look at that, the share issue. What happened? The fans didn't buy five per cent. I had egg on my face. When I went into the boardroom after that you should have heard what they said to me. My hands are clean.'

STEVENAGE, THE RETURN,
JANUARY 1998

ALAN SHEARER –
MADE OF STONE

THERE WAS NO IMMEDIATE HANGOVER AFTER ONE OF THE GREATEST nights in the history of Newcastle United.

Newcastle won three of their next four league games 1–0. It was a sea change from The Entertainers, but it was a team without a goalscorer. Heads had been scratched when Ian Rush signed in August on a free transfer from Leeds. He was 35 and had a bad knee. It was the clearest sign that the times were changing.

John Beresford scored twice at Dynamo Kiev to rescue a point in the Champions League and in October, Rush would score in a League Cup victory against Hull.

Then Newcastle got beat 4–1 at Leeds and the rest of the year became a major struggle. There were two defeats without scoring in the next two Champions League matches with PSV Eindhoven.

It meant that glorious moment Newcastle walked out at the Nou Camp was for photographs and memories only. 10,000 supporters travelled from Tyneside to the Catalan capital. It started raining before kick-off, the number of home fans was equal to those who travelled and of note was only that a young defender called Aaron Hughes made his debut and many players forgot to salute those who had came from Tyneside and got a soaking. Positive PR had previously been so easy.

December was awful. Newcastle played seven league games, drew two, lost five and scored three goals, and two of them were against Barnsley, who were bottom of the table.

The club needed a boost, and it came on 17 January.

Five days earlier Alan Shearer had played in a practice match for the reserves against the youth team. Dalglish, McDermott, Derek Wright, Paul Ferris and Rob Gregory all watched on the sidelines. He was rusty, but he scored.

'Kenny called me to see him on the eve of the home game against Bolton,' Shearer recalled in his 1998 autobiography, *My Story so Far*. 'He asked me how I felt and I said I was fine.

'"I'm thinking of making you sub," he said.'

It was 1–1 when, after 172 days on the sidelines, Dalglish turned to his number nine and gave him the nod.

'I realised how much I had missed it,' he wrote. 'With the match in injury-time I connected with a header and laid it into the path of Darren Peacock in front of goal. His effort was blocked but it ran kindly for Temuri Ketsbaia to score the winner.

'I had no right to be back so soon. I was on cloud nine afterwards. When I suffered the injury the most optimistic forecasts said I would not be back until March. I was on the pitch for 18 minutes.

'The Newcastle team I rejoined on that January day at St James' Park was certainly different from the one I played in a season earlier. Kenny had rung the changes and given the side a whole new look.

'He was slammed in some quarters for tearing apart too quickly the squad which Kevin Keegan left behind. I can't accept that. There are big financial pressures at football clubs.'

That looked increasingly the case.

There followed an unseemly row with non-league Stevenage in the fourth round of the FA Cup. Shepherd and Dalglish queried the safety of Broadhall Way. It got messy, Newcastle were derided, again.

More than that it was Shearer's first start. He scored after three minutes, you saw in his celebration the true length of the road to recovery. He added another two in the replay at St James' Park.

There was a loss at home to West Ham in the league, an FA Cup win against Tranmere and then a draw with Leeds that saw Newcastle slump to 14th in the table.

That was on no-one's agenda.

KEITH GILLESPIE – STREET FIGHTING MAN

IT WAS A SUNDAY MORNING IN TEESSIDE AIRPORT, AND SPIRITS among the group of men who had travelled down from Tyneside were high. It was not your every day group, this was Newcastle United's first team squad and they were heading to Dublin for a jolly. They had started the night before after a goalless draw with Everton. Kenny Dalglish would not be joining them.

'We had a few drinks in the airport at 10 o'clock in the morning,' recalled Keith Gillespie. 'We had a few the night before as well.

'We got tanked up at the hotel when we arrived in Ireland and then 10 of us headed into town, to Cafe En Seine. We were there quite a while.

'I've heard so many versions of what happened next and I don't understand. People said I was flicking bottle tops across the table. You don't get the bottle tops. They take the bottle top off and then they give you the bottle.

'We weren't drinking champagne either. That version is new to me too. What I do remember is I'd knocked cutlery off the table and I think I was winding Shearer up. I honestly can't remember what about. I know I'd knocked the cutlery off and the waitress rushed over to clear it up.

'Shearer ordered me to pick it up.

'"Fuck off you," I said. "Outside now."

'He stood up.

'I went, "Oh fucking hell, here we go!"

'I'm a Belfast lad, I had to back it up.

'He got up, I got up and then we started walking and I was in front of him and it's a big long narrow bar.

'You're probably walking a good 40 yards before you're outside. I could hear him walking behind me, I could hear him breathing, I was thinking, "Fuck, what have I done?"

'We were heading outside, onto Dawson Street, it's quite a trendy sort of bar.

'Then I thought, "What am I going to do?" So as soon as I got outside I ran, swung a punch at him and missed. He hit me in the side of the head and I fell and my head hit a plant pot and I was out cold.

'That was my last memory.

'As far as I'm aware, Alan pretty quickly got himself offside because he knew there'd be people about. We are talking about the England captain. It's still big news anyway. We tried to keep it covered up but somebody had got it.

'I remember waking up in the hospital and they kept waking me up during the night because it was a head injury. Every two hours I'd get woken, there was five or six stitches in the back of my head.

'I got out the next day, went back to the hotel and the first person to come to the door was Alan and Rob (Lee). We had a laugh about it in the room. It was one of those, no grudges whatsoever. These sort of things, in a smaller scale at the training ground, happen quite a lot. You just don't want to be involved with the England captain!

'I flew home the next day and the boys were staying out, not as punishment, I don't know what the reasons were.

'I was sitting at the airport and the press were there taking pictures. My lift wasn't there yet. It's one of those things.

'I didn't get a fine at all from the club, which I couldn't believe. Kenny never really said that much about it.

'Internally it was pretty much sorted between us. It was up to the club if they wanted to fine you.

'The next game was Barnsley in the quarter-final of the FA Cup. I didn't play because I still had the staples in my head.

'We won 3–1.'

Ketsbaia, Gary Speed and David Batty scored.

Newcastle were through to the semi-final of the FA Cup.

It was time to celebrate.

FREDDY SHEPHERD AND DOUGLAS HALL – TALK TONIGHT

IMMACULATE WHITEWASHED APARTMENTS, SIX STORIES HIGH, LINED the streets. In the walkways that split the expansive main roads were beautifully maintained palm trees. It was the start of the main summer season, but the weather was still warm and the clatter of those with money still filled the streets of Puerto Banus.

It was where Marbella, on the very southern coast of Spain, had created a playground for the rich and famous; a marina, filled with plush yachts, and surrounded by restaurants and shops, developed only in 1970, but thriving 28 years later.

The main street next to the harbour is called the Avenue Julio Iglesias. To get there you will travel along the Avenue Jose Banus, called after the architect who designed the rich man's paradise.

Ten minutes drive away from the main strip is the Marbella Club Hotel, a famous haunt of glamour since the 1960s. At midnight on Sunday, 8 March, 1998, a member of Middle Eastern royalty, dressed in a white jalabiya, accompanied by a flowing robe and the agal (his headdress) welcomed two businessmen to the complex.

He had a black and gold robe, worn only by members of the 25,000-strong House of Saud. There was a Rolex watch, he had arrived in a Ferrari, and he puffed away on a hubble-bubble pipe.

The pair relax on settees and were immediately given champagne and brandy. It had been a long day. The two men had watched Newcastle's victorious FA Cup quarter-final at St James' Park. They were then driven to Newcastle International Airport. A private Lear jet had taken them the two-and-a-half hours to Malaga.

There was a stop off at the villa of the father of one of the two, Sir John Hall, and then the final trip to meet the businessman whose agent had made contact with them about possible investment in Newcastle United.

What Douglas Hall didn't know was that he had made a call to Mazher Mahmood, the chief investigative reporter on the *News of the World* after the initial approach by the agent. There was no royalty. Hall was in the middle of a scam.

'Do you mind if Freddy Shepherd comes too?' he had unwittingly asked Mahmood, 'If you can't make the game on Sunday I'll fly over to Marbella straight after and meet you.'

Mahmood agreed for Shepherd to join the talks.

Champagne flowed in the private suite at the Marbella Club Hotel. Hall and Shepherd became loose lipped. What followed would create mayhem.

'We are all hommes du monde,' Shepherd was quoted as saying in the newspaper.

There were slurs against the women of Newcastle.

'Newcastle girls are dogs,' it was said. 'England is full of them.'

Hall and Shepherd called Shearer 'Mary Poppins' because of his reserved public persona.

'Shearer is boring, he never gets into trouble,' Shepherd said.

They said Keith Gillespie couldn't handle his drink.

'We're making nothing by talking to you,' Hall said, still unaware that he was not speaking to a rich Sheikh.

'We just want to be friends. We think of everything long-term, our family businesses, that's how we build bridges. If we give you any information and help you in any way, then one day you can help us.'

By 3am the pair were at Crescendo Club Puerto Banus, a lap dancing bar. There were further slurs about Keegan and about the fitness of Andy Cole, who had been sold to Manchester United.

A week later, on Sunday, 15 March, Hall and Shepherd's world would crash. The *News of the World* splashed with their exclusive story.

'Vice Girls Shame of Top Soccer Bosses,' read the headline, with headshots of the two men beside the story.

The *News of the World* made a full transcript available of the conversation on telephone lines for those who wanted to listen. It cost 50p per minute. Thousands took the opportunity to call in. Shepherd and Hall claimed they were victims of entrapment and gross deception.

It was a media circus and it would not go away.

In midweek Newcastle lost to Crystal Palace in the league. Palace were bottom of the Premiership. The calls for resignation would not subside. North East newspapers the *Evening Chronicle* and the *Sunday Sun* led comments on front and back pages calling for the two to go.

It is believed Hall, who 12 months previously had inherited the family 57 per cent shareholding (then worth £70 million) in Newcastle United after Sir John had stood down, had gone to Spain. Shepherd, who held seven per cent of the club, valued at £9.5 million, went to Barbados with his wife Lorelle.

Sir Terence Harrison, John Mayo and Denis Cassidy, three non-executive directors of Newcastle's PLC board, called an emergency meeting at St James' Park at 8am following a second round of damaging stories on 22 March.

Week two saw the *News of the World* release the rest of the transcript of the interview.

There was more on the men's alleged playboy lifestyle, mocking comments about Newcastle's fans, remarks about Formula One motor racing chief Bernie Ecclestone's wife Slavica, and mockery of Gary Lineker.

'A player, nothing more, speaks on TV, nothing else, and does adverts for crisps,' said Hall.

There was a random condemnation of Italian, French and German businessmen and comments about Harrods owner and Fulham football club chairman Mohamed Al Fayed.

'It's more important than Harrods,' added Hall. 'He's not accepted at the moment in England, and so now he's trying to get himself more involved by buying a football team.'

By strange coincidence, Alan Shearer was a columnist with the *News of the World*. His column appeared during the second week of the storm.

'It is not for me or any of the players to discuss what has gone on with the directors of the club because it is none of our business,' he wrote. 'It is not something that has been a topic of conversation around the dressing room or training ground. All I do know is that you will never get any bigger Newcastle United fanatics that Mr Shepherd and Mr Hall.

'We would not use it as an excuse for our desperately disappointing defeat on Wednesday night by Palace.

'I can't see why we should be called a club in crisis. I accept that we are in the bottom half of the table and we would obviously prefer to be in the top half but we have a great chance of winning some silverware.'

Speaking at his home in Whalton, Northumberland, Harrison, chairman of construction company Alfred McAlpine, said the allegations would be discussed at the Monday board meeting.

'It is on the agenda,' he said. 'It is a matter which affects the standing and the reputation of the business. I can't prejudge this. I need time to speak to the non-executives and discuss our position with the board."

The *Evening Chronicle* billboards that adorn the city reflected the crisis.

'Scandal at United,' read one. 'Shares chaos/Fans' Verdict,' read another.

By now the Football Association had become involved.

'The anger of supporters is utterly understandable,' said Graham Kelly, its chief executive. 'They have deserved better, much better. Our legal advice has been clear, we should await a statement then action by Newcastle United.'

Kelly revealed the FA was giving urgent consideration to proposals from Sir John Smith, former deputy commissioner of the Metropolitan Police, in a report for the association. 'His recent report called for a code of conduct by which all those active in the game can be judged,' said Kelly.

Even Gordon McKeag, the former chairman, whose family had been involved in the club for 40 years before Hall took over at the start of the 1990s, said: 'I should be very surprised if Sir Terence Harrison, who is the chairman of the PLC, has not called meetings to ascertain the truth of the allegations, and very surprised if he's not asking the chairman and the vice chairman to consider their positions.'

McKeag, either through speculation or informed information, was correct.

Denis Cassidy, one of those board members, was raging. Cassidy had grown up in Newcastle's West End before a career in business led to his appointment to the board of directors at BHS in the 1970s. He held other directorships before being appointed a non-executive director at Newcastle United when the club floated in April 1997.

'I had travelled up to St James's Park for a game against Coventry, which proved a dispiriting, lacklustre 0–0 draw,' Cassidy recalled in his book, *When the Promises had to Stop*.

'Freddie Fletcher rang to tell me he had some very bad news.

'A national newspaper the following morning was to carry an exclusive story by one of its undercover reporters with the front page devoted to pictures of Freddy Shepherd and Douglas Hall.

'Apparently, attempts had been made to serve a High Court injunction preventing publication, but they had failed.

'Messrs Hall and Shepherd's conduct was inappropriate to say the least, and had undeniably tarnished the image and reputation of the PLC and the club nationally.

'It was the mindlessly juvenile insults lavished on the fans, particularly those buying overpriced drinks and replica shirts ('all mugs'), the women of Newcastle ('all dogs'), and Alan Shearer ('Mary Poppins') which attracted most attention and caused both hurt and anger.

'I met with Shepherd's lawyer, Freddie Fletcher and Freddy Shepherd, early on 17 March, advising Shepherd there was no alternative to his and Douglas Hall's immediate resignation from all offices at the club.'

'Freddy, the culprit, exploded: "Don't fucking moralise at me."

'Sir John Hall stated: "You cannot force people who own the club to resign."'

Finally, after 10 days of turmoil, Shepherd and Hall resigned.

On 24 March, after protracted discussion, a statement was released on behalf of the two men.

It read: 'Douglas Hall and Freddie Shepherd have decided to step down as directors of Newcastle United PLC and Newcastle Football company.

'They arrived at this decision after careful consideration to ensure that the allegations made against them do not further affect Newcastle United and enable them to concentrate their energies in restoring their reputations.

'Nothing that has happened in the past week diminishes the success of Newcastle United.'

Harrison said: 'We hope these changes will enable us to put the difficult circumstances of the past 10 days behind us, and I call for everyone associated with Newcastle United to work together for its future success.'

Newcastle's share price rose six pence to 101p when the resignations were announced.

'We think, both Douglas and I, that somebody in the club, we don't know who, set that up,' Shepherd told me.

'We don't know who. We have our suspicions but we think someone in the club or close to the club set that up.

'Douglas was handling it. They got in touch with Douglas and said can we have a meeting in Marbella. We are down in Marbella we'd like to invest in the club, (but it's) not a takeover. He said, "We can help you abroad and all with other things," and we said okay.

'We went down to Marbella. That's when we met the guy. He was of Asian descent so we didn't smell a rat through that.

'We had a few drinks. There was nee knocking shop involved, as was tried to be portrayed, a load of bollocks, there wasn't owt like that involved. Purely it was a case of a few drinks and trying to impress him to get him to Newcastle.

'It was two blokes having a chat over a beer letting their mouths go. That was it. The guy was all set up in his robes. He was going to put money into Newcastle so we were trying to impress him. That's what the whole thing was about.'

Newcastle were ripe for the talks, Shepherd reveals, after more boardroom departures.

'We had just sacked Corbidge and Terry Harrison was chairman then and him and Corbidge didn't see eye to eye,' he adds. 'I remember phoning Terry and saying Mark Corbidge wants to leave and wants paid off. He went, "Well I'm in Madeira, I'll fly over immediately." He wanted to be involved. I said, "If you want to I don't have a problem with it."

'He flew over to the meeting in London with Corbidge. We did the deal with Corbidge and he left. Fletcher was back as chief executive.

'Corbidge left and this happened about three months later, a call about investment in the club, but we were always going to keep control.

'It was an unfortunate occurrence really. How many has [Mahmood] set up? He's set bloody everybody up, but none of it was interpreted correctly as to what it was. It went out of context.

'It was much ado about nothing. The reporters jumped on it. That is their job. I'm not bitter, it's their job. It did get a bit of publicity around the world.

'It was very difficult. It wasn't just one article one day. It went on for three weeks. I talked to a lecturer in law and he said, 'We use your case for students.' It was nothing but it went over for three weeks.

'It was just unbelievable.

'Then we resigned.

'Kenny was there at the time. To be fair he stood by us. We kept in touch for obvious reasons. We still had the percentage. John took over again and he wanted rid of it as quickly as possible. He had retired and he didn't want the hassle.'

This was the backdrop to the club's run to try and reach their first FA Cup final in 24 years. Only at Newcastle United.

The semi-final against Sheffield United, the first most supporters had ever seen, was truly memorable, the gigantic stand at Old Trafford and half the Stretford End packed with 25,000 supporters backing their side until it came to the hour mark, and then willing Alan Shearer's shot from close range over the line.

'Is it? Is it?'

A one of them…

'Is it? Oh, it is!!'

An FA Cup semi-final goal. You felt how special it was the second it happened. You willed that ball in.

It had been a cup run full of tribulations until then, the fight with Stevenage over the state of their ground, Gillespie missing the game with Barnsley because of his head wound, but then the goal went in and you couldn't care less. Wembley. Not for the Charity Shield, but for a Cup final.

You sang it on the train all the way home to Newcastle Central Station. Just like a team that's gonna win the FA Cup, we shall not be moved. A new song. Wembley. Joy all around you.

But still, a club with its two major shareholders hiding in the wings. It needed a rallying call, and for all the support Dalglish had in the dressing room, he was not the man for that.

Instead, after Dalglish had addressed the media in Cup final week at the ground, Sir John Hall walked into the St James' Suite, along with Alastair Wilson. Wilson had played his part in Newcastle's history by helping bring Kevin Keegan to the club but had returned to the club as director of communications on 17 April.

He didn't have to do anything that afternoon.

'I have no idea why I'm here, talking to you all now,' said Sir John, uncomfortable for once when pushed to centre stage. He complained about the upset his grandchildren were going through, he was unhappy with the coverage, he thought it was excessive.

Then his tone changed, and he was asked about Wembley and Newcastle.

'We are marching on the capital,' he said. 'We're going to do everything in our power to win the final. We will have thousands of fans who believe we can do it. The Geordie nation is on the march.'

His mood changed. It was another rallying call. He was an incredible orator. The media had a story.

More importantly, the city had a leader as it prepared for its first FA Cup final since 1974.

WEMBLEY STADIUM (PART 2), MAY 1998

SHAY GIVEN – SAD SONG

'I'M GETTING READY TO GO. I'M IN THE DRESSING ROOM AND I'M GETTING *strapped up, putting tapes on my fingers and my wrists.*

'Getting on the team bus was part of the magic as a kid and the cameras are there when you leave the hotel. We know how big it is, we're all suited and booted. We know what is happening. We know it's a huge, huge game, for the players, the fans and the club. We want to be part of history. We know how big the game is. It's massive.

'You grew up watching the FA Cup final day. You see the build up, the songs, the club suits and all the stuff that goes with it.

'You're then thrust in the middle of it, you're actually at a Cup final day yourself. It's surreal in a sense because you know how big a thing it is. When you're a kid it starts at 11 o'clock and goes right the way through to a three o'clock kick-off on a Saturday.

'Now you're part of it. You're a part of history. It's such a special tournament. To go to Wembley, the old Wembley, is fantastic.

'When you're stood in the middle of the pitch in your suit you're thinking more about the game than what you're involved in. You're trying to focus on the game. You're concentrated on the things going through your system more so than the whole occasion. You're trying to take it all in but at the same time you've got a big game coming up.

'We know what we need to do in the game.

'Time to go. Now we're in the tunnel and you can hear it. It was a wall of noise. It was special. You were amongst the Newcastle fans, right at the tunnel. It's hard to describe. You can't hear yourself think. It's electric, the noise.

'The fans are immense. There's black and white everywhere.

'Then there's the long walk from behind the goal.

'It's special walking down the tunnel behind the manager.

'There's the captain and you're walking out to show the supporters on such a big occasion. That whole walk was special.

'On the red carpet. Trying to get focused on the game. You just want the whistle to go, to get playing. You want to get underway.

'Then Overmars is through. I don't know how it broke to him, but it broke to him and I stretched myself and I think he put it through my legs. He hit it into the ground, I don't know if he meant that or not, but it doesn't matter, it's in the net.

'The first goal in a Cup final is massive.

'We were confident. It's a blow to the chin but it's early and we're still very much in the game. It's only one-nil but we're not creating many opportunities to score, a couple of half chances maybe.

'Suddenly we hit the post and it could have been one all. Mentalities change quickly in games.

'Then Anelka scores.

'I don't know why we haven't performed well. We didn't perform as we had to get to that stage. That's the disappointing thing. Its not a case of we're not trying, we're just not clicking.

'That's the frustrating thing as a player. Old Trafford was bouncing for the semi-final and we played well. It's not here today. We're not playing well.

'The fans probably think of the semi-finals as better than the final.

'We couldn't do the business on the day. Even at the end they were immense. It was just this wall of noise.

'There's just frustration in the dressing room. We know we can play better and we didn't.

'It's not for want of trying. We just didn't click on the day.

'It's a cliche, but you don't want to be there if you've lost. You have to get your medals.

'You just want to get on the bus and get out of there.

'The fans were still singing. They were unbelievable. It's a special club to play for.

'They're always very supportive of the players. They deserve great credit for that. They could have been halfway up the motorway going home but they stuck it to the end and really got behind.

'We go back to the hotel for a drink, dinner, lick our wounds, talk about the game.

'Then there's a presentation when we get back to Newcastle.

'Yeah, of course it was a surprise that so many turned out. We hadn't even done it, we weren't parading anything.

'Personally I thought we wouldn't have done the open bus because we didn't win the cup.

'When you see how many fans are there. We didn't win something. You just think imagine what would happen if we did.

'That was even more frustrating. The turnout was unbelievable. The streets were rammed like.

'We should have played better. We just didn't turn up.'

KENNY DALGLISH –
HELLO, GOODBYE

NEWCASTLE HAD FINISHED THE 1997/98 SEASON IN THIRTEENTH PLACE.
It could have been worse, Newcastle were 16th at the end of March, but it still
felt like the huge fall it was, from successive runners-up finishes, back to a past of
struggle and disappointment. Those days were supposed to have gone. Instead,
two years after fighting to win the Premiership, the club had briefly flirted with
falling out of it.

The chequebook came back out. Dietmar Hamman was signed from Bayern
Munich for £6 million, Nolberto Solano moved from River Plate for £2.5 million
and Laurent Charvet moved to Tyneside. There was also a new centre forward,
Stephan Guivarc'h, fresh from winning the World Cup with France.

Newcastle had won only two of their final 14 league games in the 1997/98
season. When the new season began with draws against Charlton and Chelsea,
Dalglish was done.

The point gained at Stamford Bridge would be his last as Newcastle manager,
on 22 August, 1998.

Talks had begun between Freddy Shepherd (still officially resigned from his
position as chairman) and Jon and Phil Smith, the agents of Ruud Gullit. When
Dalglish picked up a newspaper on the morning of 27 August, he learned that the
lure of sexy football had proved irresistible to Shepherd and Douglas Hall.

It was not something he had seen coming. He met journalists in a Durham pub
at lunchtime.

'I've no regrets about coming here,' he said. 'The only regret I have is that I've left.'

He spoke of his initial reaction to the news.

'I thought someone was "winding me up,"' he said.

Dalglish insisted that the club had been moving in the right direction during his 17-month tenure.

'On the playing staff side the club now has much greater strength in depth and has got a reasonable quantity and quality of young players,' he added. 'Given time they will push very hard for a first-team place.

'I hope the club's on the right course. They certainly deserve success and they've got enough quality players to have a successful season. I hope they have a good season, and their support for me has been very nice to hear. I made some mistakes but also some good decisions.

'To see their faces when we had the success of getting to the FA Cup final and the elation on people's faces when we qualified for the Champions League by beating Croatia Zagreb makes it worthwhile.

'I wish only success for them.'

On his future, Dalglish said: 'I honestly don't have a clue, but I'm a long time out of short trousers. However, it's not the happiest day in my life. Someone going into this job knows it's not one for life.'

Newcastle's statement said that the club was advised by Dalglish on 18 August that he wished to resign as manager.

Freddie Fletcher would later tell me Dalglish had resigned.

'He offered his resignation in the summer,' said Fletcher.

'When?' I asked.

'On 18 August he offered to go.'

We were stood at the back of Gullit's first press conference.

'Kenny is contesting this Freddie?'

'We know.'

Dalglish promptly released his own statement.

'Newcastle United PLC's press release is seriously inaccurate,' he said.

'The truth is that I did not resign. They terminated my contract without notice or any prior warning to me.

'I received first news of Newcastle United's decision through the press [and] no offer of compensation has been made.'

Newcastle lost the case against Dalglish.

After the glorious period under Keegan, they were once more getting used to defeat.

Asked about his time at Newcastle Dalglish said: 'When I went to St James' Park in January 1997, they were fourth and by the end of the season I had taken them to second and a place in the Champions League.

'During pre-season Alan Shearer picked up an injury that ruled him out for a long time, then Tino Asprilla pulled a muscle in the second game of the season.

'We then finished 13th, but made it to the FA Cup final, where we lost to Arsenal. When we were losing 1–0, we hit the bar and the post.

'Then in the next season, it was two games and I was away. My transfer record while I was there was positive as well. Everyone I signed tried their best and that is all you can ask. I thought that making it into the Champions League and to the FA Cup final was a relative success.'

Bit by bit the team Keegan built had been dismantled, through financial reasons, the sale of Ferdinand, through serious injury, Shearer at Everton, and then through sales that told you the period was over. David Ginola had been sold to Spurs, Peter Beardsley had gone to Bolton, John Beresford and Darren Peacock had been moved to Blackburn and Southampton.

More than anything perhaps, Dalglish, unlike at Anfield, could not follow Keegan, and his natural warmth and more open style. Keegan spoke as if a Geordie. Dalglish did not. The guarded approach built barriers.

Asprilla was less forgiving in his assessment.

'When Kenny Daglish arrived at Newcastle I had heard so many good things about him and I could not wait to play for him,' he said.

'Anyone who achieves so much as a player like he did you would naturally expect him to do well as a manager. This was not the case. Within months he had the team playing a style that was alien to most of us and he started to sell some of our star players.

'The stars like Ginola, Ferdinand and Beardsley were moved on. It was a team that could have gone on to win the league, having come so close in 1996, but instead we were broken up and the dream faded. I was sad to see Dalglish destroy the team. I found myself out of the side and on the bench. I did not feel that this was fair and knew that given the chance I could turn around our average season.

'I did not complain, I just did my training and waited for my chances, but they were few and far between. My departure was a sad day for me and I wish things could have been different. I have no malice towards Kenny, but with hindsight I think the club and the fans realise now that he was not the right man for the job.'

Dalglish would later talk of the unique pressure associated with the club. It was revealing stuff.

In his column for the *Mail on Sunday* he said: 'Most of my working life has been spent in the passionate football hotbeds of Liverpool and Glasgow, but for crazy, intense, obsessive and undiluted devotion to just one club in the whole city, there is nothing to compare with Newcastle-upon-Tyne.

'In 1998, as Newcastle United manager, I took them to the FA Cup final, made a couple of important signings (Didi Hamann, Nobby Solano) in the summer and started the following season with a couple of draws. Then I was sacked, still unbeaten!

'Was I surprised? The answer, in all honesty, is no because in Newcastle-upon-Tyne you have to expect the unexpected and the gossip, rumour mill and speculation run just as feverishly when times are good as when they are bad.

'I have to stress at this point that I absolutely loved my time at Newcastle. If any manager or coach was offered the chance to work there, I'd say in a flash: "Take It". The excitement and atmosphere around the place is unique.

'Of course, Celtic and Liverpool fans are just as passionate about their team as Newcastle's supporters – that goes for Rangers and Everton, too, by the way – but the bond between city and club is special at St James' Park because it is the only club in town.

'The stadium is only a few minutes' walk from the main shopping streets and even in the height of summer with no football match to look forward to, everyone still walks around in the black-and-white stripes, proud to be associated with their team.

'The irony, of course, is that this constant microscope probably works against the club in many ways. Kevin Keegan felt the pressure when his great team of David Ginola and Les Ferdinand came close to winning the title in 1995/96 (he resigned the following season), so what chance did any other manager have?

'For all this wonderful support, the flip-side is the machinations behind the scenes and in the city, which always seem to lead to Newcastle shooting themselves in the foot when things are going well.'

PETER BEARDSLEY
– PERFECT 10

YOU DON'T FORGET THE FIRST TIME YOU WENT, 'WOAH, JESUS CHRIST, what was that?'

It was against Middlesbrough, March 1984, and it was a day of great goals.

Keegan scored with a diving header.

Terry Mac scored with a lovely, delicate chip.

But it was Peter Beardsley's goal that made you stand back in wonder.

He'd scored before then, at Cardiff to start it all off, and then the three against Manchester City, who were supposed to be promotion rivals. Newcastle won 5–0 and Peter Beardsley scored a hat-trick and as it happened you knew you'd never forget that day, which was why you did it, why you went, but you didn't know then, you were young and impressionable and life stretched in front of you.

So Peter Beardsley filled it with sublime goals.

The one away at Manchester City in 84. Strength to go with the guile. The glorious, properly, absolutely, glorious chip over Joe Corrigan in 84, against Brighton, when you thought the season's brilliance meant nothing special could happen that day, but then that goal did.

His favourite, he would tell me, a lot of years later, was at Portsmouth, in that same season, when he danced and danced and Terry Mac screamed at him to put it in, so, after waiting an age, he did.

The one against Middlesbrough had come first, a right-footed shot stroked into the top corner from 25 yards. It made the dads, uncles and granddads smile in a way that you only now fully comprehend. The look of people who had watched a minefield full of mediocrity but who knew someone was pushing to join the Milburns and the MacDonalds.

He scored in the Second Division and then he scored in the First and then he went to Liverpool, and your heart broke.

You had to grow up that day and it was awful.

He won the title and then Kevin Keegan twisted Sir John Hall's arm and he came back. David Kelly went and you were gutted about that, but then Peter Beardsley came back. Keegan was a magician in the transfer market.

It was like he'd never been away.

He was the match that lit up Andy Cole, but it was not just about helping create the 41 goals Cole scored in a season.

There was a belter at Oldham, when the away end was the best place in the world to be. A roof, a big following, a night game, drunk on football, and life and how brilliant everything was.

He charged through, did the shimmy and smashed the ball into the top corner.

And then the away end burst. It did. Yes. Get in. And people jumped up, and grabbed friends, and fell over, and smiled.

Beardsley scoring goals made you smile.

He got one on his return to Everton

Thank you very much for Peter Beardsley. That was the song. Absolutely.

The goals kept coming. A superb, last minute winner at White Hart Lane. A peach at QPR, a volley after a one-two with Andy Cole on a Sunday. Dancing past two Aston Villa defenders before scoring. The one against Bolton, towards the end of the Touching Distance season, when he danced through and scored.

There were so many, 119 in total, spread over two spells, and 324 appearances.

On 27 January, 1999, the support of Newcastle United said thank you.

It was a testimonial against Celtic.

The ground was packed.

Kevin Keegan played, so did his entertainers, Kenny Dalglish played, Paul Gascoigne played and Cole got the reception he deserved for thrilling a city with his goals.

In injury-time there was a penalty that Peter Beardsley stepped up to take and he hit it over the bar.

He was allowed to take it again, and he scored at the Gallowgate End.

It wasn't one of his best, but that was understandable. Peter Beardsley had scored some of the greatest goals the old ground had ever witnessed.

He ran to his son Drew, who was a ball boy behind the goal, as he had done when he had scored against Middlesbrough at St James' Park in 1996.

A lap of honour followed. In many ways it felt like a goodbye to the team Keegan had made. Beardsley was integral to The Entertainers.

You cannot emphasize his importance and brilliance in a much more fitting way than that.

ROB LEE –
PERFECT DAY

'HE'S DROPPED SHEARER! YOU'RE JOKING.'

There are phrases you say at work that stop a sports desk.

There were only two other people on the desk of the *Sunday Sun*, then on the third floor inside Thomson House, tucked away at the bottom of the Bigg Market, and their hands did not move from their computers but their eyes were no longer looking at a computer screen.

A Newcastle player had called me at 6pm on the night of the Newcastle-Sunderland derby.

'Seriously? He's left out Shearer. Jesus Christ. Who's playing instead of him, Duncan Ferguson?

'Paul Robinson!'

Paul Robinson was a Sunderland fan who had been bought from Darlington for £200,000 by Dalglish.

It was Gullit's final throw of the dice and it wasn't a particularly sexy one.

It was a phrase he could never escape from.

'Sexy football?' said Gullit. 'Yes. It was a game between the Czech Republic and Portugal, and I found the way Portugal played sexy, smooth and nice, and I said so. After that, the phrase followed me everywhere. Journalists would ask. "Are you playing sexy football now?" – at least one phrase by me is remembered!

'As for what it is, sexy football is smooth, like the way Barcelona sometimes play. Easy, elegant.'

Dalglish cleared his things from the shared training facility at Durham's

Riverside cricket ground in Chester-le-Street, said his farewell to the players, met some journalists and then left the North East.

In the reception area at the Riverside, Carl Serrant, a young left-back, called over to David Batty.

'Hey Batts, the new gaffer's coming in this afternoon,' said Serrant.

'Me and sexy football are never going to mix mate,' replied Batty.

Within four months, Batty had been transferred to Leeds.

The Leazes End filled once more for the unveiling of Gullit.

'It's not my goal to be a hero,' he said. 'It's my goal to be successful for myself. For me the satisfaction of winning something is the smile on the faces, of the players, the board and the fans. The silverware is just the cream.

'Kevin Keegan and Kenny Dalglish did a very good job, and I'll try and continue that, and even try to do something more.

'The most important thing for me in taking the job is that I think I can do well.

'I have to see what the players can do and look at what system might suit them. I need to see the players we have here already before thinking about bringing any in.'

It felt cosmopolitan. You could never accuse Shepherd and Hall of taking the easy option. They had snared another one of the great players of his generation, on a two-year contract.

It was not particularly well known that Gullit, the dashing, dreadlocked midfielder who lit up Serie A and European football had been born in Jordaan, a working class suburb in the west of Amsterdam. His mother was a cleaner. He played football as a youngster with Frank Rijkaard and began playing for Haarlem when he was just 16. He was playing for Holland and Feyenoord just three years later.

'When I was young I was one of the second generation of black people in Holland,' he said. 'My father was the first. My mother was white, and living with a black man at that time and having a how-you-say, half-caste boy is not easy. So early on as the only black guy I was taking more attention than the rest. If people were racist, I took energy out of it. They were afraid of me, and they should have been! Because I'm gonna bust their brains out on the pitch.'

By the summer of 1988, at the age of 25, he was the reigning European and World Footballer of the Year and had led Holland to become champions of Europe.

At AC Milan he won two European Cup finals, three Serie A titles, three Italian Cups and two UEFA Cups.

He arrived in English football with Chelsea in 1995, and within a year had become player-manager at Stamford Bridge when Glenn Hoddle took over at England. Gullit led Chelsea to the 1997 FA Cup, their first major piece of silverware since 1971. Two years later he asked Ken Bates for £2 million-a-year and was sacked, leaving the door open for a move to Tyneside.

On his first day in the dugout there were supporters in dreadlocks and in the crowd stood two fans with a white piece of paper, about the same size as a scarf, and its lettering read: 'We love sexy football!'

It was 30 August 1998. The earth did not move that day, at least not if you were in black and white or were wearing a dreadlocked wig. For Michael Owen it did. Three times he scored at the Gallowgate End inside a devastating 15 minutes period. When he completed his hat-trick he rubbed his hands together in the manner of someone who had just made a lot of money. A fourth followed from Patrik Berger. Ruud Gullit, his sexy football and his new players, lost 4–1 on the opening night. It was not a honeymoon filled with fireworks.

There followed another defeat against Aston Villa that left Newcastle second bottom of the Premier League. The uplift would follow. Three victories came in succession, against Southampton, Coventry and Nottingham Forest. Newcastle scored 11 goals in those three matches. Alan Shearer scored six of them. This felt more like it, but then Newcastle bounced out of Europe, losing on away goals to Partizan Belgrade and later that month Gullit sold Steve Watson to Aston Villa for £4 million. He would later say it was a challenge to the board to see if they would give him full control. A versatile Geordie who had grown up inside the club was gone.

The following month Newcastle lost on penalties in the League Cup against Blackburn. League form remained inconsistent. Duncan Ferguson arrived from Everton for £8 million and could not hide his disappointment at having been sold by the club.

'The move was forced on me,' he said. 'Everton simply didn't want my services any longer. I knew on Monday morning that Everton were inviting offers for me. I knew by Monday afternoon that it was Newcastle, and the deal was done after the match that night. I was numb with shock really. It sickened me. I couldn't believe it. I am absolutely heartbroken to leave the club."

Two weeks before Christmas, Douglas Hall and Shepherd had returned. It felt inevitable, even to those fighting them in the boardroom.

'I was unprepared for the demand from chief executive Freddie Fletcher for a vote to appoint Messrs Hall and Shepherd to the board after I had rejected a proposal that we should consider such a move,' recounted Denis Cassidy in his memoirs.

'I said in my view it was neither in the best interests of the club nor the minority shareholders and as such was a breach of our fiduciary responsibilities. The company's financial advisers also urged him to drop the proposal.

'I was obliged to conduct the vote and duly lost by four votes to three. As I left the boardroom, I was passed in the corridor by Douglas and Freddy going in, with the latter saying smilingly to me as we passed: "We all have to lose sometime, man."

'Newcastle was now a PLC in name only, and the ruling junta were back in absolute control.

'The board's next announcement was that the satellite company NTL had acquired 6.3 per cent of the company's issued share capital, compromising nine million shares in Newcastle United, from Cameron Hall Developments. It made no mention of the fact CHD had banked a little over £10 million already from the transaction.

'Had NTL's desire to acquire a stake in the club been met, with shareholders' approval, by the issue of new shares, then the £10 million proceeds would have been banked by Newcastle United, rather than Cameron Hall Developments.'

Hall and Shepherd by now had by two thirds of the shareholding in the club.

'We look forward to working again with our colleagues at all levels,' said a joint statement from the pair. 'We have today written personally to the season ticket holders of Newcastle United, reaffirming our apologies for the events of last March and outlining our plans for the future.'

Shepherd told me: 'I think everybody was glad to see us back at the finish.

'The club was losing its way at the time. John was glad to see us back and glad to see his own son back for god's sake.'

By the start of 1999 Newcastle had found their position, 13th. They had scored 24 goals. There was no mention of a return to the days of The Entertainers, as there had been when Gullit had joined.

Behind the scenes all was similarly fractured. Stuart Pearce and Rob Lee had been banished to train with the juniors. Lee would reveal he was constantly asked by Gullit about Shearer and whether he wanted to leave. Gullit called Shearer selfish once too often in training and the Newcastle forward reacted. 'Don't call me selfish because I'm not,' he said.

Rifts were developing. Gullit would criticise Shearer for not scoring with his left foot on the training field. Shearer would score with his left foot.

The highs of the campaign, would, once more, be left to the FA Cup.

Victories over Crystal Palace and Bradford would set up a fifth round tie against Blackburn. It finished goalless at St James' Park on 14 February and the replay, with 8,000 supporters in the Darwen End of Ewood Park, providing the injection of belief that history could be about to repeat itself. A 60-yard ball from Dietmar Hamann, a first time finish from Louis Saha, on loan from Metz, and a delirious celebration. It was the first round of the competition that Shearer had not scored in. He did in the quarter-final, when Everton were brushed aside 4–1, with Georgios Georgiadis, a signing that Gillespie thought was a competition winner when he first arrived, even scoring. Shearer was captain for the first time that day. He found out when Gullit lifted a flip chart before the game in the home dressing room. Robert Lee, Shearer's friend, who had been recalled, found out he was no longer captain at that same moment.

Lee had meetings with Gullit and Freddy Shepherd to determine his future. Gullit told him: 'You weren't such a good team (under Kevin Keegan). We used to enjoy coming up here and beating your team. People in London were laughing at you when you blew the title.'

A victory in the Premier League, against Derby County at the start of April, when seven goals were scored, took Newcastle into the top 10 but it would be the final league win for the season.

Once more, it was all about the FA Cup, and the semi-final against Tottenham would unite everyone, however fleetingly.

The North Stand was once more a sea of black and white, a stunning mix of scarves and flags and strips and hats. The top tier once more bounced, moving around a foot in measurement when the game headed into extra-time and Newcastle's support turned the volume to full. It had coincided with the arrival of Ferguson from the bench. He galvanised the support. Newcastle did not look a side that would be beaten in a semi-final for much of the afternoon, but it was beyond doubt when the Scottish forward for once showed what he could do, free briefly, from injury.

The pain of Arsenal could be exorcised. It was there in the noise. A rocking football ground, a semi-final. Get back to Wembley and everything will be okay.

'Ruud Gullit's black and white army.' It was reverberating around Old Trafford. Lee was playing. Shearer was playing. The club was being put first, for whatever reason, and for however briefly. It seemed such a simple request that got lost so many times. Better United. Obviously.

TUNNEL OF LOVE

It was still goalless after 105 minutes. The noise got louder. The stand bounced more. You were in the gods up there.

Les Ferdinand and David Ginola were playing for Tottenham. There was so much on victory. Nothing left for Newcastle if it ended badly.

And then Ferguson flicked a ball from Gary Speed into the Tottenham penalty area. Speed kept running and Sol Campbell inexplicably put his hand in the air and touched the ball. His head was in both hands for 30 seconds after he did it. A penalty, in the 109th minute of an FA Cup semi-final, to be taken by the man the manager wanted out of the club.

Only at Newcastle United.

It would be at the Stretford End, where Shearer had slain Sheffield United 12 months earlier.

You were nervous now. You were willing a goal. *Just a goal Alan. Score. Please score.* That feeling never goes. Desperation and desire.

Gullit had the pendant of his chain in his mouth. He was edgy in the Newcastle dugout.

Allan Neilsen went back into the Tottenham penalty area to unsettle Shearer. Paul Durkin ushered him away.

Shearer strode forward and stroked a penalty that could have been hit on the training ground with a junior goalkeeper. It was so assured. Ian Walker went the wrong way. The ball was towards the side of the goal where more Newcastle fans were stood, expectantly. They saw it strike gold first.

Shearer wheeled away, fist in the air. He punched in triumph. Rob Lee was first to reach him and he grabbed his mate. Gullit clenched both of his fists in delight. He still chewed his chain. Shearer took the acclaim of his team-mates and then raised both fists in triumph.

And then Tyneside's version of Que Sara filled Manchester. I won't be home for tea. And then 'Ruud Hool Etts' black and white army, once more. And of course, the Blaydon Races. Oh me lads. Newcastle United were ganning. Nielsen missed a chance for an equaliser from a Ferdinand lay-off. Chris Armstrong did too.

With two minutes to go it was still 1–0. Flags were raised, the black and white chequered grand prix ones that signal a race is done. It was not then, but it would be, in the final minute, the 119th, when Lee played a one two with Ferguson, charged through the heart of midfield, fed Shearer to his left, who cut inside, played it to Warren Barton, got it back, gave to and received the ball from Silvio Maric then, from 25 yards, on the angle, crashed a right-footed shot into the far corner of the Tottenham goal.

It was over then. Gullit hugged [John] Carver and Ray Thompson on the sidelines.

Shearer ran to the black and white explosion, towards the roar. He was mobbed. By team mates and fans leaning over the front of the advertising hoarding. It was not quite Keegan's debut, but there were parallels. He kissed the Newcastle badge and waved at the support. The chant of 'Shearer' went up. It could have been 'Keegan', as it was that balmy day almost 27 years earlier.

The whistle went.

Shearer, his shirt, for once, hanging out, led the charge to the North Stand, wildly waving his fists. Again he hugged Rob Lee first. Shearer grabbed Warren Barton, Shay Given and then Gary Speed. Proper players. A proper celebration. One half of the ground emptying rapidly. The other never wanting the moment to end.

And then a walk, and a pub, and a train, and laughs and smiles and jokes and songs and life being fucking brilliant with people you thought the world of.

You floated back to Tyneside, all of you. United. That feeling. Keegan's debut, his goal, Shearer's goal, a child who queued just like you did and watched and then did it, at Old Trafford, in the semi-final of the FA Cup.

Living everyone with a black and white heartbeat's dream.

The hangover lasted for six weeks. There would not be another victory in the league, but Wembley was coming, a year older, a year wiser, less novel, more ready for business, to end the trophyless years.

LEE CLARK –
TRUE COLOURS

'WHATEVER YOU DO, DON'T WEAR ANY FUCKING COLOURS.' THEY were Peter Reid's final words to Lee Clark before Newcastle played Manchester United in the 1999 FA Cup final.

Clark was a key figure in Reid's Sunderland side, who had just gained promotion to the Premier League. In two seasons, from central midfield, he had scored 16 goals.

Before that, from the age of 10, he was with Newcastle United. He lived in Pottery Bank, in the east end of the city. His dad was a Newcastle fan. His family were Newcastle fans. So were his mates.

He was the rising star of English football as a schoolboy. Tottenham and Manchester United came to his front door. They were turned down. He saw Kevin Keegan's debut for Newcastle in 1982 against Queens Park Rangers, on the terraces. He watched Peter Beardsley score a hat-trick against Sunderland in a derby at St James' Park.

He won promotion with Newcastle in 1993 then made a space on his mantlepiece for the Premiership winners' medal that did not come with The Entertainers in 1996.

He was as black and white as you could get, and then in 1997, Lee Clark signed for Sunderland.

'I walked into the dressing room at the training ground and David Kelly was there,' said Clark.

'Going across to your biggest rivals, it was like the first day at school. It was a huge move. The opening gambit to break the ice was from Ned [Kelly]. He went, "Bloody hell, you must be getting paid a few quid to come over here!" The lads started laughing.

'Peter [Reid] designed the old training ground so it was one huge dressing room. We were all there together. The banter was relentless; Alex Rae taking the mickey out of [Niall] Quinny's dress sense. Michael Bridges getting it off Micky Gray. The black and whites versus the red and whites stuff. It brought the players together.

'I was playing with lads who were staunch red and whiters. Michael Gray and Kevin Ball, cut them open and they bleed red and white. When Kevin came to Fulham we shared a flat together. Before I went to Sunderland I never thought that was possible. Before I went to Sunderland I was usually on the end of one of his tackles. It is a friendship that you never think will happen.'

And then, after two great seasons under Reid – interrupted only by a broken leg at the start of his second campaign – Lee Clark went to watch Newcastle play in the 1999 FA Cup final.

'He knew what I thought,' added Clark. 'I was black and white. I made the move across the water and he knew there was a second Cup final I was going to. "Don't wear any fucking colours," he said again when I saw him.

'He always spoke really highly when he went across to St James' to watch games. It never went over the top. He got bait in the opposing dugouts. He went to watch an under-21 game there and popped into The Black Bull. The fans thought it was great that the Sunderland manager could go into a staunch black and whiter bar. He used to phone me on a Monday morning to ask what had been sang abut him on the terraces.

'He's a typical footballer who was brought up working class from Merseyside who ended up having a fantastic managerial career. I don't think he was appreciated at Sunderland. They'd snap your hands off for the success he achieved. Two seventh places with exciting players.

'I always felt if I played in that fixture for Sunderland, against Newcastle, it wouldn't feel right for me. I couldn't have given 100 per cent and that would have been wrong.

'I don't think any fan can have a go at any player who gives their best, even if they don't play well. As long as they're doing their best and give everything they they've got, fans can't ask for more. Players are human beings. They can't always be at their best.

'The players always used to have time to address the fans, in the supermarkets, in the fish and chip shop, in the pubs, in the streets, we had a players' lounge at Newcastle and you had family and friends and other players' friend and they were staunch Newcastle fans and you got this relationships going.

'New players who arrived at the club had to be good enough. In the North East it is more important than a London club say, you have to have a couple of local lads who know what it mean.'

It still meant something to Clark, in 1999. He was playing for Sunderland. He was supporting Newcastle. Then he went for a pint.

'We jumped out of a black cab at Baker Street and there was a Geordie who owned a pub,' Clark added.

'As I got out it was very jovial and the T-shirt, (which bore the words 'Sad Mackem Bastard') got whipped over my head. I actually had a cricket hat on and it came over the cricket hat. The cameras went for fun. People got wind of it and then it hit the media.

'Of course it was a difficult time. There was a lot of hatred towards me and rightly so. I don't blame the fans for that. I disrespected people who were paying my wages. They had to find a new entrance for me to go into training.

'We had to deal with the situation as best we could. Peter was adamant I wasn't leaving the club but it couldn't happen. I knew deep down I couldn't stay. The club made a decision I was going.

'After we had won the title I went to see the manager and said it's time to move on because I knew I would have to come up against Newcastle in the Premier League and I couldn't do it, not for Sunderland against Newcastle. The fans should always have players who give 100 per cent and I couldn't do that. People might think it (the T-shirt) was premeditated, but it wasn't.

'Being older and being a manager myself now, the incident is something I look back on and it is tinged with regret. It's difficult to go across to Sunderland to watch a game because of that, and that's sad because for two years I played some good football there.'

Reid fought to keep him. Bob Murray, the Sunderland chairman, was adamant he would not wear the red and white of Sunderland again.

STEVE HARPER –
EVERYBODY HURTS

'IT'S MY EIGHTH START, JUST MY EIGHTH START FOR NEWCASTLE, AND *it's an FA Cup final!*

'*Twelve months earlier I'm on loan at Huddersfield and I'm in the crowd for the semi-final against Sheffield United, in the main stand at Man United, and it was moving. It was bouncing. Incredible.*

'*I was cup tied in '98 so I travelled down as a fan, lived the disappointment of being a fan, watched a team, yes underperform, but also be unfortunate to face a team that was completing the double.*

'*This time on the run to Wembley I played in the third round and I had a good game at Tottenham, but I didn't play in any of the other ties.*

'*We'd trained at Northumbria Police headquarters in the week.*

'*We did a lot of work countering Sheringham playing in the hole, how he'd affect that. He didn't even start.*

'*I'd played in the last four or five games in the league but it was still undecided who was playing in goal. Me or Shay. It was up in the air. We hadn't had confirmation.*

'*Then I get picked. I'm playing. It's my eighth start.*

'*I only found out in the morning.*

'*I've always been the sort of person who doesn't like indecision.*

'*When I don't know what's happening, I don't cope as well.*

'*It would have helped to know.*

'*He put the team up. That's how I found out.*

'*I'm in and I'm delighted.*

'In the dressing room, Ruud speaks, we're going to be heros, he said. Just a pronunciation. We wanted to be heroes.

'You feel pride walking out, even more so when it's a place not far from home.

'I'm 24. This is special. I look up at Schmeichel, bloody hell, look at the size of him, he's one of the best of all time.

'Here's little me, from Easington. I've only been playing in goal for seven years.

'He's a legend.

'We start all right, and then Sheringham comes on, plays a one-two through the middle, past my centre-halves and I spread myself, like Schemeichel, and Charvet's just got the sole of his boot on it and it flicked and it's gone through my legs.

'This happened to Shay.

'The game passes me by. It did for most of the lads.

'It's 2–0 again. I'll say that to Shay. We lost 2–0 two years running and the first goal went through both our legs.

'Like Shay I played in a team which underperformed, up against a better team that did the double and more and was the best team in Europe.

'The final whistle goes. Just devastation, the flatness on the pitch.

'The dressing room is flat.

'The bus after is so flat. This is the second year running.

'Looking out the window I know how you feel. I was there 12 months before.

'I know how long a journey home it is.

'All I can see is black and white. It's unbelievable.

'And then the dinner at night. Gullit making a speech. "It's new to me," he says. "I'm not used to failure and losing."

'That's not what the lads want to hear.

'Forget it. We want to forget it.

'My family is here, the players' wives and partners are here.

'My cousin is a massive Newcastle fan and he's here and he's devastated.

'My dad was a miner in the North East.

'If you're from the area and you win the Cup final you never buy a drink in Newcastle again.

'It would have been life changing.

'The bus home and then the civic reception and it's all subdued.

'It's fitting to say thank you for the fantastic support, but it shouldn't have happened, there shouldn't have been a bus.

'We didn't win.'

RUUD GULLIT – WHY DOES IT ALWAYS RAIN ON ME

THE CUP LOSS HURT AND THE BACKDROP TO ANOTHER SUMMER OF spending – Kieron Dyer, Alain Goma, Marcelino, John Karelse and Franck Dumas arriving at St James' Park for more than £18 million – was played against the discord of a seriously unhappy dressing room.

Gullit had given new deals to local youngsters, players like Jamie McClen, who would go on to play for the club 14 times in seven seasons.

Shepherd meanwhile gave a new contract to another player, Alan Shearer. As Gullit continued his moves to oust the man he had given the captain's armband to, the chairman gave him a five-year deal.

It did not help matters either that Gullit had moved hostilities with Rob Lee to such a level that he was not even given a shirt number for the new season. Lee was told this by the club press officer and was banished to train with the reserves and, if the reserves were playing the first team, the juniors. Lee by this point was among the club's longest serving players.

Gullit actually brought himself on as a substitute in pre-season friendlies against Reading and Stoke City. By the time the season started, he may have wished he was still registered. On the opening day of the season, against Aston Villa, Newcastle lost and Alan Shearer was harshly sent off. Defeat followed at Tottenham and then Southampton away. With Newcastle bottom of the Premier League it was left to Steve Clarke, Gullit's former teammate and then player from Chelsea, to front the media, in a tiny room. He did not look the heir apparent with the manager's position now coming into question.

Newcastle raced into a 3–1 lead in their next game, against Wimbledon, at St James' Park, only for Gareth Ainsworth to score twice for the visitors, the third in the final minute. Polls in the *Evening Chronicle* showed a resounding support for Gullit, at 83 per cent.

Then, on the eve of his first Tyne-Wear derby with Sunderland, he claimed the fixture did not have the same meaning as the Milan derby because the two teams were not from the same city.

He never recovered.

It would still not be the most controversial moment of a game nobody there will ever forget. That was to come.

In training, there was a warning of what was in the wind.

'My most vivid memory was the day before in training when the bibs were given out,' said Kieron Dyer. 'The bibs were worn by players who weren't in the starting XI so they could play against the first team in the shape of the opposition.

'Duncan got his first. I thought, 'ouch' and then Alan was given one. We were all stunned, it was crazy, but the thing that struck me was how well Alan, the England captain, took being dropped for the biggest game of the season. He's a local lad. He didn't show a thing. Most players would have exploded. He trained superbly. Duncan and Alan battered us in the game, even though they were in the reserves.

'I could also see it from Ruud's point of view. He was the manager, his neck was on the block and he knew Alan didn't like him. He didn't trust him. Alan always gave 100 per cent when he played for Newcastle, he did in that training session, but you can see why Ruud made the decision he did.'

After training, he told John Carver, by then the first team coach, what he intended to do.

'We were at the old training ground at Durham Cricket Club, and I was in the room with Steve Clarke and Ruud,' said Carver.

'All of a sudden, he started talking about what the team was going to be against Sunderland. I said, "Sorry Ruud, what did you say there?" He said he was going to leave out Alan and Duncan, and this was going to be the team.

'I said, "Do you know how important this game is?"

'He used to call everyone "lovely boy", and his exact words were "lovely boy, I have played in some massive derbies. I've played in them in Holland, London derbies, and I played in the Milan derby too".

'I said, "Yeah, but do you actually know what this means?"

'He said, "I've already told you, I've played in massive derbies".

'I went, "Yeah, but you haven't played in one like this Ruud". I turned to Steve Clarke and said, "He hasn't been involved in a game like this, I'm telling you now".

'Then we just walked out of the room. I continued the conversation with Steve, because he half understood where I was coming from because of the relationship we had, but I don't think Ruud did. He just seemed set on the fact that was what he was going to do, and that was the team he was going to put on the pitch.

'I talked about it being a motivation for the opposition. Reidy was the manager at the time, so I said it will be a motivation for Peter when he sees that Alan Shearer and Duncan Ferguson are not on the team sheet, but he had no concerns whatsoever.

'I actually thought if we don't win it, he's gone.'

By six o'clock a team sheet had been pinned to the wall in the home dressing room at St James' Park.

Alan Shearer, the Newcastle captain, born in Gosforth, who stood on the Gallowgate End as a child, who turned down Manchester United to come home, whose family and friends lived in the area, looked and could not see his name. It was the first he knew of it (playing for the second team in training had seemed to him a test that he had emphatically passed). There could not have been a more brutal act from Gullit.

'I found out an hour-and-a-half before kick off on the board in the dressing room,' said Shearer. 'I was captain at the time and he didn't even tell me I was left out of the team, which I thought was disrespectful.

'I was having rows with Gullit, he didn't want me at Newcastle and he made that plain for me.'

About then, the football gods of Tyneside showed Ruud Gullit what they thought of the decision.

It rained, and it rained, and when you thought it was impossible to be any more wet, it rained some more.

The Leazes End and the Milburn Stand were still without a roof. There was no hiding place.

Paul Robinson, the man to replace Alan Shearer, was a 20-year-old Sunderland fan; a former Sunderland season ticket holder. He knew before Shearer.

'I was in training on the Monday and still had my bib on when I was called to one side and told I'd be starting against Sunderland,' he said.

'I just remember phoning my dad and him saying, "I'm happy for you, just don't score". It was quite a strange feeling. To think that I was keeping an absolute legend and England centre-forward out of the team, along with Big Dunc, was surreal.

'However, they both shook my hand and wished me the best. There was no nastiness at all from them.'

Gullit was in meltdown. Having paid £800,000 for the Dutch goalkeeper, John Karelse, he dropped him for the 36-year-old Tommy Wright, who had left Newcastle six years earlier and returned on loan as cover from Manchester City.

Sunderland should have taken an early lead, Quinn sliding in at the far post at the Gallowgate End to narrowly stab a Kevin Phillips cross wide. There were only 850 supporters from Wearside in the ground. You did not hear them then; instead, the name of Shearer tumbled down from the stands in the immediate aftermath of the opportunity.

Then Newcastle scored, a fine move involving Nolberto Solano, Maric, Robinson and then Dyer, dinking the ball over Thomas Sorensen, in front of the sodden masses at the Leazes End.

The rain still fell.

The home fans stayed with their team, their Shearerless team.

Another chance came for Quinn, from a Nicky Summerbee cross. That should have been a warning.

Gullit replaced Robinson with Ferguson. The Sunderland fan was applauded off.

The weather got worse. You got more wet. Everything was wet. All your clothes, all the fans, the pitch was flooding, water dripped through the stands. It was the Toon in a monsoon. This relentless rain, getting heavier and heavier. It was the eye of the storm by now. The plastic raincoats had washed away, some people were taking shirts off. Clothing had become pointless. The rain would not relent. Your face dripped. Mini waterfalls cascaded down the stairways.

The balls started slowing on the turf. It had to. It was flooding.

Solano gave away a free-kick, Summerbee struck it low and Niall Quinn, with a glancing header, into the ground, equalised. A tiny pocket of the ground celebrated. The cry for Shearer rose again. Then he emerged, replacing Maric. Momentum was against him, and his team by now. The ball was starting to stop. It needed air. That suited Sunderland. Shearer took the ball on the touchline. Kevin Ball went in with two feet. Graham Poll waved play on. The ball broke and was crossed to Philips, who was all alone eight yards from goal, Wright blocked the first effort with his body, Barton ran to the goal-line, Wright readied himself for the shot, but it was a chip, and it went over both men.

There were 15 minutes remaining, 15 minutes for Gullit to save himself. Solano curled one narrowly wide from a great position. At the death, Kevin Ball challenged Ferguson and the ball ricocheted, clipping his own crossbar from 30 yards.

It was not meant to go in. Newcastle were not meant to get anything from this game. There will not be another game with such an apocalyptic feel. They had not lost at home to Sunderland in a league game since 1979.

Roads flooded all around Tyneside. You could not get home. You could not escape. Newcastle United were marooned. Marooned in water. Marooned in misery.

In the Newcastle boardroom Bob Murray, the visiting chairman, paraded in a Sunderland strip, having ditched his wet clothes.

Gullit was unrepentant.

'No one complained when we were 1–0 up,' he said after the defeat. 'I didn't gamble. It paid off. Robinson played very well.

'I'm always considering my future. I am still the coach of Newcastle. You are suggesting I have no heart. I am putting everything I have in. We put the two substitutions on and we lost the game.

'When we put him [Shearer] on in the second half we lost. What conclusion do you draw from that? You saw what happened when Shearer and Ferguson went on. That's when the game slipped away from us, so make of that what you will.'

Both men fumed.

The following morning, Gullit had to face the anger.

Ferguson almost knocked the door to his office of its hinges.

'It was crazy, just stupid, to leave Alan out of that game,' said Ferguson. 'He didn't win but then he had the cheek to tell the media Newcastle were winning before he sent on Alan and me – the inference being that if he hadn't made those substitutions we might well have won.

'I wasn't having that and I stormed into the manager's office the next morning to let him know he was bang out of order. The door was still just about on its hinges when I came out – and Alan Shearer was the next man in. To play anybody instead of Alan in any game is just silly. It just showed he had lost the plot.

'It was adding insult to injury, it was really was a disgrace. I wasn't even fit at the time and the manager knew it. It was obvious he was trying to make a point about Alan but if you make a decision like that, to leave out Alan Shearer against your biggest rivals from down the road, then you've got to win the game if you want to keep your job.'

Shearer was next in.

'I got my kids up nice and early, dropped them at school half an hour early so I could be first in the office,' he said. 'I get to the training ground, still raging, and I burst into the office to have a word with him and Big Dunc is already there tearing the wallpaper off the walls because he had also left him out also. So he beat me to it!'

But still, in an interview with *FourFourTwo* magazine in 2006, Gullit refused to accept he had made a mistake that night.

'I still think I made the right decision,' he said. 'Look at the way things have developed. It's still the same situation. I spoke to fans on the radio recently and asked if it had improved since I left. They said no, so maybe I was right.

'The coaches since me have tried to do the same thing and they couldn't, because he [Shearer] is so beloved there. That's why I thought, "I cannot change this, it's better for me to go." I'm sitting here now, and I know I was right. It was six or seven years ago, and nothing has changed. Nobody can prove that I was wrong.

'It just hadn't worked. You can't be successful all the time. I wanted to leave. I loved the people there and the fans. But the press felt, "Oh, you're that boy from the city – so you're going to have to tell us what to know, city boy." Like I say, I know what it takes to win things. You have to get also players who know how to do that.'

There weren't enough of those sorts of players there? he was asked.

'Like I said, I know exactly what it is to win.

'As everybody knows, I don't think that Alan did his best when I was coach here. Therefore, if he didn't play well, then I had to substitute him.

'The problem was that he had too much power. In the end, it became a battle I could never win. He was England's favourite, England's captain and he was playing for his hometown team.

'All of that meant he was bigger than the club itself. I told him to his face, "You are the most overrated player I have ever seen", but he didn't reply. Maybe that's why they call him Mary Poppins, because he is so innocent, but I know how powerful and ruthless he can be.'

Alan Shearer had scored 87 goals for Newcastle United when Ruud Gullit left St James' Park.

'If Ruud had stayed at Newcastle then I would have had to leave,' said Shearer.

It was a different emotion after Gullit's departure.

'There were tears of joy when he went,' said Rob Lee.

'What was his biggest problem? Ego. His coaching was decent. The lads quite enjoyed it. He had good ideas, different ideas which the lads like but his ego was huge.

'He was bigger than anybody at the club. It was as if he was the top player. You'd think, "Ruud, you're not playing any more. It's your job to make the players that are here better."

'He didn't seem to want that. All he kept talking about was Chelsea and Milan, everything he'd done in his career. You'd think, "That's over now. You're manager of Newcastle. You should be helping players here."

'From the word go he wanted Alan out. There was no question about that. He saw him as a huge threat. I was captain at the time and Alan's best pal and I was used. Even the captaincy became an issue. He offered it to Alan and said, "If you don't take it I'll offer it to someone else."

'It never came up before because he left me out. I was still captain when I played but I hadn't played all season and then he had to bring me back against Everton because he had no players.

'The whole cup run he had no players. Even when I was playing I played well, he still didn't want to pick me for the Cup final.

'He was playing me out of position on the wing. He was desperate not to play me in the Cup final. He got me back for Everton, the team sheet was there and it had captain next to Alan.

'I wasn't expecting that. He said to Alan, "If you don't take it, I'll offer it to someone else." I think he wanted him to turn it down so he could make a rift. Alan spoke to me, he said, "If there's a problem I'll turn it down."

'I said, "No problem, I'd rather you had it than anyone else." He would say in training to the defender marking Alan, "Keep him on his left foot, he can't shoot with his left foot." That was his top striker he was talking about. He did it after Alan had turned a defender and scored with his right foot in training.

'The next time the ball came to Al, he turned the defender the other way and smashed it in with his left foot.

'He used to play the foreigners against the English in training. He used to say you'll never win anything with the English. He had stopped me and Stuart Pearce training with the first team. Before the game, Pearcey said, "Lay one between us," so I did, and he smashed him all over the place when he tackled him.

'What annoyed me was he never once confronted me. He got the press officer to tell me I didn't have a shirt. He didn't come up to me, he never said a word.

'He got Steve Clarke to tell me I wouldn't be training with the first team anymore and that Wolves were interested in me. The only time I spoke to him was in his first season and he said, "I don't want to play you in all the games."

'I was playing for England at the time. I said, "That's not a problem if I'm playing badly." He said, "I want to keep your legs for the big games."

'I said, "I'm playing for England, you're going to kill my career." It's not like it is now. If you didn't play for your club, you didn't play.

'By the end the club was in disarray. There were two different camps inside the dressing room, the fans were up in arms.

'Would Newcastle have got relegated if Ruud Gullit had stayed? Without a doubt.'

Gullit did not stay. On Friday morning following the derby defeat, he handed Shepherd his resignation. There would be no compensation, as Shepherd would reveal, no messy splits. There was even a resignation press conference and statement.

'I want to notify everyone in this room that I resigned from Newcastle United,' he said. 'The reason for my resignation is partly for the bad results we have had in the last couple of weeks but the biggest reason is something that I am going to explain to you now.

'I am as disappointed by the results as any other person who loves Newcastle United and therefore I take full responsibility for the bad results. The fans' expectations have not been fulfilled and therefore I would like to apologise to them.

'I know there are still a lot of people who want me to stay and there are a lot of people who want me to go but I think that the moment has come to resign.

'The main reason why I came to England four years ago was that I wanted to have my own private life back.

'The feeling of walking along the street minding my own business, being able to shop, being able to go to the cinema, being able to go out, being able to be like anyone else.

'The moment I came to Newcastle the journalists asked me if I understood how big the job was and I thought I knew, now I know what they really meant by that.

'In this last year my private life has been invaded in a bad way. During the last year I have had reporters, photographers constantly around my home in Newcastle, people following me where I go to eat, go out, go to the cinema.

'The moment I came to Newcastle the journalists asked me if I understood how big the job was and I thought I knew, now I know what they really meant by that.'

In truth, Gullit never really got Newcastle United.

It was time to find someone who did.

SIR BOBBY ROBSON
– WHY AYE MAN

'I HAVE NOT BEEN APPROACHED BY NEWCASTLE, AND NEITHER HAVE I spoken to them,' said Bobby Robson on the morning of Monday, 30 August.

But then came the pay off.

'That's the truth but I'm free as a bird and I didn't come home to England to retire. I am looking for the right ball to bounce. This is the right ball. It's the sort of job I want.

'I turned the job down two years ago because I couldn't take it. It was the right job at the wrong time for me then, but it's always been the right job for me. I'm a Geordie, a Durham boy, and I bleed black and white. I have got no contracts with anybody else that would prevent me taking it; as far as I'm concerned it's the right job at the right time.'

That alone had Robson in pole position, as names like Glenn Hoddle, Terry Venables and Ray Hartford were mentioned. Robson was everyone's favourite.

Kevin Keegan, by then the manager of England, backed Robson.

'I think the whole idea of getting stability to the club will help all the players, not least Alan Shearer,' he said. 'I think the people want someone to relate to as well. He's a Geordie and there are less and less Geordie players at Newcastle.'

That was early in the day.

By team-time the situation had become far more perilous and pending. Newcastle had lost 5–1 at Manchester United. Nikos Dabizas had been sent off and Andy Cole, the former Newcastle forward sold by Keegan, had scored four.

Steve Clarke was in charge for the game. He recalled Rob Lee and gave him the number 37 shirt (Kieron Dyer had the number 7).

'The size of the job caught myself and Ruud by surprise,' said Clarke. 'This is a very big club, the focus of everything in the North East. It takes a certain type of person to handle the job. Football is people's life here.'

Life was not good. Newcastle were nineteenth of the 20 Premiership teams. Played six, won none, lost five, points one. The goal difference was already at minus 10.

Alex Ferguson said it could be turned round, but there was a warning. 'Every club has bad periods but Newcastle can get over it,' he said. 'They've got some good players but they need to get out of the limelight. They have been on the front and back pages for the past few weeks and they need to get back to playing.'

That was on Monday.

By Wednesday contact had been made with Robson, who by that stage was aged 66, and Freddy Shepherd and Freddie Fletcher flew to London to meet him. It had been 30 months since he was first interviewed for the position. This time there was nothing to stop the appointment. It felt right. The Newcastle board was acting on thought, not just whims.

The next day, Newcastle released a statement from Fletcher.

'Newcastle United can confirm that a meeting was held between Bobby Robson and the club in London yesterday [Wednesday]. A press conference has been scheduled for tomorrow morning at 10.00.'

It would be Robson's first position with an English club for 17 years, since he had left Ipswich to take over England. He played for Fulham and West Brom and won 20 caps for England. As a manager there was a brief spell at Fulham, before he transformed Ipswich Town into one of English football's best teams during the 1970s and early-1980s, leading them to the FA and UEFA Cup wins. He became England manager in 1982.

After England, and the agony of a failed penalty shoot out in the semi-final of the World Cup in 1990, he moved to PSV, Sporting Lisbon, Porto and then, to Barcelona, where he had won the Cup Winners' Cup. There was another spell at PSV, and then finally, Bobby Robson was the manager of Newcastle United.

By nine o'clock, on Friday morning, Bobby Robson was on his way to St James' Park. A group of supporters had gathered outside of the stadium but it was not the grandiose displays that had accompanied the unveiling of Shearer or Gullit.

In Harvey's restaurant, which separated the Gallowgate End and the Milburn Stand, there was the usual jostling for space, cameras were put in position and then a man in a dark grey blazer, his hair white, his chest out, walked to the head table.

Robson had fought cancer three times by then. It did not show. He had the glow of a man 20 years his junior.

One of the first questions came from a female reporter, and it was laced with the controversy that had unfolded in Marbella.

'Those in charge of the club have said the region's women are dogs,' she said. Robson did not even stutter in his response.

'If they are all as lovely as you are my dear,' he said, 'then we shall be fine.'

That issue was closed.

He spoke about his father's love for Newcastle United. He spoke about why the club mattered. More than anything he made sense.

Robson had ben born in Sacriston, in County Durham, but moved to Langley Park when he was young. He had four brothers. His father, Philip, was a miner. He grew up with an outside toilet.

He played for Langley Park Juniors and went to Waterhouses Secondary Modern School. He worked as an electrician's apprentice for the coal board. There were approaches from Middlesbrough, Newcastle and Fulham to sign a professional contract. He chose Fulham. Some 49 years later, he was finally back in the North East.

'I have got a massive job ahead of me,' he said. 'It's a great challenge and I am up for it. There is no need for panic here. I thought Barcelona was a big club but I think this has just pipped it.

'As you can see its a lovely day so its a great day for me to be announced as the new manager of Newcastle United Football Club. I'm very proud of that, I'm very honoured about that. I'm absolutely thrilled. I realise I have a massive job ahead of me. It's a great challenge. I'm up for it. I don't underestimate it. I'm not afraid of it. I'm going to really enjoy working in the North East again. We have to bring about a set of results the fans and the board deserve.

'It didn't sadden me I couldn't come here two-and-a-half years ago. It was unavoidable. It was for me the right club at the wrong time. I was under contact at Barcelona. I'd just got there and I had to fulfil my contract. There was no way I could get out of it.

'I was born and bred here. I played my early football here. I maybe should have signed as a boy at 17 but didn't. I used to come and watch the team play, Shackleton and Stubbins and Milburn and Joe Harvey and Cowell and Fairbother, those guys were my heroes.

'The public are aware I'm one of them. I came here with my father; first in the ground at 12 o'clock outside waiting for the gates to open. It's always been my love. It's always been the first club I've looked for wherever I've been. How have United got on? I've never lost my devotion to it. I'm just thrilled to be back.'

There came the obligatory photos with the fans who wait so patiently at these events.

Lots of lads and a few lasses and all with smiling faces. His car was mobbed as he drove out of the car park at St James' Park, heading down onto Barrack Road.

By half past 12, Robson was where he was always happiest, out on the training pitch, in an Adidas Newcastle tracksuit, Copa Mundials on, BR on his sweatshirt, ready for business.

Robson called the entire squad into the centre circle. Everyone sat down and Robson started talking. He was taking control. He told everyone to stand up and follow him. He walked to the touchline and picked up a football. Then he called Gary Speed out of the group. 'Stand 10 feet away from me Gary,' he said.

Speed went and stood 10 feet away from his new manager.

Robson put the ball behind his head and took a throw-in. The ball went into Speed's midriff. He cushioned the ball and then passed it back to Robson.

Robson picked the ball up.

He told Speed to stay 10 feet away.

He picked the ball up again, put it behind his head and threw the ball, once more, at Speed. This time it was to the midfielder's feet. Speed half volleyed the ball back to Robson.

'Which throw-in gets us playing quicker?' Robson asked his players.

'The second one,' they said.

'Good. Right, everyone over here.'

Robson walked over to the six-yard box. 'This is how we're going to do goal-kicks.'

It was all so simple.

By the end of the session Newcastle had worked on throw-ins, goal-kicks, corners, free-kicks and kick-offs.

The players, the press and the public, all done in one day.

'Aah, Bobby, where do you start?' pondered Steve Harper.

'He always wanted three options at throw-ins, somebody forward, somebody square, somebody back. He was obsessed with them. At the time you could see people thinking, this is tedious but he would say, "It's a set piece, it's an opportunity to regain possession."

'If we ever lost possession from a throw-in we knew about it, it was real bugbear of his and he loved video analysis.

'If you did something wrong in a game on a Saturday, you knew you'd have to sit through it with the team on Monday morning.

'You got over it as well. Bobby was brilliant.

'He is the only manager in my time at the club that in his first couple of days there was a schedule went up and he had 10 minutes with every player.

'It was, "How are you son? Can you play for me? It's a big club, will you be okay with that?" This, that and the other. He just probed, in his way, for ten minutes and when you left the office he probably had a box; needs a cuddle, needs an arm around his shoulder or needs a kick up the arse or needs a bit of both.

'He found out in the first few days. he didn't wait six weeks, or a couple of months or six months even to find out about you as a person. He did it in the first week. He's the only man who ever did that and I think it was vitally important.

'That really set the stage and his man management was brilliant.'

His first game was away at Chelsea, an awful opening fixture. The night before the game Robson went to Alan Shearer's hotel room and the pair talked for hours. Bridges were built, damage was repaired. The next day, Newcastle were unlucky to lose one-nil.

For his home bow, Newcastle faced Sheffield Wednesday at St James' Park. By half-time Newcastle were four-nil up.

It finished eight-nil. It was a remarkable afternoon. Shearer scored five times. His fifth, like his second, was a penalty. Paul Robinson asked if he could take it because Shearer had scored four. Shearer told him to get lost.

Hierarchical structures were being put back in place.

JOHN CARVER –
YOU GOT THE LOVE

'I FIRST MET BOBBY WHEN HE ARRIVED TO REPLACE RUUD GULLIT AS *manager at Newcastle United.*

'At any club when a manager leaves and a new one comes in, it's always a very unsettling time for all the staff.

'You have no idea what to expect. Will the new man like me or get rid of me? What kind of a manager will he be? Will he consult the staff before making decisions? Will he be a dictator and go it alone? You think all of that.

'We were getting a manager who's managed some of the biggest players in the world, who managed his country with distinction, who won trophies at Barcelona, one of the biggest clubs in the world.

'To say I was a little nervous about meeting him, and about my future, would be a very big understatement.

'I had a genuine fear that he would bring in his own staff and at best I would go back to the academy. He didn't know me and owed me nothing.

'How wrong I was. He greeted me with a warm smile and a firm handshake and offered me a cup of tea. We talked for two hours about me, my family, the players, the fans, and the history of the club.

'He never once talked about his achievements as a player or manager with England, Ipswich, PSV, and Barcelona. Instead, he talked about growing up in Langley Park, his wife Elsie, his kids and most of all he talked about his lifelong affection for Newcastle United, football in general, and the people in the region.

'The time passed in the blink of an eye and I could have stayed with him the whole day.

I left the room floating on air.

'He made me determined I would do all I could to help him bring success to the football club.

'Whatever he had about him, I wish we could bottle it and let everyone have the privilege of that moment I shared with him back then. It is something I cherish and will never forget.

'I'd gone from apprehension and fear, to determination and belief in less than two hours. I haven't met anyone in life, or football, before or since, who has had such a profound effect.

'The amazing thing about him was that he did that with everyone else at the club as well.'

ROB LEE – HALLELUJAH

NEWCASTLE WERE STILL, HOWEVER, NINETEENTH. THEY LOST AT Leeds, beat Middlesbrough and were hammered at Coventry. There was still much to be done. Then came three wins and three draws in the next six games and Newcastle were fourteenth.

Everybody breathed out.

The season still needed a hook, another story other than Ruud and the rain. At White Hart Lane on 12 December, Gary Speed scored with 13 minutes remaining against the Premiership's seventh-placed team to earn a deserved draw in the third round of the FA Cup, which was staged in December that year in an attempt to ease fixture congestion. In the replay at St James' Park 10 days later, Newcastle smashed Spurs for six. Tottenham's reply, a consolation, came from David Ginola.

It seemed implausible that for the third successive season, and from the ashes of Gullit's reign, where Alan Shearer had nearly left, that another run to Wembley would unfold. Shearer scored twice in the replay against Spurs, and in the fourth round, on 8 January, he managed another, in a comfortable win against Sheffield United.

The league form fluctuated, a 5–0 win against Southampton followed by a 2–0 defeat at Wimbledon, but the Cup remained steady and dramatic. The Darwen End at Ewood Park was full to its 8,000 capacity once again with travelling supporters at the end of January. The stadium was full. Shearer was jeered. In the 21st minute Steve Harper launched a clearance, Duncan Ferguson flicked on and Newcastle's number nine opened the scoring and changed his celebration. This time he pointed his right finger at the badge on his strip and the left finger into the air. It was not quite lift off. Not yet anyway. Within four minutes Matt Jansen, a Newcastle fan who had started his career at Carlisle, equalised.

When an away end is full, when the quarter-final of the FA Cup is a step away, you want the magic in front of you. Didier Domi just kept running down the Newcastle left, the roar grew with each stride and then he hit the perfect low, drilled cross into the Blackburn six-yard area. You could see the ball and the low cross, and then you could see Shearer arriving and he smashed it into the goal and slid on his chest in celebration. The away end went berserk. People fell over seats. Shirts were taken off and waved in the air, in triumph. Black and white was the colour of celebration.

Afterwards, Shearer, who had scored 112 Premier League goals in 138 league games at Ewood Park and led the team to their first domestic title in 81 years, finally bit.

'I've taken a lot of abuse here for what reason I don't know after the service I gave them,' he said. 'I waited a long time and those goals are a bit special. I said if we go through this round we can talk about Wembley.'

There was a draw in the first ever derby at the Stadium of Light, back in the league, on 5 February, 2000. Domi, a Newcastle player, scored the first ever goal in the fixture at the new stadium. The on-loan Portuguese defender Helder quickly added a second but a Kevin Phillips brace, the second late, meant it finished 2–2. Shearer scored twice himself in the next game, a memorable 3–0 win against Manchester United that took Newcastle to thirteenth.

Then came the cup, at Tranmere, on a Sunday, and in front of the television cameras, Newcastle held on, just, to win 3–2, and book a third trip to Wembley, where the FA Cup semi-finals were now staged. After Arsenal and Manchester United it was Chelsea. The easy ride never came. In the other semi-final it was Aston Villa and Sam Allardyce's Bolton. Beat Chelsea and the final would be a breeze compared to what had gone before in the previous two seasons, when the visiting dressing room at Wembley housed two of the greatest sides English football had seen in the modern era.

The form going to Wembley was good, four wins from six games, eleventh in the table, the threat of relegation long since forgotten.

Newcastle's fans were in the same tunnel end, if anything more boisterous. Everyone there had seen Newcastle win semi-finals. It gave you confidence. Wembley Way felt less nervous, less novel. Taking it to Wembley didn't seem to take the magic from the day.

Chelsea's support turned up at the last minute. That's how it felt. Another home game for them. Another shot at glory for the visitors, the hordes from Tyneside.

Robson looked stately when he walked out. You could feel his pride. It wasn't a Cup final, and thankfully, Newcastle played like it wasn't. They did not freeze.

They attacked, and then they went behind, when Gustavo Poyet flicked the ball with the outside of his right foot over Shay Given's head after 17 minutes. This was familiar. Overmars 23 minutes. Sheringham 10 minutes, and now Poyet.

Except this time it was not over. This time Newcastle found courage from the backing behind that goal. *Just a goal.* That was all we wanted. *A goal.* Before half-time, Shearer knocked a ball down and Nobby Solano shot just over the bar. That felt different.

Then, in the 66th minute, Shearer went wide, down the Newcastle right, and he toyed with Frank Leboeuf, and then he went past him, with a feint, and then he whipped over a superb, right-footed, cross. Everybody behind the goal went up with it, but none like Rob Lee, who came charging in to smash his header past Ed de Goey.

Everyone from Tyneside's heart burst with pride. You stood up, you jumped up, you fell over, you waved a fist. Christmas had come, at last. It was pandemonium in the Tunnel End, pandemonium. A lifetime's worth of celebration. Breathless.

The tunnel end of Wembley in explosion; delirium and unbridled joy inside a black and white kaleidoscope.

Robson left his seat and waved a giant fist in celebration.

'You don't realise what it meant to the fans who had been there so many times and not seen a goal until much later,' said Rob Lee, who would be given a testimonial 12 months later for absolutely sterling service to the club following his transfer from Charlton.

'It's well known Alan was the best crosser at the club, he was battering Frank Leboeuf all game and as he got the ball I knew what he'd do. I'd seen it so many times in training. He teased him in and I could see him going down the line.

'I looked around me and thought Speedo was behind, I'll get in the box, I got in the box and I wouldn't tell him but it was a great cross, Dennis Wise was tracking me and he didn't think I would go past him but I did.

'I've always been decent in the air. It's all about timing and I always tried to hit the target.

'I caught it plum and put it straight in the top corner. As soon as I hit it I knew it was in. It was so sweet. There was no way the 'keeper could get there. You know it's going in.

'I wish I had changed my celebration. It was such a momentous goal. You don't realise it at the time. You get lost in it. It only registered later.

'The fans hadn't been able to celebrate anything. Suddenly they had a goal. People come up to me now and say, 'I was there, we went mad, I was squashed,' then you realise how significant it was to everybody. When they say that you feel very proud.

'I went to run to behind the goal to the fans and then I remembered Alan had crossed it, and I gave him stick when he scored goals I set up and he ran off with his arm in the air, so I started to go to him and stopped and that's when the lads got me and that's why we celebrated by the goal.

'I would have probably gone straight to the Geordie crowd, straight up to the seats, and made it more momentous. I didn't know where to go really. Nikos Dabizas grabbed me and that was the celebration. I didn't realise the significance of it.

'You're just pleased to be back in the game. We'd scored and we'd equalised and we had momentum. We the had the chance to get to the Cup final.'

This was it. This was the game to win. To get to the final. Where just Aston Villa waited, not a giant, not the champions. Just Aston Villa, who had beaten Bolton on penalties a week earlier.

Newcastle went looking for a winner, Didier Deschamps and his waterbags clattered into Kieron Dyer, near the edge of the Chelsea penalty area. No one stopped. The ball ended on the right side of the Newcastle penalty area, where Jon Harley fired over a cross and Poyet, who had clashed with Steve Howey, jumped and looped a header over Given and into the Newcastle goal, like a knife into your side.

Three times as many shots. Five times as many corners. Half as many goals.

There was a late chance for Dyer, denied from a tight angle by De Goey.

And then the whistle went.

Robson spoke of devastation.

'This ties with the World Cup semi-final defeat because of the disappointment and because I'm from the North East,' he said. 'I will get over it but the players will find it hard. When you are young it is difficult to get over such things and hard for players.

'I have had a few of these so I am used to it, but even so it is still a huge blow. The players are a bit numb to be honest. They know they played well and didn't deserve to lose the game, they deserved to win it.

'They can take consolation from the fact they did play well, which they haven't done in their last two visits here, but it isn't really consolation when you're out of the semi-finals of the FA Cup.

'At least the players showed they are now an accomplished team. I always thought we were the better team and at 1–1 Chelsea were visibly wilting, but then they got their second goal so close to our equaliser and we couldn't come back even though their 'keeper had to make the save of the match from Kieron in the last few seconds.

'We tried to go out and play and at least we did that. I just feel sorry for the fans, they were superb and I'm heartily sick and disappointed that we haven't given them the marvellous result we nearly did.

'We've come a long way. Back in September it would have been unrealistic to even think about getting to a semi-final, never mind play the way we did against a team like Chelsea.

'Now we have to finish as high as we can in the Premiership and not let the season die.'

There were seven league games left. They didn't mean much. Newcastle finished 11th and Shearer, a player who was about to be sold at the start of the season, ended up with 30 goals. Chelsea beat Aston Villa in the Cup final. Of the three years to get to the FA Cup final, 2000 was it.

FREDDY SHEPHERD – WE'VE ONLY JUST BEGUN

'ARE YOU COMING UP AS WELL FREDDY?'

'Am I shite.'

The second major transformation of St James' Park had finished in 2000.

It had cost Newcastle's board more than £50 million and for that they had created, in their eyes, the best stadium in the country.

The all-seated capacity had grown beyond 52,000. Newcastle United had the second biggest stadium in the country and the world's biggest cantilever roof.

Shepherd had sat in his office as we talked figures, and what it all meant. It was a sign of ambition he told me. It put Newcastle on the map.

There were issues for another day, like the fact it made St James' a bit lopsided – the club could not build on the East Stand because of the listed Georgian terracing behind it. That part of the ground had remained at the same size as when it was built in 1972 (with seats replacing executive boxes) and the Gallowgate End remained at the same size as when it had been developed in 1994.

The other half of the stadium, however, was mind-blowing. Especially when you stood on the roof.

'Are you sure Freddy?'

We both had hard hats on – the redevelopment was nearing completion but work was still going on – but Shepherd, this time, was remaining grounded.

'No chance, you're on your own.'

From the roof, 150 foot high, you can see all of Tyneside. They should stick new players on it and point, 'See all those houses? Well all the people in those houses care about what you do when you put a black and white shirt on.'

At its end, you can see down onto the pitch. From up there, you could also see the sea.

Newcastle would no longer be having any size issues. The ground was huge and it felt huge.

From the back of the stadium, as pictures from the air would later confirm, it looked like half of the San Siro in Milan, with spiralling entrances to the car parks to its side, huge roofs, a monolithic addition to Tyneside's skyline.

The football club had always cast a shadow on the city below it.

Now it was impossible to ignore.

When Kevin Keegan had scored on his debut, 18 years earlier, the noise was such that you could have heard the explosion of joy from the moon. Now, if you were in space, you would be able to see where the racket was coming from.

Expense had not been spared in the decoration inside the stadium. It felt luxurious. Harvey's was a fine restaurant, there was the Bamburgh Suite, which could house 1,000 banqueting guests, and a huge kids area behind the executive boxes (of which there were now 98 in total) in the Leazes End of the stadium.

Newcastle had started the season well, and after four games and three victories against Derby, Tottenham and Coventry were top of the Premiership. It never looked like it would last. By December Newcastle were tenth after a heavy defeat at Arsenal. They beat Leeds, drew with Manchester United and lost to Spurs, and then, on 17 January, they lost an FA Cup replay at Aston Villa through a goal from Darius Vassell.

A win followed at Leeds which took the team to sixth but from there came a run of two points from seven games.

By then Newcastle were thirteenth and drifting. The season had been disappointing. Newcastle had spent £16 million under Bobby Robson on Carl Cort, Christian Bassedas, Diego Gavilan, Lomana LuaLua and Clarence Acuna. There had been injuries but that did not hide the underwhelming transfer activity. Another calm after the storm.

That was the backdrop to another afternoon with Shepherd, in a restaurant at the very centre of the new development, in the executive facilities, between the Milburn Stand and the Leazes End. It was the new heart of the club. Open the doors of those facilities and before you stretched a beautiful stadium and a life time of dreams. Empty of people, not a noise, but still filled with hope. The pitch was beautiful. A field of dreams.

You can stare at the stadium of your football club for hours if it means everything to you.

'Things would have been different if we hadn't lost that 12-point lead and the title in 1996,' said Shepherd. 'This time, though, our challenge will be different: under Keegan, there was a bit of all-fur-coat-and-no-knickers about it.

'It would be ridiculous for me to give a 68-year-old guy a two-or three-year contract because you guys would be constantly saying, "He's only got three months left, who is going to replace him?" Instead, I've given Bobby a 12-month rolling contract, which means that every morning he wakes up he's got a 12-month deal in front of him.

'I've never worried about Bobby resigning out of frustration. Sure he gets down after defeats, but then he's back out there rallying the troops.

'Dalglish and Gullit didn't come here to bugger the club, but unfortunately things didn't work out and, thankfully, Bobby has stabilised the situation. He's been unfortunate with injuries, but we've created a stable platform and the team is poised to strike back.

'If we get European qualification we can attract anybody here,' he said. 'It's difficult to attract top signings if we don't get into Europe, but we would still be well placed. Look at our manager. Who is better respected than Bobby Robson? I believe Bobby will attract top players. This is where it all takes off again.'

Then Douglas Hall turned up.

'I've hidden in the background because I got more than I could stand from the newspapers and it's taken me a while to come back,' said Hall.

'Although I've been in the shadows, it's not as if I haven't been doing anything for this club. I've been abroad looking after my business and investments in Newcastle United. The newspaper thing was unfair, but it's history now and my intention is to pass my shares on to my children.

'There is no debt at the club that is not manageable. The ground is being paid for over 17 years, so it's like a mortgage. You don't see yourself as being in debt just because you've got a mortgage.

'For the first time in a lot of years, there is cash in the bank to spend on the team and we will not let our fans down. We are ready to invest heavily in either transfer fees and/or wages to provide a winning team.

'We've invested heavily in the stadium and we've got the best ground in the country, so now for the players. Newcastle fans can look forward to an exciting time next season. Our signings won't be small, they'll be large.

'We'll make sure we compete at the highest level in the Premiership and, hopefully, in Europe. I've every confidence we can compete with anybody.

'Newcastle is better placed than most Premiership clubs and most European clubs to compete. We've had to be financially prudent over the past couple of years because bad purchases were made, but the manager has done well in selling players, the board has had a good year financially and we're ready to compete again.

'We haven't yet got as big a turnover as Manchester United, but we've possibly got a larger stockpile of cash than Manchester United because we haven't gone crazy in the transfer market over the past couple of years.

'In my opinion we're already bigger and more financially stable than the likes of Barcelona. We might not be as successful on the pitch, but we are more financially stable. Freddy Shepherd has run the club in difficult circumstances for the past three years without any credit at all.

'The most important thing is to try to win the Premiership. We'd love to qualify for Europe in May and have a good UEFA Cup run next season, but the Premiership is the priority and our ambition is that Newcastle will attract players of the highest calibre.

'My dream in the past was to see Rivaldo play here and it is that type of player we will try to get. This club should attract players of the quality of Rivaldo.'

That Newcastle's next signing was Andy O'Brien, an English central defender from Bradford City, was the usual punch line after the bold talk, but Newcastle have never been that simple.

The next victory would not come until April, against West Ham, which took Newcastle to thirteenth. There was a derby draw with Sunderland, when Andy O'Brien scored, and then a late victory against Leicester and a draw with Southampton that took Newcastle into the top 10.

Four points from the final three games ensured an eleventh placed finish. Few hearts were racing.

(A group of supporters, under the Save Our Seats title, would lose their battle with the club at the Court of Appeal in June after being moved to a different part of the redeveloped stadium, despite buying the ten year bond, the court finding small print in the contract which meant the supporters could be moved).

In that summer, however, the club bought a forward with pace and goals and a wide man with a left foot to pick pockets. It was the most simple of combinations and solutions, but it had worked in the past.

It might not have been Rivaldo, but for £16.5 million Newcastle had bought

Craig Bellamy and Laurent Robert.

The team was back alive.

'It was fantastic,' said Steve Harper. 'The thing with Bobby's team was it had pace in it. Bellamy was a great foil for Shearer, Robert had pace, Dyer had pace, Jenas joined later on and he was a great athlete.

'It had that mix. Gary Speed was an unsung hero. Bobby said he was a rock. Pace worries teams. The opposition will drop five yards and give you more space to play.

'We had multiple outlets of pace and teams were scared of that.

'The first two years under Bobby we had Mick Wadsworth and we finished eleventh. Mick was a self-confident guy, but he was quite negative. I remember us changing formation at home to counter teams. That wasn't the Newcastle way.

'When Mick left it almost seemed to unshackle Sir Bobby. John Carver replaced him. JC was young, enthusiastic, vibrant and knew the club.

'The lads responded to his training and John was a better foil to Sir Bobby. Mick was reluctant to unleash the team.'

Carver, had been on Newcastle's books when he was 14. By the age of 20 a serious thigh injury had curtailed the hopes of a local who had been brought up in Cruddas Park of playing for the club.

'A lot of people think because I was an ex-player and a young player I got an opportunity,' said Carver. 'I had to work extra hard. I was working part time in a school in the west end of Newcastle. I started doing that voluntarily. Then for £60-a week, which was less than dole money, I started a community programme scheme, 20 hours-a-week coaching for the city council.

'To get my badges and experience of coaching I would get on a bus with a bag of balls. I used to go to Scotswood Sports Centre, then up to West Denton, then across to the Lightfoot Centre in Walker. I had no car then.

'I had done the ground work. It wasn't handed to me.

'Ruud promoted me. He came in with Steve Clarke and they wanted someone who knew the club inside out. I was quite young, I was 31, it was quite a big responsibility. I didn't understand the job and what it entailed and how I had to be the link between the manager and the players. I made lots of mistakes and learned by my mistakes.

'Bob had a big staff so my job was to go and watch opposition and report back to the players. At the time I really wasn't keen on it but it was the best thing I ever did. It gave me the opportunity to go and watch all the teams in the Premier

League, foreign teams, systems and how to play.

'It actually was beneficial to me more than anything else. It was a big test for me. He got his trust in me. I gave my first team talk to experienced players, it went so well before we played Sofia in Europe. Gary Speed came to me after and said that was as clear as daylight because we know nothing about the opposition.

'That was nice of him. I eventually went on to work with him. Maybe that planted a seed. Bobby got to know me and through the week I would start doing coaching work, on the training ground, about how we would break down the team we were playing in the next game. We used to video it and the guys would take it on board because they trusted me with what they had seen in the lecture room. I enjoyed that role.

'All of a sudden out of the blue Mick Wadsworth had the offer to go to Southampton. I went to see Bob, I said, "I know Mick's going, will you consider me for assistant manager, as your right hand man?"

'He said, "Absolutely John, I've had 96 applications for the job but I want to give you a month to see how you adapt." I said, "Okay that's great, that's all I want."

'We went to Trinidad and Tobago and I sat down with the guys. I just said, "Give me an opportunity, I've learned by my mistakes. If you still feel I'm part of Ruud's gang and all that then that's fair enough." In fairness to the senior pros they said okay and they were great after that. I never looked back.

'After a month Bob said, "There's a new contract for you son, I want you to be my number two."'

By then, Newcastle were on their way.

SIR BOBBY ROBSON
– DIGNITY

ON 10 JANUARY 1996, NEWCASTLE PLAYED ARSENAL IN THE QUARTER-final of the League Cup, at Highbury.

Lee Dixon kicked David Ginola and then he grabbed David Ginola and when he was tired with that he started kicking him again. After an hour of this Ginola booted Dixon. Ginola was sent off and Arsenal won and Dixon was applauded for doing his job.

On the evening of 17 December, 2001, Newcastle were third in the Premiership, with 30 points from 16 games and a goal difference of plus eight. Liverpool were top (+10), with 33 points (though they had scored less) and Arsenal were second, with the same points tally as Newcastle but a better goal difference (+16).

Nobody had foreseen a challenge from Newcastle. They were the upstarts that would not go away.

It had been a real slow burner to get there. The season had started in mid July in Belgium, in the Intertoto Cup, at Lokeren. That particular trophy would end in yet more penalty pain, just over a month later, against Troyes.

The first league victory did not come until 8 September, at the Riverside Stadium but it was 4–1 and it was emphatic and it was a sign of what was to come. Shearer scored twice, and Robert broke away for the third. It was a first show of his speed.

It triggered a good run. Brentford were hit for four in the League Cup in the next game and Manchester United got whacked for four in the next in a seven-goal seesaw of a match.

One-nil up, 2–1 up, 3–2 down and finally, with seven minutes remaining, Shearer's shot was helped into his own goal by Wes Brown.

That was not the end of it. With the clock ticking down, Shearer ran the ball out at the Gallowgate End. Shearer put a hand in front of Roy Keane as he gestured to take a quick throw in. Keane bounced the ball off Shearer, the pair squared up, the Newcastle captain did not move. Keane, who would later claim that Shearer called him a prick, was first held back by David Beckham and then shown a red card. 'I fell into the trap,' Keane said.

Newcastle went third with the win. They were still there at the start of November, after beating Aston Villa at St James' Park. Bellamy scored twice and Shearer scored a quite exquisite volley at the Gallowgate End. He would later say it was one of his best ever. There were more wins, against Derby and Blackburn, and then Newcastle went to Highbury.

It was a red and white storm in the first half, and after 20 minutes Henry overhead kicked the ball to Ashley Cole at the far post and Pires prodded in a deserved lead. Then Bellamy was sent off for catching Cole with his arm. It looked harsh. Bellamy looked devastated.

The second half was a different story. On the half hour mark LuaLua sent over a right wing corner and O'Brien, unmarked two yards out, headed an equaliser.

Newcastle came to life.

Ray Parlour tripped Shearer, it was his second yellow card offence and he too was dismissed, despite the protestations of the Newcastle captain.

With four minutes remaining, Robert charged through, Sol Campbell clumsily took him down and from the resulting penalty, Shearer put the visitors ahead with his first ever goal at the old ground.

He ran to the Newcastle fans, arms outstretched.

It had not finished, in injury-time, and with Arsenal pressing, Lualua sent Robert charging through again, this time he had the finish, calmly slotting a left-footed finish past Stuart Taylor.

3–1.

Newcastle United were top of the league.

In the visiting dressing room they slumped onto their seats. It had not been easy. Hard work, dogged, determined and with flair. There was delight as well.

'It's an amazing feeling,' said Robson. 'It was our first victory in the capital in 29 attempts. We've done it, we've won in London and we've gone top of the league.

Arsenal did not take kindly to being beaten, not that anyone on Tyneside cared. Memories still lingered at being kicked out of the League Cup by Bruce Rioch's side in '96. Geordie Karma.

Thierry Henry rebelled against defeat.

'After the final whistle Henry descended on Graham Poll and hardly left him alone,' added Robson. 'It was acrimonious. He was complaining about anything and everything. He's some player, and a smashing boy I'm told, but on that occasion the defeat got under his skin and I didn't like the way he conducted himself. Arsene was moody afterwards.

'They didn't take defeat gracefully. I said so. "This is a great club they've got here, and what great clubs have to do is learn to lose sometimes. They're bigger as a club if they learn how to lose."'

Arsenal didn't. Arsene Wenger spoke of sorcerers, rather than scorers.

Four days later, Newcastle played Leeds.

Newcastle went one-nil up, and then 3–1 down.

Robbie Elliott scored with a header to make it 3–2.

That made it interesting.

In the 71st minute Newcastle were awarded a penalty when Gary Speed flicked the ball off Eric Bakke's arm.

From 12 yards, Alan Shearer smashed the ball into the home goal, in front of the support from Newcastle, around 5,000, and raised two arms in triumph.

Bellamy followed the run of Shearer. When the ball went in, he jumped on his shoulders.

The away end went a bit crazy.

There was no love lost with Leeds.

Robson kept calm.

And then, in the final minute, Nobby Solano went through on the right.

Kieron Dyer, who had run Leeds United inside out, waited, and waited, and then finally slipped his pass through to his Peruvian team-mate.

The ball was perfect for Solano.

He took it in his stride and then tucked his finish beyond Paul Robinson, with the same delicacy as a parent putting his child to bed.

Five thousand Newcastle supporters watched that ball, and willed it in.

Then they went wild.

When they had stopped celebrating, the game was over, the comeback was complete.

Jon Champion, the commentator, read it so perfectly.

'Bobby Robson does a jig of delight on the touchline and then remembers he's 69!' he enthused. 'Joy unconfined amongst the traveling hordes!'

He didn't say it.

He shouted it.

Newcastle did that.

They touched the neutral.

Newcastle were 3–1 down and then 4–3 up. A complete turnaround.

Robson pointed, even he didn't know at what.

He grabbed Carver and smiled a massive grin.

'One up, 3–1 down, they stay top of the Premiership thanks to the most remarkable of recoveries,' shouted Champion.

'December was a smashing month for us,' said Robson. 'We led the Premiership at Christmas. We were very proud.'

On Boxing Day, in front of a crowd of 52,127, Newcastle comfortably saw off Middlesbrough at St James' Park, Shearer, Speed and Olivier Bernard all scoring. The win took Newcastle three points clear at the top of the Premiership.

Happy Christmas.

Back to back defeats to Chelsea and Manchester United in the space of five days followed. Down to fourth, but then the team started winning again, a lot. Leeds were beaten, Peterborough were beaten in the FA Cup and then Newcastle scored nine times in 12 days to beat Spurs, Bolton and Southampton. Newcastle were joint top on 9 February, behind Liverpool only on goal difference (+18 to Liverpool's +20) and with a game in hand.

Manchester United were a point behind.

It was starting to get serious.

KEVIN KEEGAN
– THANK YOU

THEY WERE THERE BEFORE THE MANCHESTER CITY TEAM BUS ROLLED underneath the Milburn Stand, more than 500 supporters, black and white wherever you looked.

They were waiting for the proper farewell that had not been afforded them, the chance to say a heart felt goodbye and thank you.

At half past five the Manchester City manager Kevin Keegan walked down the steps of that coach and he looked taken aback. His name filled the concourse and echoed off the concrete pockets that help keep the giant structure in place.

It was breathtaking when he finally took his place in the City dugout, through the scrummage of photographers, just before kick-off. He seemed lost in the moment, and that was understandable. He looked high to the summit of the imposing stands, as if trying to see if any one of the 51,020 there that day were not on their feet, clapping and singing his name.

He would not have found them.

He looked moved by it all.

It was the least Kevin Keegan deserved.

His team, on their way to being Division One champions, lost to a Nobby Solano goal.

He was knocked out the cup, but he did not look like a loser.

NIKOS DABIZAS –
I WANNA BE ADORED

'I'M TAKING MY SHIRT OFF. I'M WAVING IT AROUND MY HEAD. I HAVE *lost my mind. I am a mad man. I am possessed. This is sheer joy. It does not get better than this. I am at one with the fans.*

'I am jumping in front of them. I'm waving their shirt. I have scored against Sunderland. I'm half naked. My teammates are jumping on me. It is a magical feeling.

'I headed the ball and I remember seeing it go in. Cheering. Shouting. The lads jumping on me. It is crazy. I will never forget this moment. This is as good as it gets. A hero.

'I did not dream of this.

'I did not dream of being a footballer.

'I was planning from a very young age to follow the footsteps of my father, to continue our family position business, a milk factory in Greece.

'I enjoyed playing football but I was training to succeed my father.

'I had the chance to join a Third Division club. I said okay, I'll move from my home town. Things went well. I was there for three years. I went to Olympicaos, the biggest club in Greece.

'It was something big for me going there. I didn't plan it but it came. I was always pragmatic. I was always down to earth. I was excited but I said, okay this is my chance, I have to grab it. I started playing for the national team and suddenly it came alive.

'I won the title once and I left in March so almost twice! I got a medal. I had a chance to renew my contract but I didn't. I wanted a new challenge and the offer from Newcastle came.

'My agent told me the scout will come from Newcastle, they were looking for a central defender. They watched me in the Champions League against Real Madrid. They watched me for Greece. They liked what they saw. Kenny was the manager. My ambition was to play in the Premier League. It suited me.

'I knew Kenny as a player and he was a manager for Liverpool. He was in charge for Newcastle United. I knew Newcastle but I was not ready for England. It was a shock. The first three months was very difficult to establish myself. Kenny was alongside Bobby the best man manager I had in my career.

'He was not very close to you but you had this sense he was with you. He was backing his players in public. He was very low profile. I really appreciate this personality.

'The first season was reasonable. Newcastle had challenged for the league but we were thirteenth. We were in a semi-final against Sheffield United.

'It was like throwing me in the middle of the ocean and asking me to swim. I had the ability in a way, like a chameleon to adapt to the new challenge I had.

'The feeling you have playing in a Cup final, at the old Wembley, it was a huge, huge memory for me. It still is.

'Leaving the stadium empty handed it was disappointment. When we first came back after the Cup final and the bus parade, people cheering outside on the street was remarkable. That was the time I realised it was all about the people and what it meant being a fan of Newcastle United. Also, what it means to be a player of Newcastle United. It was huge disappointment but the people were still out there trying to give us a positive approach.

'Ruud was tactically very smart. He was a great player at Milan. What he was really lacking was the man management with the players inside the team. It's a different philosophy. Ruud had an inside battle, his personality as a character was good, but it got him in trouble in terms of his coaching.

'If you judge him for me he was a good tactical reader of the game but his personality was not close to the players. He compared himself with the players we had at the football club. Some of his decisions you can raise an eyebrow.

'I played the first year in 80 percent of the games under him. He bought four central defenders ahead of me. I knew that I didn't have a chance with him.

'No. I didn't have a clue what Bobby was all about. The very first day he walked into the dressing room and, how can you say this, he had this aura. He was the most charismatic manager I've worked with. He was very clever. In my eyes he could be a politician.

'He was unbelievable in that sense. His language, his body language. He transformed us. He signed some players, but the same players that were still there under a different regime were transformed. We were playing exciting football. We were top of the league at some stage, unbeatable. We had a very healthy squad. In every department he was there. He was the key, he was the main reason the same players and those he brought in brought success to the club.

'He was so charismatic.

'Sometimes I was left out and he was very clever, he was always trying to share a joke with me. When I was playing he was not so close. He didn't have to do it then. In a way he knew exactly what players needed to hear and to feel in different circumstances.

'One day after the Sunderland goal and performance and he said Nikos was a mammoth. You hear that and he is like a father.

'He was so, so clever to read the body language. He knew what was exactly in your mind, he was spot on with his approach all the time. He was very close to the players.

'I realised straight away from the first derby I played what is the special meaning of this game of the region.

'I was always in town. I was not staying somewhere miles away, outside of the town. I'd go for a coffee in Kafeneon in the Bigg Market. It was popular with the people of Newcastle at that time. I was very close to the fans. I have these feelings and was sharing these feelings all the time. I was not living somewhere and being distant from them.

'Then the game. The ball came over and I headed it over Sorensen into the Sunderland goal. It wasn't just scoring the goal, I scored the winning goal and it put us to second top in the Premier League at the time.

'It was a huge feeling for me. I went completely blank you know.

'I was possessed with joy and happiness. I was watching the fans jumping on each other half naked. I tried to share my joy with them.

'The feeling is still there. I have a huge banner in my house. Me, celebrating that goal half naked. Gary Speed is jumping on my back, so is Jermaine Jenas and Sylvian [Distin]. It is something that will always stay in my mind. It was the highlight of my career.

'You just lose the feeling around you. You are like in another dimension. Pure joy. Pure joy. This 15–20 seconds that you lose your head. That feeling is exactly that. It stays deep inside you. That makes the moment so special.

'The sheer joy of this achievement, of sharing that with the fans, with your teammates, knowing exactly what it means, it was what made the moment so very special, and still is.

'That 15 seconds marks you inside. It stays deep inside your brain. You have this feeling inside you for the rest of my life.

'Of course I was lucky to celebrate with the Newcastle fans. They have moved them now. You can live that moment with them, from a very small distance.

'Sharing that feeling, that joy, happiness with them and seeing the expression in their faces.

'I could see how mad they were going. I was at one with them. One unit. I could see their face. I could see my face in their face.

'It was complete. I scored a goal but it was like every individual in that stand scored that goal. It was very, very deep, inside us all.

'The memory is still very strong. When I go back to Newcastle, people keep reminding me all the time. It was the first goal to win a derby at the Stadium of Light. Even all these years later, it is still the same. That makes this moment so special. That will never change. This will never be erased. It will be the same with the same volume in my head and in my heart, that strong feeling, of me, with the Newcastle supporters.

'It will never go away.'

SIR BOBBY ROBSON
– ALTOGETHER NOW

'OH THE GAFFER WILL HAVE YOU FOR THAT.'

It was the second shot on the seventh hole at the old Close House golf course.

A five iron had done spectacularly well and bounced through the green, splitting the four ball in front of us.

'He'll wait for you at the end!' Craig Bellamy was laughing when he spoke but I wasn't sure if he was joking.

It turned out that he wasn't.

'Was that you?' said Sir Bobby Robson, at the green, next to the 18th hole. 'That ball bounced right past us. I wasn't happy with that.'

'I'm really sorry,' I repeated. 'It was a five iron, I didn't think it would go so far.'

'You should have waited son.'

'I know, I'm really sorry.'

And then a moment's contemplation.

'A five iron!? From there? Mind, that was some shot!'

He could do that, Robson.

It was a golf day for Carl Liddle, a North East sports writer, ahead of his wedding.

Robson played the entire round with Carl's uncle. He got his name wrong for 18 holes. He watched a tee shot and went, 'Wow, what a strike lad' put his arm around him on the tee and walked away pulling the wrong bag of clubs.

No one said a word.

In the club house there were all kinds of goodies given by companies for the day. There were donations to charity as well. A firm had handed over a washing

113

machine as a prize. Robson did that. He got people on stag dos brand new washing machines.

At St James' Park the Sunday journalists would congregate around his desk once the rest of the press conference had finished. He would make formations out of Dictaphones, he'd grab a notepad and draw four defenders and then show you how a midfield should slide across when the opposition full-back had the ball. I kept that bit of paper for years.

He told a story that his precious England caps had been stolen and it became a front page story, a national disgrace. There was a hunt to find them. The FA talked of replacing them. It was kept quiet but they were found in his loft. No one kicked up a fuss.

He had that status by then.

He would tell stories about Barcelona, about how Hristo Stoichkov would sometimes walk off the training field, mid session, and Robson would let him go.

'You have to know how your players work,' he would say.

He made Newcastle's players eat together, sit together, bond. Phones were banned. If you were late, you got a £5 fine. Robson was a stickler for timekeeping, and togetherness.

'We had a player's common room where we used to sit and play darts,' said Steve Harper. 'One day me and Alan and Speedo, Shay, Rob Lee and Bobby's in there and he's holding court and he's slaughtering Bellers to us.

'"I'm sick of him, he's a pest, I told Charlie (Woods) when we signed him he was a risk, I've had enough of him, he's doing my head in." As he's talking, who walks in? Bellers.

'Straight away, "How are you son? How's your hamstring? Are you fit for the weekend? I need you, get me a goal son." He made a right fuss of him.

'As Bellers has walked out the other door, he switched again, "He's still a pest, I'm fed up of him. I've had enough!"

'It was a priceless example of his man management. It was brilliant. It was absolutely brilliant.'

Bellamy always railed against the story that he had been locked in the team bus toilet on the way back from an away game by team-mates when he was at Norwich.

'If you were married to him you'd want a divorce every day,' Robson once said, but he was smiling when he said it.

'I'm aware there are many people who believe that I had no respect for Bobby

Robson,' said Bellamy in his autobiography. 'From a lot of the coverage of my time at Newcastle, you could be forgiven for thinking that I spent my years there trying to undermine him or simply mocking him. The impression that was conveyed was that I was an unruly kid taunting a wise old teacher.

'The truth is that Bobby Robson was the best manager I ever worked with. Another idea has been allowed to take hold that the players at Newcastle viewed him as a soft touch and took advantage of his kindness and his age.

'Again, that isn't true. He could be kind and he was the best man-manager I have ever come across but he had a ruthless streak, too. He wasn't soft. No one who lasts in management as long as he did can be weak. He was clever. He had learned to treat every individual differently.'

Newcastle really were flying. High octane, high work rate, high maintenance even.

The team bus that rolled back into Tyneside early that Sunday evening after victory over Sunderland was looking up. For the first time since Kevin Keegan had been at the club.

It was incredibly tight. Newcastle were two points behind Manchester United with a game in hand and a point ahead of Arsenal having played the same number of matches. Liverpool were just one point behind them.

Newcastle were, however, the form team of the division, having won five and drawn one of their previous six games.

There was just one problem, and it was a major one. Craig Bellamy's season was all but over.

'We had a chance of winning the title,' added Carver. 'We were convinced inside the camp we had a chance.

'We went to Sunderland and won 1–0. That made it eight wins out of nine. We went second.

'That sticks in my mind because that is the day we lost Craig Bellamy to the patella tendon injury. That's when I felt the wheels fell off a little bit.

'We lost against Arsenal and Liverpool and drew with Ipswich.'

One point from three games, two of those without scoring. It was a bad time to stumble. Any dreams of silverware went in that period. Newcastle were eight points behind Manchester United in the blink of an eye.

There was an FA Cup loss to Arsenal in a replay at Highbury and then another unbeaten run, winning four games and drawing three. Shearer scored six goals in the seven game run. Newcastle had won 21 games by then, and were guaranteed fourth place, and a Champions League qualifier. The season would finish with a loss at Southampton, but it was a success whichever way you looked at it.

'We edged up to the elite and we blew some teams away,' said Robson. 'We had an exuberant, pacy style. Shearer, Bellamy, Robert and Solano were knocking them in. We got 71 points and finished fourth. We had secured a Champions League qualifying spot less than three years after I had inherited a bottom placed team.'

Robson was in control. He went back to Ipswich, on the recommendation of Charlie Woods, his chief scout, whose back garden in Suffolk you could watch Ipswich train from, to sign Titus Bramble for £5 million. Eyebrows were raised. Bramble was prone to errors, and to get him Newcastle let Sylvain Distin, who had been on loan, go in a row over salary.

There was, however, the incoming Hugo Viana, an £8.5 million buy from Sporting Lisbon. 'We have signed Hugo and we're delighted to have got him,' Freddy Shepherd said. 'The consensus is that he's the best young player in the world. He's a left-sided midfielder, just the player Bobby Robson wants to spearhead our Champions League bid.'

It was harder to argue with that.

There was ambition, and youth, and speed, and excitement.

It felt the club was on the cusp of something special again.

There was surprise in a link between Liverpool and Alan Shearer. Robson and the Newcastle captain were both aware of the interest. Gerard Houllier spoke with Phil Thompson about the possibility of a deal. Shepherd put down a new 12-month contact.

There was the possibility of a return to the Champions League group stage for the first time since the 1997/98 season. To get there they had to beat Zeljeznicar over two legs in a third round qualifying tie. Newcastle won the tie five-nil, Viana scored the third in the second leg. Dynamo Kiev, Juventus and Feyenoord were the reward.

That felt special.

The 2002/03 league campaign, however, had not started well. On 14 September, Newcastle lost 3–0 at Chelsea. It was the third defeat in five games. Newcastle were second bottom, and then lost the first group game in the Champions League to Kiev 2–0.

There was a comfortable win against Sunderland but then another loss in Europe to Feyenoord. Two games in and Newcastle had not scored.

Robson called a meeting in his hotel room, before Newcastle faced Juventus at the Stadio delle Alpi.

'We had our dinner and we went to Bobby's room at 8.30,' said John Carver.

One of Newcastle's great managerial partnerships, Terry McDermott and Kevin Keegan have much to ponder.

Kevin Keegan's uncertainty with the Sporting Club championed by Sir John Hall is clear to see.

Newcastle's players line up at Wembley alongside Terry McDermott before the Charity Shield in 1996.

Alan Shearer and
Les Ferdinand celebrate
Newcastle's fourth goal
against Manchester United
during a memorable
Sunday in 1996.

Philippe Albert admires his work as the ball climbs over the head of (out of shot) Peter Schmeichel for Newcastle's fifth and final goal against Manchester United.

The author (blue polo shirt with hand against his mouth) listens to Sir John Hall in the build up to the 1998 FA Cup final.

Everywhere you look there is black and white. At the tunnel end at Wembley before the 1998 FA Cup final.

Newcastle's players line up for Abide With Me before the 1998 FA Cup final.

A dejected Alan Shearer applauds the Newcastle fans following the loss to Arsenal.

Tens of thousands of Newcastle fans wait at the city's Civic Centre to welcome the players back from the FA Cup final.

Faustino Asprilla completes his flip after scoring against Barcelona in the Champions League at St James' Park.

Big pants but it was filling
the big shoes left behind
by Kevin Keegan that
proved more problematic
for Kenny Dalglish.

Alan Shearer accepts the
Carling Player of the Month
from Ruud Gullit,
but the pair's relationship
was fractured throughout.

John Carver, who was
Newcastle coach under
Ruud Gullit and
assistant manager to
Sir Bobby Robson.

Back beside the red carpet before the 1999 FA Cup final against Manchester United.

'We were talking about how we were going to beat Juventus. We were sitting there and we started saying what we thought the team should be and what changes we could make, and then we were talking about the opposition, they had Alessandro Del Piero and he was in the number 10 area, and how their midfield rotated.

'We got to 11.30, me Davie Geddis, Simon Smith and Paul Winsper, I looked and Bob had dropped off. We looked at each other and didn't know what to do. We were giggling.

'We carried on, he woke up and went, "Right, I know what we're going to do, I'm going to play this way with this team." It was the team we started off with at 8.30!

'We lost the game 2–0. Del Piero scored both.

'After the game it was in my head to go and see the gaffer. Bob is in the office and I knock on the door, "Gaffer can I come in?"

"Yes, come in."

"Listen, I want to give my opinion!" I said on the first day I would do that. "We've got some talented players in our dressing room. They would run though a brick wall for you. I think we should concentrate on ourselves instead of the opposition."'

Robson listened.

There was a punishing 5–2 loss at Blackburn before the fourth Champions League group game, against Juventus, at St James' Park. No team had ever qualified from the group phase after losing the first three games.

'We played Blackburn in the league and got beaten 5–2 in a monsoon and Shay had had a tough afternoon,' added Steve Harper.

'We were playing Juventus in the week in the Champions League and the gaffer told me I was playing.

'Shay had a tough day but I was like, "Wow".

'We had lost three Champions League games and then he threw me into a no lose game against them. Gianluigi Buffon was playing for Juventus and he's one of my heroes, to meet him, never mind play against him, was a special thing.

'I did the press conference with Sir Bobby and I sat next to him and I remember he was asked what the chances of qualifying were. He went, "Well, you know, it's up to Stevey, if he makes a mistake then we'll be out. He has to do his job, he's the goalkeeper, if he costs us a goal we'll probably be knocked out."

'I was sat there, thinking, "Is he challenging me? Am I not focused?" I just thought it was unusual for him. Maybe he used it to get me switched on ahead of the game. Bobby was very good at testing you. He would do it to keep you on the money.

'He was a very clever man as well. Sometimes when he got names wrong you weren't sure if he was putting it on or not and he was messing with you. The passion and enthusiasm he had for football just oozed out of him.

'He was infectious. Everybody loved him. He was like Kevin Keegan in that respect. He filled a room. Everybody wanted a piece of him. He had time for people and they appreciated it.'

Newcastle, with Harper in goal, beat Juventus 1–0. The right back Andy Griffin scored. They were still bottom of Group E. Kiev and Juventus had seven points, Feyenoord had five. Newcastle had three, but then, in the fifth game, Newcastle beat Kiev 2–1 at St James' Park. Juventus beat Feyenoord.

Going into the final game, at the De Kuip stadium in Rotterdam, Newcastle were third.

The group was suddenly wide open. Juventus were top with 10 points and through and there were concerns what effort they would raise in the Ukraine. Kiev had seven points. If they won it did not matter what Newcastle did in Holland.

If Newcastle won and Juventus did the same or drew, however, then history would be made.

It was some carrot.

JOHN CARVER
– UNBELIEVABLE

'WE'RE DRIVING INTO THE STADIUM. WE'VE GOT A GREAT FOLLOWING.

There's been a bit of trouble, it was a bit naughty. Friends have told me.

'Going into the stadium we know what we have to do.

'We have a chance of going into the second stage. If we can achieve this it will be fantastic, historic.

'Bob looks like royalty. He looks like the King of Holland.

'He'd worked in Holland, everyone wants a piece of him. He's a hero here.

'He's a big man. When he's in Holland or Barcelona it's as if he's grown another six foot.

'He was so proud. It looks like he owns Holland.

'He's doing his team talk. Same structure each time. He's got the flip chart. He's making his points. He's got the coloured pens. He's got it on his hands.

'The guys know what he's delivering. He's gone through the set plays, where we should be. Thorough. Detail.

'"Do you want to come in with anything John?" he says.

'The technology is down to me. I show the lads how we can win. We've won two games. This is how we win the third. We make history if we do, if we go through.

'I look around the dressing room. I look at the players. It's in their eyes. They smell the situation. You can tell.

'"Craig, and Kieron and JJ, the young lads. You can see their faces.

'Look at Shearer. Look at his focus. Speedo. They were winners.

'We've got good players here. We've bought good players.

'It starts.

'We're 2–0 up and we're in total control, in Feyenoord, in the last game. We've got Ray Thompson, the kitman, telling us the score in Kiev. Juventus can't lose.

'From nowhere it's 2–2. Feyenoord have got two goals back.

'We need to win this game. We've got to win. We were watching Juve against Kiev. Juve are winning.

'Bob's cool. He's keeping a cool head. He's scanned the game. He's not panicking.

'Kieron's through. It's right at the death. Then it's saved. Then Bellers pops up and gets that ball over the line. Yes! What a feeling. What a feeling of emotion and excitement and joy.

'That was the goal that was taking us into the next stage of the Champions League.

'We charge off the bench. It's the best celebration I've ever seen or been involved in. We celebrate on the pitch.

'It's a great feeling. Honestly. Everybody in the dugout is going crazy, apart from one man, apart from Bob. He's calm, and cool and he has that little swagger he had. He's so calm about the situation, we're going crazy.

'He's telling us to calm down.

'The dressing room is celebrating.

'It's as if we've just won the cup.

'We go back to the hotel after the game. Everyone's so happy.

'It was one of the greatest days of my life.'

BUCKINGHAM PALACE, NOVEMBER 2002

SIR BOBBY ROBSON – DESTINY CALLING

EIGHT DAYS AFTER THE DRAMA OF FEYENOORD, BOBBY ROBSON WAS knighted at Buckingham Palace.

The Prince of Wales said to Robson, 'I hope the job's not too taxing for you!'

Robson, who was 69, received his knighthood with his wife Elsie and two of the couple's three sons, Andrew and Paul.

'She has been a solid support for me throughout 47 years of marriage,' he said. 'She made sure I got out of bed every morning and went to work, and always had a warm welcome for me on my return. I've always had a great family around me.'

And then back to football.

'We are doing very well,' he added. 'But it's a long time since Newcastle won something. I just hope we can bring in some silverware at some stage.'

Newcastle were beaten more comfortably than the 5–3 scoreline suggests, in their next game, at Old Trafford.

Inter Milan, in the following game, and the first in the second group stage of the Champions League, put four past Newcastle. Domenico Morfeo scored after 65 seconds, Craig Bellamy was sent off after five minutes and Shearer was caught on camera elbowing Matias Almeyda.

It was a punishing night.

Newcastle lost their next European tie, 3–1 in the Nou camp. The game had been put back 24 hours because of rain.

The league campaign needed a lift. It came. Following the loss, Newcastle went on a 12 game run in which they lost just once, on Boxing Day, at the Reebok

Stadium, 4–3 to Sam Allardyce's Bolton. Jermaine Jenas, signed for £5 million from Nottingham Forest in February 2002, was increasingly influential.

'The best Christmas party I have been to as a footballer was the first one I had at Newcastle in 2002, when Sir Bobby Robson was manager,' said Jenas.

'All the players had gone out in fancy dress to the Quayside in the city centre. I was Superman, Carl Cort was Batman and Kieron Dyer was Austin Powers. Then we found out that the club's directors were having their own party at St James' Park, a black-tie do with their wives.

'We decided we would gate-crash it, so we all piled into taxis to the stadium, ran upstairs and burst through the doors. It was a bit surreal. We were all running about this posh dinner and ball dressed as superheroes, then found Sir Bobby, said "all right, gaffer" and sat at his table. Someone had his pint.

'He just looked at us and said: "Right, have one drink and get the hell out of here." Nobody ever had a go at us for it. Even the next day Sir Bobby just laughed about it and said, "You lot are a nightmare!"'

Jenas was just 19 when he was plunged into the derby at the Stadium of Light, when Dabizas scored. Robson had just paid £5 million to sign the youngster from Nottingham Forest.

'My first two weeks on Tyneside were hard,' he said. 'I was nervous, and I was rubbish in training. I remember thinking: "What have I done? I'm just not the player I was at Forest."

'Then on the Thursday before the Tyne-Wear derby Sir Bobby Robson came to me and said: "You're playing on Sunday by the way." I was shocked.

'There's no bigger game at Newcastle, but the minute I played that game, those two weeks of training were irrelevant. I performed well and that earned me the full respect of my teammates.'

Robson remained a fan of the player.

The unruly element of the dressing room, however, was causing concern.

'Some of the younger players we bought were little shits and they destroyed Bobby Robson,' Sir John Hall would tell me, much later.

Hall had been snubbed by Carl Cort, Griffin, Kieron Dyer and Bellamy for a meal in his honour in Malaga in November 2001. The quartet instead went on a bar crawl. They were sent home and fined by Shepherd.

'Were they a handful?' replied Carver. 'No. After what happened when we signed so many foreign players under Ruud, French, Spanish, Croatian, Bob came in and said, "We're going to sign British players."

'We had Dyer, we signed Bellers, Jenas, Bramble, we already had what he called his blue chip boys, Shearer, Speed, Rob Lee, Warren Barton, Harper, Given, Hughes, blue chip, British.

'We had a mentality.

'What I will say about these guys is that, yeah some of them were lively. The city was a goldfish bowl but we could control them. As long as they were performing Bob had their back. He had the knack of managing players. Rather than confront every issue. Sometimes you have to mollycoddle them.

'The biggest thing was all the young players respected Bobby and me and when you have that they don't give you as much hassle as they could do. They were good players as well. You can get away with it sometimes when you're performing well.'

Leeds, Chelsea, Spurs, all beaten, as were Bayer Leverkusen, both home and away in games three and four of the Champions League second group stage. Newcastle, third in the Premiership, were back alive there as well. It had helped signing Jonathan Woodgate, a quality central defender, from Leeds for £9 million in January.

A fixture had been missed, when Middlesbrough shamelessly called off a match at the Riverside in the same month, at lunchtime on the day before it was due to be played, because of a snow forecast. Robson was furious, and phoned Steve McClaren, the manager of Middlesbrough, to tell him.

'I am absolutely furious,' he said. 'How they can call a match off on the Friday beats me. There's been very little will shown by Middlesbrough to play the match and they even turned down our request to play it on Tuesday.'

The *Sunday Sun* ran a front page picture of the area around the stadium at 3pm on the Saturday when the match should have been played. The conditions were perfect. There was no sign of a snowflake. When the game was played, and Juninho and Ugo Ehiogu were fit and Michael Ricketts had signed. Middlesbrough won 1–0.

Thankfully, for 12,000 Newcastle supporters there was a trip to Italy six days later to think about.

ALAN SHEARER – THE BLAYDON RACES

'WE'RE ON THE BUS, GOING TO THE SAN SIRO, AND ALL WE CAN SEE *is black and white flags and black and white strips. There are Newcastle fans everywhere. The hairs on the back of your neck go up.*

'We've come so far under Sir Bobby.

"To walk out the tunnel, at the front, with the arm band, and to look to my right and to see a sea of black and white. This is something else.

'It's one of those moments. The sheer volume of people.

'There's 12,000 there, to our right.

'We're confident. It was a confident mood in the dressing room.

'We're all looking forward to it. We believe we can get something out of the game. There's no point being here if you don't think you can.

'We know the height of who we are playing, their stature. We think we can get a result.

'We have a bit of everything. We can mix it if we have to and we can play if we have to. We have technical ability. We have pace. It's a good team.

'When I signed for Newcastle it was for nights like this. It's a shame we didn't have it every season. That is what I hoped I had signed for. It's great to be a part of.

'These are the best defenders in the world. The Italians are the best. The way they mark.

'To these guys defending is an art. It means so much to them. I loved that. I loved going into battle anyway. This is what I like, the battle.

'Scoring goals anywhere is a great feeling, but here, this is special, in the first half. It's very, very special. I will never forget it.

'I score again in the second half. It's at that end where there's 12,000 fans from Newcastle.

Just incredible. Brilliant. If I could have written the script that would have been it.

'We put in a great performance. They equalised again and we draw. We gave everything we had. The atmosphere, the fans, the passion, when you do that and put everything in, you come off the pitch satisfied.

'That's how we felt.'

JOHN CARVER AND CRAIG BELLAMY – WE CAN WORK IT OUT

NEWCASTLE BEAT CHARLTON ON THEIR RETURN TO THE PREMIERSHIP, and then lost 2–0 at home to Barcelona. Robson had thought the 2–2 draw in Milan was not enough, and he was proved right. Juventus had beaten Bayer Leverkusen. Newcastle this time could not quite pull off another miracle, finishing third in the group with seven points.

There were three defeats on the trot, including a punishing 6–2 loss at home against Manchester United. It was a reminder of the size of the final step. Newcastle slipped to fourth after a 1–1 draw with Aston Villa.

There needed a final push, and it duly came. Newcastle beat Sunderland at the Stadium of Light through a first half Nolberto Solano penalty. Hugo Viana scored the winning goal against Birmingham at St James' and in the final game Jenas and Viana scored in a 2–2 draw. Third. The highest finish since 1997.

At the start of the following season, John Carver was sitting in his hotel room, for the third successive day. He had left it only once, to watch Paritzan Belgrade and make notes. He went straight back as soon as the game was finished.

'I never left the hotel for the three days I was there,' he said.

'I flew over to watch them. The game was on the Saturday night, against Borac Cacak. It was one of the most intimidating stadiums I've ever been in my life. The team didn't fly out till the Tuesday night.

'I've never been so pleased to see them driving down the street. I ran down the stairs when I saw the team bus. I gave them all a big cuddle because I was so pleased to see them.

'In the game we got a result, Nobby scored, we won 1–0. Happy days.'

Newcastle lost the return leg 1–0 on Wednesday, 27 August. Partizan scored through Ivica Iliev five minutes into the second half.

It went to penalties.

'Alan took the first penalty and missed it,' added Carver. 'When he missed it I knew we were in trouble.'

Newcastle missed their first three penalties. Shola Ameobi scored the fourth to make it 1–1. Radovic scored to make it 2–1 but LuaLua levelled it again and Iliev then missed.

Jenas scored to make it 3–2, Ilic kept his side in it and then Aaron Hughes missed. Lazar Cirkovic scored the goal that put Newcastle out of Champions League football.

You walked out of the ground that night and it felt different. A corner had been turned, for the worst. It was a long, long way back.

It was a shadow that neither the campaign, or indeed Robson, could ever shake off.

'It took us a long time to recover from it,' added Carver. 'It wasn't just the Champions League, it was financially massive. The amount of money you lose from not qualifying for the Champions League meant to get knocked out was absolutely devastating.

'All I remember was it was probably one of the lowest points. We had got ourselves into such a great situation. 1–0 in Belgrade. Then thinking we were just going to qualify and we didn't. We dominated the game, they didn't have too many chances but that's what happens when you only have a 1–0 lead.

'We had the big characters and we need to try and pull ourselves around. We had the UEFA Cup but getting knocked out of the Champions League, yes, it was hard to take.'

Newcastle had only signed one player in the summer, Lee Bowyer, on a free transfer. That was a major surprise, especially after finishing third. Bowyer returned to his old club Leeds on the first day of the Premiership season and drew 2–2. Then Newcastle lost at home to Manchester United, and at home to Birmingham, after Belgrade.

That was three home defeats in a week. Everything was cranked up after that. Newcastle were joint bottom of the table going into September. There would be no league victories that month either. Not until the first week in October did it come, a 1–0 win, after a Shearer goal, against Southampton. Form finally returned.

There were three wins in a week in October and a UEFA Cup run that was slowly coming to life after beating Basel 4–2 on aggregate.

A 4–0 win against Spurs in December, when Laurent Robert and Shearer both scored twice took Newcastle to fifth in the Premiership. There were further victories against Leeds and Fulham to stay there and then a disappointing fourth round FA Cup exit at Liverpool, after Laurent Robert had scored a screamer, his eleventh of the season.

Newcastle flew to Valerenga in the third round of the UEFA Cup. Shearer was rested, Bellamy scored in a 1–1 draw and the Newcastle captain voiced his displeasure before a flight back to Tyneside was diverted to Manchester because of the weather. He scored in the return leg and Newcastle won 3–1 and a win against Charlton kept Newcastle fifth, level on points with fourth-placed Liverpool but a massive 16 points behind Manchester United, who were third.

On 24 March, Newcastle were flying to Mallorca for the return leg of their fourth round UEFA Cup tie with Real Mallorca. The game was already over (4–1) but thousands still flew from Newcastle Airport for some sunshine. Craig Bellamy had parked in Carver's spot at the airport. The two began rowing in the executive lounge.

'There had been things said and it came to a head in the lounge at the airport,' said Harper. 'They had a roll about. They had a bit of a wrestle rather than punches being connected.

'A chair was thrown. Bobby was in the next room and he heard a bit of a commotion and was trying to get in and me and Speedo were blocking the door and holding the handle! We were refusing to let him in. It was an unfortunate incident but it was a storm in a teacup.

'I don't think anybody landed any blows. Bellers said something not very complimentary about Geordies to which JC took offence to and Sir Bobby tried to get in and we rightfully didn't let him in!

'We tried to keep it in house but by the time we landed it was common knowledge and John Carver subsequently found out which player it was.'

Robson took Bellamy for a walk after the row.

'Bobby told JC to get on the plane,' added Bellamy in his autobiography, *GoodFella*. (The friendship with Carver was such that Carver went to his wedding). 'He gave him a real rollicking and asked him what the hell he had been doing, confronting me like that.

'I arrived at the training ground and he wasn't there. He's a coach. He should have been in before me so I parked in his space. I knew it would wind him up.

'I walked past him later that morning and said, "Hiya", all proud of myself because of my little stunt, and he just walked straight past me without saying a word.

'It made me smile. I thought, "Job done".

'By the time we got to Newcastle Airport to get the flight to Majorca, he was at snapping point and we had a confrontation. I was angry and I threw a chair out of the way so I could go and argue with him.

'We ended up wrestling stupidly on the floor. The manager came in and yelled at everyone to get out and get on the plane.

'I had lost my rag totally by that point. I was saying, "I'm not going, I'm not getting on the plane, I'm going home to see my missus."

'I was still saying I was going home. I was adamant. The manager put his arm round me.

'"Walk with me, son," he said. So I walked with him and he started asking me how my kids were, how they were doing at school, how was my missus.

'The next thing I knew I was on the plane. I was thinking, "How the fuck did I get here?" If he'd told me straight that I had to get on the plane, if he'd ordered me to get on, I wouldn't have done it.

'That evening, Sir Bobby came round to my room and brought Carver and Alan Shearer with him.

'I thought they had come to gang up on me so I was ready to have a right go back, but then Sir Bobby sat us all down and started blaming everything on John Carver and made him apologise to me.

'Alan had to say how much he rated me, too. I could tell Alan was saying that through gritted teeth. It was killing him. The next thing I know, I'm shaking everybody's hand and we're all friends.'

Carver and Bellamy were pictured laughing pitch side before the game.

'Sir Bobby put me on the bench for the game,' added Bellamy. 'I came on and scored with practically my first touch and we won 3–0.'

A 4–2 win at home to Everton in April took Newcastle fourth, but it was the last time they would occupy a Champions League spot for the season. A goalless draw at home to Arsenal, sandwiched in between a tight UEFA Cup quarter-final with PSV Eindhoven (more than 86,000 watched the two legs) saw the team drop to fifth.

Another goalless draw at Aston Villa, after Liverpool had done the same the previous day against Fulham, was a big missed opportunity. The two teams, on

Sunday, 18 April, were level on points (50) and goal difference (+12) but Liverpool had scored more (48 to 45).

Still, there was the first leg of the semi-final of a European competition to look forward to, and the stadium was rammed full and raucous, for the visit of Marseille. There were big players missing, Bellamy, Dyer and Jenas, but chances still came, for Shola Ameobi, Shearer and Gary Speed. They were not taken. Didier Drogba hit the post for the visitors. There was still hope.

'We know we can go to Marseille and give them just as tough a game as we have done here,' said Robson. 'Can we score there? I think we can.' Shearer added: 'This is far from over.'

There was a win against Chelsea and then a loss at Manchester City before all eyes shifted to the South of France.

MARSEILLE, A WALL OF SOUND, MAY 2004

SIR BOBBY ROBSON – CUM ON FEEL THE NOIZE

IT WAS THE NOISE THAT HIT YOU. LIKE SITTING ON THE TARMAC with an aeroplane taking off over your head.

They had told you, in the bars and taxis, about what Olympique de Marseille meant to the people of the region, but they always say that. Everybody's club means more than the last person.

And then you got the bus to the ground, watched as the best part of 60,000 squeezed themselves into a true, football stadium that was only covered on one side.

You watched Newcastle United walk out in the deciding leg of the semi-final of European competition, and you were taken back to names that always slipped into conversations at the ends of meals when you were little. Names like Moncur and Arentoft and Barton and Gibb and Craig. Names that had seeped into the subconscious of your family. Names that made your dad and your uncles happy.

You remembered it only briefly, when the walk began, for then the noise blew through your senses.

In the Virage Sud there was suddenly a beautiful mosaic held up by supporters, their own piece of paper, white, or blue, or silver, depicting the Marseille badge and the UEFA Cup at its side, and to the right was the red and yellow stripes of the province.

When the noise increased and the chants rocked throughout all four sides of the ground, it was a sensory overload.

Newcastle's fans, around 1,700 of them, had a far corner of the far terrace. They might as well have been sat in a bar in Byker watching the game.

You could barely see them. You could not hear them.

All around was an intoxicating welter of sound.

It had been so calm 24 hours earlier, where the twinkle in Robson's eyes had sparkled in the sunshine of Southern France. There was apprehension at who he was without. No Bellamy, no Jenas, no Woodgate, a spine broken, no Dyer too, but it did not stop the 71-year-old from standing tall.

He revelled in such an occasion.

'It is an ordeal. It is a task but we must not be afraid,' Robson said.

'We have to go for it, we have nothing to lose. Our enthusiasm must be spot on, and our commitment cannot be in question. It cannot be in doubt.

'We have to be positive about it. Our motivation has to be high, our work ethic must be exceptionally high.

'We know what we are playing for, we are playing for the chance to reach the final of a European competition, but we need to score a goal and to do that we must play better in Marseille than we did in the second half at Manchester City.'

It sounded like Robson meant business, but the gnaw was at four of the previous games in which Newcastle had failed to score, it was at the menace Didier Drogba had presented in the first leg, at St James' Park.

And then, as the players went through their sprints, your heart dropped at the sight of actors from the forthcoming 'Goal' film (about the son a of a gardener offered a trial at Newcastle) similarly being warmed up pitch side. Separating fact and fiction was hard enough at Newcastle. The lines seemed way too blurred on the eve of the biggest night abroad for 35 years.

You wanted concentration and then celebration. Instead it was celebrity.

Injuries meant it was a half a team, and in the heat of that battle, Newcastle needed more than that.

At the front of the Virage Sud and Virage Nord, behind each goal, were moats, about 10 foot deep, and you did not know why they were there until the 21st minute, by which time Andy O'Brien had received a booking that would rule him out of the final, if Newcastle were to reach it.

Then the game was stopped because of fires caused by the flares, which were dealt with in those pits at the front of the support. It felt like the team from Tyneside would melt in the cauldron.

The opening goal came from a Newcastle free-kick, the ball was headed clear from the Marseille penalty area and they broke with real speed and intent. The ball was passed to Drogba, who charged into the Newcastle half, cut inside Aaron Hughes, evaded his challenge and dragged his shot low, past Given. The ground exploded. Drogba slid on his knees. You couldn't see a way back, not really, although Ameobi did curl a shot wide.

Then a second half free-kick in front of the Newcastle fans, struck low, to the penalty spot. Drogba checked his run, using team mates Habib Beye and Abdoulaye Meite as a decoy. Newcastle's defenders didn't notice. He was free, from 12 yards, almost a penalty, and from there, on home soil, the centre forward struck a shot that went straight down the centre of the goal.

He dived full stretch to the corner flag, stood up, and was mobbed. Celebration was all around you, in the terraces, behind the goals, in the seats, to the side of Newcastle's fans. That pocket of the stadium got even smaller. Flags were waved, flares were lit, the noise got louder.

Shola Ameobi and Lee Bowyer went close, but it was over before Lubos Michel blew his whistle.

Then the scarves came back out. The stadium bounced, Marseilles's players hugged each other and waved to all four sides of the ground.

Then they walked to the Virage Sud. It was a celebration, another one you had to watch, like after the FA Cup finals, where you had been invited to a party and refused entry at the door.

All dressed up and not allowed in. To watch celebration. To feel the intensity of a club's joy, back within touching distance of dreams.

It was getting harder and harder to take.

Sir John Hall raged at Robson in Marseille Airport.

'I was very, very annoyed that night,' said Hall.

Robson's time, as the front man, was coming to an end.

It was a tiring club. It left your knuckles white from holding on.

The drops were becoming longer.

There had been two league victories away from St James' Park all season. Fifteen goals scored in 17 games. The away support who trudged back from France was weary. The team was weary.

The fall out would tumble into Tyneside.

Newcastle drew their next game, at home to Wolves. It was the final game at St James' Park of the season. Laurent Robert was substituted in the 80th minute and he was booed off. Hugo Viana, who replaced him, was booed on.

The estimations were that around a quarter of a crowd of 52,139 waited for the lap of honour, as the final act on home soil of the campaign took place. Newcastle were five points behind fourth placed Liverpool, who they would face on the final day, and two behind fifth placed Aston Villa.

The reaction hurt Robson, who spoke to the media after the game.

'I can't stop the reactions of the fans,' he said. 'They are what they are. We thanked the ones who stayed behind. The club have played 28 times in Europe over the last two seasons.

'When was the last time this club did that? People have forgotten that. The expectation here is so high. Five of our big players did not play here today. All five would have played and you have to remember that.

'My policy has not been to talk about the injuries but we've lost first-team regulars and we're not complaining. We'll need to have resolve and commitment to qualify for the Champions League now. My message to everyone is to get your head up and your chin up. There are still two games to play. In football you always have a chance. You have to believe that.'

It was not the end of what Robson said that day.

Behind the main stage at the St James' Park media suite are the rooms where television interviews take place. Robson had finished his piece for *Match of the Day* and assumed the feed was switched off. It wasn't. When Robson ranted about Newcastle's supporters going home and Leeds' staying behind at Elland Road, despite relegation, it was beamed to the hospitality areas inside the stadium. In the corporate boxes, in the 1892 club and in the boardroom they listened as Robson let rip. It was damning stuff. It wasn't supposed to be televised.

Debates fluctuate in press rooms in such circumstances but it was pretty unequivocal that it would not be used, that it was out of the public domain, that it was very much off the record. It ran the risk of those outside the media room who had heard leaking the severity of what Robson said, but the decision was made to leave it alone, until, that is, a journalist from the *Evening Chronicle* broke ranks and printed Robson's response in its entirety the following day.

Then the sands of time for Robson started moving that bit quicker.

The 2003/04 season would close with two more draws, the first a bizarre night at St Mary's, where Newcastle led once, trailed twice and equalised in the 90th minute through a 30-yard strike from Darren Ambrose, another youngster signed from Ipswich. At Anfield, Michael Owen cancelled out Ameobi's first-half strike, and that was enough, with Aston Villa losing at home to Manchester United for Newcastle to qualify for European football, once more.

It was the UEFA Cup, again, and, at the time, there were no laps of honour for that.

THE STOCK EXCHANGE, AUGUST 2004,

WAYNE ROONEY – IS IT REALLY SO STRANGE?

ON MONDAY, 23 AUGUST, 2004, THE STOCK EXCHANGE ANNOUNCED that Newcastle United had made a bid of £20 million to sign Wayne Rooney, who was then 18, from Everton.

'I went to Bill Kenwright,' said Freddy Shepherd.

'We were bidding for Rooney, we went to London and I saw Bill.

'I seen him and agreed the money, it was £20 million. He said, "Yeah, speak to Philip." I said, "Philip who?" He said, 'Philip Green.' 'I said, "I don't know who the fuck he is."

'He says, "Philip Green, he helps me at Everton."

'I spoke to him and he said it would be £30 million. I went, "We're not paying that". He went, "You're not going to get him."

'I said, "Well one thing's for sure, you're not going to let him go to Man U."

'I said, "You're mad at £30 million."

'Then the shit hit the fan.'

Manchester United matched Newcastle's initial bid of £20 million. Newcastle returned with an offer of £23.5 million.

Chelsea stayed out of the bidding but Jose Mourinho, the newly installed manager at Stamford Bridge, said: 'Wayne Rooney is a good player. Newcastle and Manchester United are fighting for him because they have the support and economical potential and the club who wins the fight will get a good player. That's normal.

'Maybe they do it because they are not happy enough with what they have but in my case, I am more than happy with the strikers I have at the club.'

On 31 August, 11 days after Newcastle's initial offer, Manchester United agreed a £27 million deal with Everton. Rooney signed a six-year contract. It was claimed Pro-Active Sports Management, his representatives, could receive up to £1.5 million for their part in the deal.

'I'm very excited,' said Sir Alex Ferguson, the Manchester United manager. 'I think we have got the best young player this country has seen in the past 30 years. Everyone is delighted by this signing.'

Newcastle, who had already signed Patrick Kluivert a month earlier from Barcelona, were well off for forwards. They also had Alan Shearer, Craig Bellamy and Shola Ameobi.

Three days before the bid for Rooney, Jonathan Woodgate had been sold to Real Madrid for £13.4 million. Robson would later claim he knew little of the sale. The next player to sign for Newcastle after the failed move for Rooney was in fact Ronny Johnsen, who was 34 and available on a free transfer, having left Aston Villa at the end of his contract.

THE NEWCASTLE BOARDROOM,
A PHOTOGRAPH
SEPTEMBER 2004,

FREDDY SHEPHERD –
NEW DAWN FADES

THE BOARDROOM INSIDE ST JAMES' PARK, ON THE FIFTH FLOOR, WAS lavish, airy and expansive, its table, firm, sturdy, with seating for around 12 and a freshly polished mahogany finish.

Freddy Shepherd was not worrying about the room or its furniture, instead he was staring down at a picture. Things were not good.

The season had ended disappointingly. There would be no Champions League football for the first time in three years. The support was restless.

And now this. A picture of a Newcastle United player, one of his Newcastle United players, an international, on the training ground at Benton, sticking two fingers up behind the back of an unsuspecting Sir Bobby Robson.

It was there in full colour, in front of him.

He had already been visited by two first team players. It was a private meeting. They told Shepherd of their concerns that Robson had lost the dressing room.

Things were mounting up.

There had been the failure in Marseille, a league season that had never been able to follow the highs of the previous two. Robson had been caught criticising the fans after the final game of the campaign at St James Park, senior players were that concerned they were coming to see him. Newcastle had not won a game in the new season, and now this, a picture of Robson being undermined in the extreme by one of his players.

Shepherd decided the picture could never come to print.

He agreed a deal to buy the negative. He would not say how much but the figure is believed to have been around £10,000.

'Can I write a player was photographed putting two fingers up behind Bobby Robson?' I asked Shepherd.

'There was,' he said. 'You can write that.'

'Can I say who it was?'

'No, don't mention who it was. There was a player and I had to buy the negative, the whole thing off a certain photographer.'

'It was definitely a picture?'

'I don't want to get into it too much and I don't want you to print who it is because that person is still alive and I don't want to get his character.'

Things were spiralling quickly.

During the summer, after Newcastle had finished fifth, Shepherd had drawn up a plan to ease the 71-year-old Robson from the direct firing line into a more senior role at the club, like the one he had taken at Barcelona.

'We asked him to come upstairs that summer, but he didn't want to,' added Shepherd. 'We wanted Shearer to be involved.

'We didn't approach Alan. It would have been wrong to have gone to him first. We wanted Bobby's clearance so we spoke to him.

'We wanted him to take Shearer as his number two and he wouldn't do that.

'He didn't give a reason why. He just said he wanted to do it himself.

'I think he thought perhaps Shearer might be poking his nose in too much but it didn't happen.'

It was not going to be easy.

'I said in an interview in Dubai that he was only going to stay on until the end of the season,' added Shepherd.

'Two players came to see me and they said, "He is losing the team." It wasn't a case of control, the words they used were losing the team.

'I think at the time some of the players there were a bit hard too handle. There wasn't any shrinking violets.

'You had the Brambles and the Dyers and they were a handful for anyone to handle. All that got on top of Bobby. He was 71. He was feeling the pressure. He was successful. The crowds loved him and all that, but at the end he got a bit tired of it, as they all do.

'All the fans walked oot at the Wolves game. They all went.'

Newcastle drew the opening game of the season at Middlesbrough. Dyer refused to play on the right side of midfield and was put on the bench. Bellamy and Shearer scored and Jimmy Floyd Hasselbaink's late equaliser went in off his arm. Luck had gone.

Newcastle lost at home to Tottenham in front of a crowd of 52,185 and in the next game threw away a two-nil lead against Norwich. When they went to Villa Park, for the fourth game of the season, Robson dropped Shearer. It was not quite the suicide note of his predecessor, but it still felt a gamble, to overlook Shearer for Patrick Kluivert, a summer signing from Barcelona, who at just 28, had already enjoyed the best days of his career.

Kluivert cancelled out Olof Mellberg's early opener and then Andy O'Brien scored before half-time. By the time Shearer came on for Kluivert, Newcastle trailed, and a fourth goal from Juan Pablo Angel finished it.

Sunday, 29 August, would be Robson's final full day as the manager of Newcastle. The call came in the afternoon from a contact that it looked like he was on his way, but it was not confirmed.

Robson insisted he had gone to St James' Park the following day believing he would be discussing new signings with the Newcastle chairman.

'We did offer him to stay on as director and he refused that,' said Shepherd.

'We wanted him to stay on as director of football because we had to pay him anyway. We had to pay his contract anyway so we wanted him to stay.

'The rest is history.

'Four games into the season I called him to come to the ground.

'Somebody has to do it. You can't get Lee Charnley or Russell Cushing to do it for you.

'You couldn't get them to do it. That wasn't acceptable. I had to do it myself.

'Douglas lived in Gibraltar then. He went there in 2000. It was left to me to sort them all out. Keegan I had to sort out, then Kenny, then Gullit, then Bobby.

'In some ways he was relieved of handing over. To be fair when he did go I think he understood. He was near the bottom of the league, and we had gone four without a win.

'We got hammered for it, or rather I got hammered for it, for sacking him.

'I always said it was like shooting Bambi.

'It was very emotional.'

Sir Bobby Robson got in his car and drove out of St James' Park. He would never work for Newcastle United again. It is debatable that he ever fully recovered.

'I call it bereavement,' he would say 12 months later. 'During the three preceding seasons we'd never finished outside the top five. Then, four games into a new season, I'm gone. I hadn't even lost two consecutive matches so I was devastated. I say I'm almost over it but it will always rankle. I'll never forget what they did.

'When I came in as manager Freddy Shepherd said he still thought we'd be relegated. It was not some psychological ploy to gee me up. There was this feeling that Newcastle were in free fall, but of course we ended up playing Champions League football and the expectations climbed again. There were a few other difficulties as well.'

He spoke of the aftermath of the Wolves game.

'I got the shock of my life that day,' he added.

He called the decision to print his off the record quotes a 'despicable act'.

'If the chairman had made a small gaffe like that it wouldn't have seen the light of day,' added Robson. 'His influence would have carried the day inside the paper's office, but it became a huge local talking point.

'I couldn't believe it, but everything was done in secret at Newcastle. The players' contracts were always kept upstairs. Shepherd didn't want to show me anything. Hall was a recluse to me. I was kept in the dark with contracts and even transfers. Alex Ferguson, Arsene Wenger and Jose Mourinho know exactly what's going on at their clubs. That doesn't seem possible at Newcastle.

'I've heard it all before but one stupid remark made by the press – claiming I'd lost the dressing room – hurt me more than anything. I finished third and fourth with those boys. I handled Bellamy for four years.

'I didn't like dealing with Bellamy in the week because he's a strange and awkward character who can start an argument with anyone, but I liked him in that black and white shirt. I thought Bellamy was better than Michael Owen, so I put up with him.

'They're all moody, difficult characters but they could play, and Lee Bowyer never gave me a moment's trouble. I think he felt remorse over what he'd done in the past and he kept his nose clean with me.'

When Robson left St James' Park after being sacked, he drove straight to the Benton training ground four miles away. He would be pictured with his putter as he cleared his office, but before that, he stood in front of his Newcastle players for the final time.

'We were in the same room as where the Bellers thing was,' added Steve Harper.

'There had been whispers going around and I remember him walking in to tell us that he had lost his job.

'It was awful. Awful.

'I've likened it to looking at your grandfather when your grandmother has just passed away. It was like his reason for living had been taken away from him. I can still vividly picture exactly where he was and how he was and how he looked and how he was talking.

'I can still remember it. It burned in my memory. It was a sad, sad day.

'Some of us were in tears. He wasn't in tears but he was visibly as emotional as you can be without crying.'

Harper insisted the decision to announce it was Robson's final season, which was also done in a newspaper interview, was a major mistake.

'Once the statement was written that he was leaving at the end of the season then it almost became untenable,' he added.

'It puts it in the back of your mind wondering about it. Players need to be 100 percent focused on the job in hand. Any sort of distraction will detract from performance, so knowing that he was going, if your contract situation is on the horizon, he won't be the manager. There will be a new manager. That will be at the back of your mind. That will take an edge off your performance.

'Speculation about a new manager that you might or not want to play for or has turned you down in the past, that will detract form your performance. Any sort of uncertainty at Newcastle, any sort of instability is going to affect performance. That is beyond dispute.

'Newcastle fans are a fantastic bunch and they're demanding and they want to see people put a shift in.

'There was quite a group that wanted him out at the end of the season when we finished fifth.

'That seems to have been forgotten. There are fans definitely rewriting history. Fourth, third and fifth and there was significant group of fans who wanted him out.'

What was without question, as of 30 August, 2004, Newcastle United and Sir Bobby Robson were a thing of the past.

'You know what's incredible? I never knew anything about it on the Monday morning,' said John Carver. 'I never knew anything about the rumours.

'Bob never rang me. We never spoke to each other. For whatever reason, I don't know what I was doing that day, I had no inkling when I walked through the door of what was going on.

'I walked into my office at Benton. I walked into the office and the secretary came and got me, I think it was Judith Horey. She said, "I've got Freddy Shepherd on the phone."

'He said to me, "We've relieved Bobby of his duties, you're in charge until further notice and I'll speak to you later."

'I was gobsmacked. I didn't know what to say. I put the phone down.

'I walked into the office. All the guys were there, I said, "Shut the door, listen, this is the situation, they've sacked Bobby. I don't know who's coming in. We've got to take training and be as positive as we can."'

GRAEME SOUNESS
– BIG RIVER

THE SUITE ON THE SEVENTH FLOOR AT THE MALMAISON HOTEL IS designed to let you inhale much that is good about the city of Newcastle; certainly its dramatic river at night. It was early evening and it was dark and the Tyne Bridge was lit up in all its glory. It is a striking piece of architecture, finished in 1928, allowing people easier access to the city.

The Tyne's riverside is always a welcome sight for sons and daughters of the region returning home: in total seven bridges crossing the water, the Quayside lurking underneath, the Tyne Bridge its crowning glory.

It was to that backdrop that Graeme Souness stood at the window and overlooked the city to whose football club he had just been appointed manager.

'I think I'm ready for a big challenge, and they don't come much bigger than this,' he said. 'I don't need to be told by anyone that Newcastle are one of best supported clubs around. Everything is geared to be successful, and I hope I can bring success.

'I just can't wait to get started. Everything is here. I can't describe how excited I feel.'

He would be the man to succeed Sir Bobby Robson. That alone was not an easy ask.

He had not been an outright choice to fill that void. There had been moves for Steve Bruce and Sam Allardyce. Compensation packages were being put in place, but both men decided the timing was wrong.

Souness, as Shepherd admitted at the time, showed no such hesitation.

'It was a hard job because of what was in the dressing room,' said Shepherd. 'But he wanted the job and he told me wanted the job and that was impressive.'

There are no regrets today that he did.

'I was like everyone else who takes the job, you think you can be the one to win a trophy for the first time since 1969,' he told me. 'You look at the stadium. You look at the passion of the supporters and you think you're the one, like Kevin did, like Kenny did, like Ruud Gullit did, like Bobby Robson did, that will bring success.'

As a player he was one of the most powerful midfielders English football had seen. Hard, talented, an outstanding footballer; highly decorated. The Edinburgh-born Souness won three European Cups, five English titles, and four League Cups with Liverpool (they had signed him from Middlesbrough), a Coppa Italia with Sampdoria and then three Scottish titles and four Scottish League Cups with Rangers. It was there he made the switch to management and he was fearless then as well, buying the Catholic Mo Johnston (the first the Protestant club had signed) and taking England internationals to Scotland.

He returned to Liverpool as manager in 1991, underwent heart surgery and lifted the FA Cup in 1992. He went to Galatasaray and planted his club's flag in the middle of Fenerbahce's pitch after winning the Turkish Cup in 1996 (the president of Gala's rivals had called him a cripple because of his heart operation) and almost sparked a riot.

Southampton, Torino and finally Blackburn (where he won the League Cup in 2002) followed before an agent made an approach to join Newcastle. He took a few days to think about the offer and agreed to take over.

'The approach came through an agent and we started work,' he added. 'I felt I was the right man to do it. I was happy at Blackburn. I thought about it for several days when I had the opportunity to speak to them and ultimately having lived and worked in the North East before I knew a bit about the passion of the football clubs up there and it was very attractive to me.

'I quickly realised it was a monster of a job. You never get a job if everything is right and rosy in the garden.'

It did, however, start well enough. Newcastle won seven and drew two of the first nine games Souness was in charge. There was even a victory at his former club Southampton, a place where Newcastle had not won a league game since 1972.

By the end of that run Newcastle were joint sixth in the table, through to the fourth round of the League Cup and going well in the UEFA Cup.

Still, the rumblings of discontent had started, at Charlton, on 17 October.

Newcastle drew 1–1 and Craig Bellamy was substituted. After the game he clashed with the new manager. Bellamy said he was the best player at the club.

Then came a run of one win and three draws in ten league games. As 2005 started, Newcastle had sunk to 14th place. Souness went into the transfer market. The club signed Celestine Babayaro from Chelsea and he went back to his old club Rangers and paid £8 million for the defender Jean-Alain Boumsong.

'He is a communicator on the pitch and you can never have enough of them,' said Souness when the deal was finalised. 'That is something we have been lacking. We do not have enough people who are talkers, and he will certainly help us in that department. I think the supporters will enjoy watching him play.'

There was an improvement in league form (seven points from nine) and an FA Cup win over Yeading.

Still, Souness had walked into a dressing room that looked like it was on the brink of meltdown.

At Arsenal, on Sunday, 29 January, it would implode.

Souness had already clashed with Bellamy about his best position in the side. The Wales forward saw himself as a central striker. Souness saw him as a wide forward.

On Friday, two days before the trip to Highbury, the pair's relationship ended.

'Bellers was Mr Angry from Monday to Friday and on match days,' Souness told me. 'He trained properly. He always wanted to improve. He always wanted to better himself but yeah, I fell out with him and it was about him wanting to play down the middle. He threw one in one day when he said he was injured and he wasn't.

'I walked out onto the training ground and he was walking in.

'I said, "What's the matter with you?"

'He said, "I'm feeling my hamstring."

'I walked over and the senior players came over and said to me, "There's nothing wrong with him, he's just thrown one in. He had said he would do it before training."

'I went back into the dressing room and said, "You and I are going up to see the chairman."

'We got to the chairman and he repeated what he had said.

'That was the end of our relationship.

'I'm sure if he had his time again he wouldn't be going down that road.

'It was frustrating, it was annoying and it was a new one on me that someone didn't want to play, that he wanted to make a point to that extreme. 'I will throw an injury,' it's not just himself he's letting down, it's his teammates.

'Whatever you think of the manager you have to think of your teammates.

'It was when we were playing Arsenal at Highbury, one of the biggest games of the season. It wasn't something I'd ever experienced.'

The story began to break before the game at Highbury had started. Bellamy, a brooding figure of discontent, was pictured in the seats behind the visitors' dugout at Arsenal.

He was Mr Angry then all right.

Newcastle lost 1–0 to a Dennis Bergkamp goal. It should have been more. Shay Given was outstanding. Souness was still angry afterwards. He then went public on why Bellamy had not played.

The player was not slow to respond.

'How can I fake an injury when I didn't know I was going to be playing or where I was going to be playing?' said Bellamy.

'I couldn't believe it. I was in shock. I just thought: "Not only has he gone behind my back, in front of my face, he is lying."

'I'd do anything to play for this club, even if it's in goal.

'I'll never ask for a transfer request to leave this club. This club mean so much to me. To leave this club? I couldn't do it?'

It was revealed then that Bellamy had asked for assurances about possible signings coming to the club in his position, including Ayegbeni Yakubu, when he had spoken with Shepherd and Souness. He was told the forward would not be signed.

Finally, after Bellamy's outburst, Freddy Shepherd reacted. The player was fined two weeks' wages, around £80,000.

'I wish to put the record straight regarding the Bellamy situation,' said Shepherd.

'Craig walked off the training ground saying his hamstring was tight (on Friday), but what he failed to reveal was that he had told other members of the squad before training that he intended to feign injury.

'When Graeme discovered this he immediately ordered Bellamy to attend a meeting in my office.

'At that meeting Bellamy admitted to Graeme and I that he had told the players that he was going to 'fake' an injury in training and walk off.

'He also agreed at that meeting to apologise to his teammates for his behaviour. He didn't do this, which resulted in the action taken by the manager at the weekend, which I fully support.

'In my book this is cheating on the club, the supporters, the manager and his own teammates. He is paid extremely well and I consider his behaviour to be totally unacceptable and totally unprofessional.

'It is not about money. It is about a player thinking he is bigger than this club.

'No individual is, be it the chairman, the manager or a player.'

Bellamy wasn't finished: 'I won't apologise because I have done nothing wrong,' he insisted. 'There's no doubt about it, I am out of here.'

By 25 January, Newcastle had another FA Cup tie to play, with Coventry.

'Craig Bellamy has been a disruptive influence from the minute I walked into this football club with his attitude to the coaching staff, to me and to his teammates,' Souness wrote in his programme notes.

Finally, on 1 February, Bellamy signed for Celtic on loan until the end of the season.

'I knew this club was right for me as soon as I heard they were interested,' he said.

'This is a big thing for me; to come and play for an incredible manager and be part of Celtic football club is a great honour.

'I'm still emotionally attached to Newcastle. I didn't really want to leave and the way it has happened, I have found it very difficult.

'I do love the club and I am still coming to terms with life without Newcastle.'

Souness said then: 'He can't play for me ever again. He can't go on television and accuse me of telling lies.'

Bellamy would score nine times in 15 games for Celtic and lift the Scottish Cup.

Souness, talking of that volatile period with the player, said: 'When he did that I had to get him out of the club. That was the most difficult moment. The chairman agreed with me and supported me. Then he went. We loaned him out to Celtic.

'Bellers was difficult to deal with. I think if you sat down with Bellers now and put it to him I think he may accept he was a difficult animal to deal with. I always felt his biggest threat was in the wider area breaking in. He wanted to play through the middle.

'Kieron Dyer I found no problem at all. Lee Bowyer was no problem at all. He was a good lad. Being a player I could relate to what they were like. They were rascals. They needed a firm hand.

'I think Dyer was really unlucky because of his ailment that prevented him being fit all the time. He was a super player. Lee Bowyer gave you everything he had every time he went across the white line.

'Was I surprised at how difficult the dressing room was?

'No, no. I think my style of management was right for that time.'

Next came an 11-game unbeaten run that included two excellent FA Cup victories against Chelsea and Tottenham at St James' Park. 97,000 watched the two ties. Patrick Kluivert scored the winning goal in each game. They were through to the quarter-final of the UEFA Cup and through to a semi-final of the FA Cup at the Millennium Stadium against Manchester United. As ever, it was proving impossible to keep up.

Then, on Saturday, 2 April, Newcastle played Aston Villa at St James' Park. And all hell broke loose.

Sir Bobby Robson, who would lead Newcastle back to the Champions League.

Robson shows his vitality and love of the game never wavered as he goes for a header in training.

Wembley Way is dominated by black and white before the semi-final of the 2000 FA Cup against Chelsea.

Alan Shearer leads Newcastle out of the tunnel at Wembley before the semi-final against Chelsea, with Shay Given at his side.

Sir Bobby Robson walks pitch side past the Newcastle support at Wembley.

Robert Lee cannot hide his joy after equalising against Chelsea with an excellent header.

Nikos Dabizas takes off his strip in celebration after scoring the first winning Tyne and Wear derby goal at the Stadium of Light.

An emotional Kevin Keegan gives Newcastle fans the thumbs up as he returns as the manager of Manchester City.

Peter Beardsley in his first spell at the club shoots for goal against Manchester United in the snow of St James' Park.

Freddy Shepherd pours the water as Douglas Hall looks on.

Sir Bobby Robson, back at Barcelona's Nou Camp, with his Newcastle players.

Graeme Souness stands to the side of the dugout as Newcastle face Crystal Palace.

Lee Bowyer (left) and Kieron Dyer are held apart after fighting each other during a 3-0 defeat to Aston Villa.

Glenn Roeder congratulates Tim Krul for a clean sheet on his debut in the UEFA Cup at Palermo.

Sam Allardyce in the away technical area at the Reebok Stadium during his first game in charge of Newcastle.

Joe Kinnear.

Chris Hughton takes charge of Newcastle at West Brom following Joe Kinnear's heart attack during the early hours of the morning.

Alan Shearer swaps the number nine shirt for a suit as he becomes manager for the final eight games of the 2008/09 season.

Mike Ashley, who took full control of Newcastle United in July 2007 for £134 million. (Getty)

KIERON DYER AND LEE BOWYER – BORN OF FRUSTRATION

THE HOME DRESSING ROOM AT ST JAMES' PARK WAS SILENT. STEVEN Taylor was sat on his own, only his thoughts to contend with, and they were racing.

'I'd been sent off and I was very low,' he said. 'I thought, "I'm 21. I'm not established in the first team. This was my big chance and I've blown it. I wanted a career here. This is my club and it's my family's club. I handled the ball and I've been sent off. The manager won't put up with what I've done."'

Then Taylor heard a commotion outside the dressing room. The silence was smashed.

'You punch like a fucking girl.' It was Lee Bowyer's voice. His shirt was ripped. There was a member of the club's backroom staff with him. Kieron Dyer came next. 'You've always been shit, that's why I didn't pass to you.' There was a Newcastle official with him as well.

'I quickly realised what had happened,' added Taylor. 'It was unbelievable but they'd had a fight on the pitch. I knew then people would forget all about me!'

In the 82nd minute of a quite unforgettable afternoon at St James' Park, Kieron Dyer ignored the call for the ball from teammate Lee Bowyer.

Bowyer, now ignoring the game in which 10-man Newcastle were already losing 3–0, began shouting at Dyer. Dyer began shouting back.

What happened next still feels remarkable.

Bowyer ran at Dyer, 10 yards in front of the Newcastle dugout, and the pair began grappling, in front of 52,306 people. Bowyer threw two right-handed punches at his teammate. Dyer, appearing the more surprised of the two in the fight, eventually aimed one back.

'There's a fight between two Newcastle players,' said the Sky commentator, losing control of his voice. 'Kieron Dyer and Lee Bowyer are having a fight. Goodness me, what on earth is going on? I have never seen such a thing!'

Gareth Barry, who had already scored two penalties for Aston Villa, jumped in and grabbed Bowyer, who was still snarling. Stephen Carr was the next to get in between the pair and he grabbed Bowyer. Nicky Butt then came in to keep the two men away from each other.

Bowyer, whose shirt was hanging off, ripped down the middle, was then taken in hand by Shearer. As he was doing so, the referee Barry Knight was raising a red card to Dyer. Knight then walked over to Bowyer, and pointed the red at him as well.

The pair were tracked by backroom staff into the dressing room.

'We were playing Aston Villa at home and we were going for our sixth straight home win on the belt,' recalled Souness. 'The run we were on shows it wasn't all bad.

'We started off full of confidence. They got a goal. We had a penalty shout not given. We had a goal disallowed.

'Then they make it 3–0 and the incident was a show of the frustration among each other.

'I was on the touchline and I could see the two of them ignoring the ball. Someone has said you should have passed to me, the other one said fuck off and then I could see them walking to each other and shouting at each other and the game was going on and I was shouting at them, "No! No!"

'I wasn't that far away. I almost stepped onto the pitch; I could see the two of them were going to go for it. I've been there. I've not committed it on the pitch, but it's certainly happened in dressing rooms where I've been, but not on the pitch.

'We were going really well and it was a game we were expected to win.

'Of course it was frustrating. You look at it afterwards and the personality of both of them. Lee always gave me everything when he went out onto the pitch.

'Kieron was an extremely talented young footballer. He would have been frustrated permanently because he couldn't keep himself fit for every game.'

Shearer charged into the dressing room once the game had finished and let rip at both players. Boumsong weighed in next and said the pair should fight each other there and then.

It was suggested that Souness said to both Dyer and Bowyer that if they wanted a fight they would have to have one with him, an offer that they could, and did, refuse.

He laughed at the story.

'I don't think that happened,' he said. 'I can't remember. I might have said that but I can't remember that.'

Dyer recalled he did.

'We were playing the game, he [Bowyer] came short and wanted the ball and I passed to someone else,' said Dyer.

'He was like, "Give me the ball" and I was like, "I haven't given the ball away, what you talking about?" Five minutes later he came again and I gave it to somebody else.

'He said, "You never pass to me!" I said, "The reason I don't pass to you is because you're shit basically."

'There were a lot of swear words, and that was it then, you just saw him lose his head. He said, "You what?" And I said, "You heard me."

'As he was walking towards me I just thought he was going to grab me or push me. When he was raining the punches in I thought, "You need to get on the weights because they aren't hurting."

'Secondly, I was thinking, "I can't believe he's doing this in front of 50,000 people."

'I didn't know you could get sent off for fighting your own teammate, so when the red card came out I thought, "What the hell!"

'I was sent off first and I was waiting in the tunnel to get some revenge. He came in, and we had two massive masseurs and they just dunked us on their shoulders.

'It was like a cartoon when your feet are dangling off the ground and we were trying to get at each other. We were sat in the changing room and they were in the middle of us.

'I was thinking how I could get to him. Then we heard the final whistle. Boumsong came in and said, "If you want to fight, fight now." I was wanting to fight and get the revenge.

'Then Souness came in and said, "If you want to fight I'll beat both of you." Al came in and I never saw him lose it like that – he went mad and called us selfish and a disgrace. He knew we'd have a three-match suspension and miss the FA Cup semi-final that was coming up.'

Bowyer added: 'It was a moment of madness. Everybody regretted it afterwards, but we are winners. When you play football, you have to be that way. You have to want to win. Sometimes it goes too far, that's what happened that day. I'm sure if we'd been winning 3–0, it would never have happened.'

What Souness did do was to tell the pair they would be frogmarched up to the media suite and forced to apologise to the supporters on camera, with the incident still flashing across the globe.

As the pair sat, humiliated and offering contrition, Kath, the tea lady who began working at the club in 1966 handed Souness a cup.

It was the first touch of normality at the club in two hours.

Upstairs Shepherd plotted his own punishment, an £80,000 fine for the two men.

'The two players fighting on the pitch was a low point,' said Shepherd. 'I got them both in. I was a bit hard to say the least. I just couldn't believe it at the time, I couldn't believe it.

'You know what it was over don't you? Dyer wouldn't past the ball to Bowyer.

'Nobody on the park could believe it. The two of them getting stuck into each other.

'It wasn't a case of handbags. I couldn't fucking believe it. I fined the pair of them.

'Graeme still trained every day in the gym. He was fit as a butcher's dog.'

Souness sat between the two in the media suite.

'I took them into the press room,' he added.

'The first thing you're disappointed with is you've lost the game and they've embarrassed the football club.

'Then they've embarrassed themselves, then they've let their teammates down, it's all those things. I don't know what comes first in all of that.

'It was just a very frustrating day. You know Newcastle attract headlines without trying on a daily basis.

'You just know you'll be dealing with that when really you should be dealing with the next game. It was everything. It just compounded the problem.

'If you don't win two games at Newcastle the storm clouds are gathering. It was just another thing you could do without.

'Bellers throwing that one in. There will be a week of that. It will run into the next game. That is Newcastle. That is what you are always fighting against.'

Players fighting against each other in public was, however, a new one.

Five days later Newcastle had the first leg of a UEFA Cup quarter-final.

Breathless, once again.

GRAEME SOUNESS
– FALLING DOWN

FIVE DAYS LATER, JUST FIVE, NEWCASTLE PLAYED SPORTING LISBON at St James' Park. Kieron Dyer started. Lee Bowyer was a substitute. He was cheered by sections of the support when he came on, for Dyer, just past the hour mark. There were times you were scratching your head and bewildered by it all. He had been jeered when his name was read out before kick-off.

'I couldn't have asked for more,' Bowyer said of the supporters. Earlier in the day he had apologised publicly through the local paper. 'I'd die for this football club,' he said. 'All I can do is to plead with the Newcastle United fans to forgive me.'

After the game Souness said: 'The reception was fantastic; it tells you our supporters have forgiven him. He's a buoyant character around the place but since Saturday he has been extremely low. He'll be happier now.'

It was left to Alan Shearer to bring goals and football back to a Newcastle match report. In the 37th minute he headed a Laurent Robert free-kick past Ricardo, a really good goal. Robert also hit a post. Bowyer and Dyer shook hands when one replaced the other. The action of another substitute looked more important. James Milner shot over when well placed. Aaron Hughes was booked and faced suspension.

'I'm pleased to get the 90 minutes out of the way really,' added Souness. 'It's been a particularly stressful week.'

When Robert was substituted for Milner, he walked straight down the tunnel. 'We need more from him, a lot more,' added his manager.

Another storm was brewing.

Three days later Newcastle went to Tottenham. It was not a squad for this kind of schedule. They lost 1–0. Jermain Defoe scored. The following Tuesday, outside of the main entrance to Newcastle's training ground, players were interviewed ahead of the return tie in Lisbon. There was a sense among the more senior players of what was on offer here. No outstanding teams were left in the competition. CSKA Moscow looked likely to reach the last four and then it was Parma or Austria Vienna in one quarter-final and Villarreal or AZ in the other.

There was still a nucleus of players who had suffered the Wembley disappointments. They knew a door was opening, an opportunity to make history.

Outside of that training ground Laurent Robert, a player who scored some quite wonderful goals for the club, was interviewed by newspapers. Having been substituted in his last seven games, his mood was not good. He did not hold back in his criticism.

'We have been awful,' he said. 'We are not playing good football. We have not played well in the last three games. We have been very, very bad. We were awful against Villa and lost at Tottenham.'

Asked if the current Newcastle team was better than the one that had reached the quarter-final of the UEFA Cup 12 months previously, he replied. 'No, I don't think so. Are we the same? No, probably worse. I don't think we are playing as well this season as last. Our form is awful.

'It is difficult to explain why we are playing so badly, but we have to get out of it quickly.'

The story was used on the morning of the return tie in Lisbon. Souness was furious.

'We've had to take our eyes off the ball because of the selfish attitude of one of our own players,' he said.

'Once again, we've been side-tracked by a selfish player at a time when this club is playing its two most important games for 35 years.

'That is totally unacceptable, not only for the management team of Newcastle United and its players, but also the supporters.

'These two games are not about Laurent Robert, they are not about Alan Shearer or Graeme Souness either, they are about the cause, and that cause is Newcastle United. What Laurent Robert has to do is to look at himself first and if he is not playing well, he should try harder. He always seems to blame someone else.'

As the team bus waited to go to training on the morning of the game, Souness marched on. His mood had not calmed. 'Where's Laurent?' he shouted. He marched over to his seat, threw the papers at him and called Robert a disgrace. The pair argued. Robert was kicked off the coach.

Souness went back to his seat.

Later that day the same bus drove the squad to the Estadio Jose Alvalade for a European quarter-final.

Twenty minutes into the game Kieron Dyer burst through. He cracked a shot through Ricardo's legs. Newcastle were 2–0 up in the tie. Souness and his staff – Dean Saunders, Terry McDermott and Alan Murray – grabbed each other. They could not contain their joy. It was the perfect start. Dyer almost added a second, shooting wide from a similar position. Newcastle were playing well. Souness spoke much of 'proper players' and right then it looked like he had them.

Five minutes before the interval, poor defending allowed Niculae to equalise on the night, but there was still an away goal in the bank. Jenas was replaced by Milner and then, in the 60th minute, Dyer's hamstring went. He limped off. It was a huge blow.

Eleven minutes later, the scores were level: Shay Given parried Barbosa's shot only as far as Sa Pinto, who slotted in the second. Titus Bramble had also gone off injured by then. With 13 minutes of the tie remaining, Beto headed Fabio Rochemback's corner into the Newcastle goal. The corner taker then scored a fourth, at the death. A place in the semi-final of a European competition had gone in the space of 19 minutes. It was hard to comprehend.

'For 60 minutes we were comfortable,' Dyer said. 'Then we blew a gasket.'

Souness had to somehow rally a disintegrating dressing room, one physically and mentally exhausted.

'We can't feel sorry for ourselves,' he said. 'I think we have done an okay job and, if we'd been able to keep our starting XI on the pitch, I'd be sitting here telling a different story. When we started to lose our better players, we knew we were under pressure.'

Souness now cannot even remember what Robert, who was left out of the squad for the quarter-final, said.

'What did he say again?' he said. 'You expect that. How did his career pan out when he left? Unfortunately there are people like him in football, occasionally.'

His job was to lift his players to face Manchester United, who had played one game in the time Newcastle had played three. None of their players had fought each other either.

'The UEFA cup was a great opportunity for us to get to a semi-final and then you never know,' said Souness.

'You know they're down. As a manager you have to put on a front.

'Onwards and onwards. We were playing against a Manchester United that were the best team around.

'They hadn't been playing in Europe on the Thursday night. They hadn't been travelling.'

There was a flight to Bristol. A bus ride to a hotel. More change, more upheaval. Injured players, suspended players. Newcastle were limping into an FA Cup semi-final. They needed a lift.

The Newcastle team coach, unable to move as it neared the Millennium Stadium through the sheer volume of supporters in black and white, would provide it.

'I remember speaking to them when we saw how many were there,' added Souness. 'We were going through the Newcastle supporters. They were everywhere. I said to the players, "Look at that, look at how many there are, look at what it means to these people. You've got to give them everything today. You have to do it for them."'

He was talking to half a team. Bowyer was suspended, Dyer was suspended, Bramble and Jenas were injured, Robert was recalled to rally numbers.

Ant and Dec were there, so was Sir Bobby Robson ('I never felt in his shadow,' Souness said). The Blaydon Races was really belted out across Cardiff. It was a battle cry from 35,000 supporters, in hope rather than expectation.

It was the longest of shots and it was not helped by the FA Cup being Manchester United's last hope of silverware or of their previous two games being a defeat to Norwich and a goalless draw with Blackburn.

Newcastle had lost every cup-tie they had ever played to Manchester United. Ruud van Nistelrooy scored first, after 19 minutes. Paul Scholes added a second and in the 58th minute, when Nicky Butt lost the ball, Manchester United broke and van Nistelrooy had his second. Newcastle replied through Shola Ameobi, but it was a mismatch of a team and a mismatch of game. With 14 minutes left Cristiano Ronaldo scored the fourth, 4–1 again, twice within three days. The season was over. The fight in everybody had gone at that point.

'We had two 18-year-olds and a 19-year-old on the pitch,' said Souness. 'We did it on Thursday trying to win a UEFA Cup quarter-final and again trying to get into the FA Cup final. We didn't get started in the first-half and the game was won in the first half.

'In the second half we got a goal and I would have liked another to make it

3–2 but it wasn't to be. I can't be critical of any of my players. We've been bashed physically and mentally on Thursday night and sometimes it takes you 45 minutes of football to get your legs going after that. I think that was the case with us.'

Craig Bellamy was less understanding.

'I felt bad for Newcastle when they lost their 2005 FA Cup semi-final to Manchester United,' he wrote in his autobiography, *GoodFella*. 'They had loaned me out to Celtic but I still had a lot of affection for them. They lost 4–1 and afterwards Alan Shearer did a television interview.

'He mentioned shortcomings in defence, which made me laugh. He wasn't the player he had been and now he was trying to pass the buck. I had seen how poorly he performed personally. So I got my phone out and texted him. "Fucking typical of you," I texted. "Looking at everyone else yet again. You need to look at yourself instead. Your legs are fucking shot. Concentrate on yourself and let the team take care of itself."

'I got one back straightaway. "If I ever see you in Newcastle again, I'll knock you out." "I'm back in Newcastle next week," I texted back. "Pop round and say hello." His 'Big, hard Al' act wasn't for me.'

(Bellamy played against Newcastle the following season, having moved permanently to Blackburn. He went nowhere near Alan Shearer. For that he was taunted by another large traveling support. Newcastle also won 3–0).

Before then, and another summer to plot and repair yet more damage, came a month of football that no one really wanted.

'We have seven hard games left and we have to somehow regroup,' said Souness. 'I don't think it's psychological at this stage.'

It felt it.

Two defeats followed, another one against Manchester United, this time at Old Trafford. There would be just one more victory, away at Fulham. Patrick Kluivert scored in a 3–1 win. Nothing said more of that period in Newcastle's history than Kluivert. It was said he had a disco upstairs in his house in Jesmond.

He was an expensive forward whose best days had come too young. Newcastle seemed unlikely to make that mistake again.

GRAEME SOUNESS
– ACQUIESCE

'I WANTED NICOLAS ANELKA.'

In the summer of 2005, Graeme Souness was about to find that the manager of Newcastle United did not always get what he wanted.

He told Freddy Shepherd he wanted Anelka and Luis Boa Morte, who had scored eight league goals for Fulham in the previous campaign. He got Michael Owen and Albert Luque. The Owen deal, all in, would cost Newcastle more than £40 million. Luque, a Spanish winger with Deportivo la Coruna, would cost £10.5 million. They were staggering deals.

'I initially wanted Anelka,' said Souness. 'He was keen to come back from Fenerbahce.

'We ended up with Michael Owen. Boa Morte and Anelka were the first choices that I wanted. We got Luque and Owen.'

The season had started, in Slovakia, on a pitch with a running track around the edge, in the Intertoto Cup. That was short lived, over by the first week in August. The first five league games did not yield a goal, just one point. Then came pockets of form, Newcastle beat Blackburn away, and Shearer and Owen scored. They beat Manchester City at home and moved up to 11th. There was a barnstorming win against Sunderland, an Emre free-kick settling a thrilling five-goal game, and then another three wins on the trot. Newcastle were joint eighth, two points off third place Arsenal.

Newcastle would beat Arsenal at St James' Park and then Owen would score a hat-trick at West Ham in a 4–2 win. Shearer scored the other. There was a loss at Liverpool, and then Newcastle went to Spurs.

'It was right on half-time,' said Souness. 'It was the goal to the left of the tunnel at White Hart Lane.

'Michael going for it with Robinson, their goalkeeper, and he stayed down. The half-time whistle goes. Tottenham, then, were one of the few clubs to have an x-ray machine in the stadium. So, at half time he goes off to have his X-ray. Ten minutes into the second half the doctor stands in front of me, "It's bad news, it's his fifth metatarsal. He'll be out for six to eight weeks."

'I said to the guys, "That's us finished. We might as fucking well resign now. We ain't going to be scoring any goals. We're done."

'That's exactly as it turned out.

'I had made a bit of a mistake with Alan Shearer. He was a very, very special player, but he was coming to the end.

'He had single handedly at Newcastle, with his goals and his attitude around the place, dragged on lesser lights to heights they normally wouldn't have got to. He was fantastic in his time at Newcastle. Him coming to the end, I knew all that when I took the job. I knew I'd never be able to replace him. That was a big issue going forward.

'He wanted to retire, but I persuaded him to stay another year and then we got Michael Owen. If Alan Shearer hadn't decided to stay for another year we would have had to get two strikers.

'Ultimately when Michael Owen got injured right on half-time at Tottenham, when he did his metatarsal, we were finished. Alan was finding life very difficult at that level because he was at the end.

'But Alan was so strong for me in the dressing room, so good and so on side with me, as was Shay and Harps, the bigger personality in the dressing room, that I felt it was a gamble worth taking, but it backfired a bit in that respect.

'After that the chairman wanted me out.'

Newcastle did not win another Premier League game under Souness. There were two FA Cup wins and then a 3–0 loss at Manchester City. Shepherd made his mind up that night.

'Tony Toward came down with a letter,' added Souness. 'He knew what the letter was. He's a nice man but I could tell by his face. He brought it down to the training ground.

'That was pretty classless.

'I opened it and it said I was relieved of my duties.

'In many ways it was a relief.

'My relationship with the chairman had long since broken down. Maybe it was best for everyone that it happened.

'By a letter? I would have preferred it face to face. To be fair, by then our relationship had broken down. That was his way of showing that.

'It had been good. In the first year I enjoyed it.

'Freddy Shepherd was critiqued a great deal for different things. I found him to be really passionate about his football club. He had a real passion for Newcastle. He took losing very badly which was a good sign.'

Souness was schooled at Liverpool, a club that won things, like Dalglish. His verdict on the club bore a haunting theme to his old teammate.

'I've been at big clubs,' he said. 'There was no major surprises.

'The supporters' frustrations are quickly shown. That surprised me a bit and I'd been to Glasgow with Rangers, been to Liverpool and been to Galatasaray and Benfica, all monster football clubs. The supporters there didn't allow their frustrations to show as quickly as they do at Newcastle.

'You know when you're doing well, no matter how well, at any club, that there is a train coming down the track. It can be one game away. It can be five games away but you know it's coming when thing start to go badly. At Newcastle you knew it was never five games away. It was three or two and sometimes one, and you knew it was always on its way, coming down that track.'

GLENN ROEDER – IN THE HEAT OF THE MOMENT

THE FIRST TIME GLENN ROEDER MET ARTHUR COX HE WAS GIVEN A lasting piece of advice. 'He said to me, "Glenn, Geordies love three things, Newcastle United, betting and beer,"' said Roeder.

'I went, "That'll do fine for me, I'm not a big drinker, but I'm happy with the other two!"'

He recounted the tale to a packed Stanley Club in 2006. There was laughter and there were cheers. By then he was the temporary manager of Newcastle United and the talk-ins and the run of form was building up a head of steam.

Roeder's relationship with the club had started in 1983. He had played in the second last league game of the season at St James' Park in May 1982 for Queens Park Rangers when just over 10,000 had turned up. He missed the next game between the two teams through injury, when Keegan changed everything at a football club, and this time 10,000 were locked out.

He drew an FA Cup final against Spurs and missed the replay through suspension.

When he met Cox for the first time, Newcastle were pushing for promotion. Roeder could play, a central defender as happy carrying the ball from the back as he was raising his arms and marshalling those around him.

It was a natural fit.

To a team that bristled with Keegan, Peter Beardsley, Chris Waddle and Terry McDermott was added the Roeder shuffle, a stepover with the right foot and then a touch with the outside of his left and a charge away from an opponent, it always seemed to work, another stamp being made indelibly in the history of Newcastle United; passion and heart and style. It would remain at the core of both the values and the expectations of the supporters for decades.

It worked and Roeder worked.

Like Beardsley he had travelled north as a player for the first time with Keegan. 'You'll be the final piece of the jigsaw,' Keegan told him as they drove up together, and he was right.

By the time the 1984/85 season started, the first in England's top flight for six seasons, Keegan had flown off to his retirement in a helicopter and Cox, appalled that the club's board did not share the fundamental ambition and desire of the city's people, had also gone.

Roeder was given the captain's armband by Jack Charlton, the new manager. For the first game, a friendly at Queen of the South, Charlton picked an ambitious 4-4-3 formation. Roeder was left with the shortest of straws to inform his new manager of the mistake. He was left out.

It did not matter. He marshalled and he cajoled and he was a good servant of the club. In the following five years he played 193 times. He got what the club meant. When he finally left it was 1989 and he had spells with Watford, Leyton Orient and Gillingham.

He also managed Gillingham and Watford, coached England under Glenn Hoddle, managed West Ham, suffered a brain tumour, came successfully through surgery, lost his job at West Ham before one day, in the summer of 2005, he got a call from his old Newcastle team-mate, the left back Kenny Wharton, from Cowgate, who asked if he would like to return to the club to take charge of the academy.

Roeder took it.

'I came in as the director of the academy,' he added. 'We worked together. Kenny took the under-18s. Freddy Shepherd gave me the role. I enjoyed it very much. It didn't last very long. When I look back now, we got to the semi-final of the FA Youth Cup that year. I'd left at the quarter-final stage because I was needed at the first team.

'There can never have been a youth team that had two international goalkeepers like Tim Krul and Fraser Forster! We had Andy Carroll as well and they ended up putting him to left-back when I arrived. It was the last position, they'd given up a little bit because he was tall and gangly and lacking coordination, as someone of his height at that age would.

'Things are a bit more scientific now. If someone as big as that and has ability, which he had but it didn't always come together because of ungainliness, if you're patient, then that will all fall into place.

'He's ended up with a couple of big transfers. He's doing extremely well for himself and without doubt there isn't a better header of the ball in the British game.

'It's just his injuries he keeps having. He did really well for me. We went to Brentford in one of the Youth Cup rounds and we beat them in extra-time. He played the whole two hours, he was 16 and he was getting an absolute lashing from their two big centre-backs. He took it and came back fighting and I thought, "You've got a chance". Those games help make a player. David Edgar and Paul Huntington had careers, two very honest lads.'

Then, on 8 October, Newcastle United's academy, managed by Roeder, played Sunderland's academy, managed by Kevin Ball. Ball had joined Sunderland in 1990 from Portsmouth and stayed for nine years, developing from a central defender into a combative midfielder.

Like Roeder, Ball had left and then returned to the North East.

The pair clashed during the game.

'We both ended up with a fifty quid fine for having a go at each other,' he added.

'Kevin's Sunderland teams were pretty aggressive. He brought them up in a hard and tough way and they were playing Newcastle. We were a younger team and they wasn't shy in getting stuck in. That is fair enough, but there is a difference between getting stuck in and being ten minutes late and putting one of our young lads down where he needed to come off.

'I might have complained to the referee and I got the abuse back from Kevin, which I expected anyway. It wasn't a big surprise.

'We got reported because it's not good at academy level when the two coaches are kicking off a bit. It's not a good example.'

On 2 February 2006, Roeder received a more encouraging call, from Russell Cushing, the Newcastle secretary.

'Glenn, Freddy Shepherd would like to see you in his office please,' he said.

Newcastle had lost 3–0 to Manchester City. Shepherd's mind had been made up as he sat in the directors' box at the City of Manchester Stadium as he watched another insipid display.

Souness roared into Tyneside when he succeeded Robson. His team meekly sent him from football management. He never held another role.

By the time he was receiving a letter from Shepherd, Roeder was being called by Cushing.

'Russell said, "The chairman wants you to take the game on Saturday because of last night, it's getting uncomfortable that we're sinking completely the wrong way down the table."

'I literally had an hour on Friday. I knew the players. I'd worked with some of them. Graeme was very good to me. The training grounds of the first team and the academy were separate. He would say, "Come over for a breakfast, you're welcome any time at the training ground." That was a decent thing to say.

'I had worked with some of them in the England squad as well.

'A young manager might have thought, "I'll show how good a coach I am by putting on a long, complicated session."

'I knew, because of how things had gone for Graeme, whichever way he wriggled, and I call it Sod's Law, he couldn't get himself off the hook. It's always disappointing when someone loses their job, but when they came in on Friday, my idea was, "I know they're good players when they play well as a team."

'We knew we could beat Portsmouth. I kept it a very light-hearted training session.

'Even the warm up was in teams and we did passing drills, it was all in competition and suddenly the players relaxed. I was thinking the players wouldn't be physically tired but they would be mentally tired. 'It ended up with an eight versus eight, one and two touch. I can remember standing on the side at the training ground thinking, "How did this lot get beat three-nil on Wednesday?"

'They were popping it around really well. That gave me confidence. I did a long team talk and I reminded them of a few factors. I reminded them as a group, the fans are hurting, the chairman's hurting, the directors are hurting, the staff are hurting, but the people hurting the most are your families.

'They have to live in Newcastle. Your kids are going to school in Newcastle and the other kids are saying, "Your dad's no good". Horrible. I said we don't want that today. We want the kids to go to school and say your dad was great on Saturday.

'We played Portsmouth. We were five points ahead of them and they were third bottom. If they'd beaten us the five becomes two. It turned out to be a fantastic day.

'We won the game two-nil and Alan Shearer broke Jackie Milburn's record with the second goal. It was one of those things, as soon as he got the ball and it broke to him and he was on the other side of the defender with only the 'keeper to beat, you never thought he would miss. There's not many strikers you think that of. It was with Alan.

'To win the game was huge and of course Shearer scored the goal. It was amazing.'

Newcastle won four and drew one of their next five games. Shearer scored twice in the run, Shola Ameobi scored twice and Nolberto Solano struck four times. They conceded just twice.

They lost the next four, against Manchester United, Liverpool, Chelsea in the FA Cup and then Charlton, where Scott Parker scored against his old club in a four-one defeat to suggest momentum had gone but then came another five game unbeaten run. Game four was at Sunderland.

On 17 April Newcastle headed to the Stadium of Light, and in the 32nd minute of the 126th Tyne-Wear derby, Justin Hoyte scored and Sunderland were leading one-nil.

Newcastle's record on Wearside had been imperious. It had been more than a quarter-of-a-century since they had lost there. Newcastle had never been defeated at the Stadium of Light. It was one loss in almost 39 years of football between the warring clubs when Newcastle United were the away side.

When Hoyte, a loan player, scored, Kevin Ball, by this stage the caretaker manager of Sunderland, joined in the celebrations. He did not hold back, jumping around Roeder in the opposite technical area.

More than 36,000 Sunderland supporters danced with him. It is a dark place when the opposition scores in a derby, lonely and bleak, and for those from Tyneside half-time came and Newcastle had not scored.

'Sunderland go 1–0 up and he did a little rain dance around me,' added Roeder. 'He came over to where I was standing and it was like, "What are you doing?"

'Anyway, I told the lads at half-time, "Listen, we're only a goal behind. The next goal has to be ours. That changes everyone's feelings in terms of motivation. We can get them on the back foot."

'Usually I'm a very calm person, I don't like jumping up and down like a lunatic because I don't think you make good assessments, but if I've ever jumped up and down like a lunatic it was during that half-time. I stripped the walls. At least what I said to them, which I can't repeat, they took on board.

'It was 15 minutes before we got back in the game. I took Lee Clark off. He was playing a holding role. We needed to gamble. Having played for Sunderland and the problems he had with the picture with the tee-shirt he obviously got a lot of stick. I did it when we had a free-kick. He came off but the player I put on, Michael Chopra, it was his first touch, and he scored.

'The game completely changed. Alan gets a penalty which he scores, just a minute later and now the lads behind the goal (the 3,600 from Newcastle) are taking the roof off. It was fantastic. Charles N'Zogbia got the next one. Three goals in six minutes. Then Albert Luque got the fourth and he didn't get too many! It was such a good day.

'The press asked me afterwards what Kevin Ball was doing when he did a jig around me. I said I was very surprised, I don't know what he was doing, I told them I'd said, "Kevin, I've got to remind you, a game is 90 minutes and not 32."'

The goal for Shearer would be his 206th for Newcastle, in front of the travelling support, at the Stadium of Light, before he was forced to limp off with ligament damage after a challenge by Julio Arca.

'I wanted to go the full distance,' he said. 'But if I have to finish then it's not a bad way to go, coming to your local enemies and scoring a goal that helped us get a 4–1 win.'

There were few problems for Roeder for the rest of the season, but he could not build on that goal from Luque for the player. The Spaniard had cost £10.5 million when he arrived from Deportivo La Coruna in 2005.

The dressing room had been bedevilled with internal issues under Souness. Only Luque brought trouble for Roeder.

'There was one who was particularly difficult, of course,' he added. 'Then he proved that in his whole career, he wasn't just difficult with me. He went to Holland and had a proper punch up in his own dressing room (with Luis Suarez).

'He didn't train properly. You get paid to be a professional footballer so be professional Albert. Detach from the football from being a normal human being and you don't earn your living as a footballer. He was a decent human being but when you factored in that he was paid for this, he was difficult to manage.

'You couldn't use him. There was a few times I had to use him but he let himself down. Could he play? Yeah, if he wanted to. Of course. We signed him from Deportivo.'

Roeder's biggest battle had been with the League Managers Association [LMA]. He did not have the required UEFA pro Licence. He had started it when he was at West Ham, but the course had understandably taken a back seat when he was forced to go into hospital for surgery on his brain tumour.

Alan Curbishley led the call of those who said he should not be allowed the position.

'It bothered me,' added Roeder. 'It was nasty. It was wrong. In other European countries, as long as you're doing the licence at the time, that was okay. Bearing in mind I had signed up and was about to start my Pro Licence at West Ham when I had the brain tumour. I do think the coaching badges are important.

'I had a brain tumour and it's still working. As the surgeon said to me, "When those idiots shout you're brainless refer them to me. I've seen your brain."'

'When you've had a life threatening situation, most people, 13 years later, aren't here anymore. Seve Ballesteros, a great sportsmen, didn't survive more than a couple of years. It is life changing. You go out in the pouring rain and everyone is moaning, I'm not, I can feel it.'

Joy would come on the final day of the season. From nowhere Newcastle were on the cusp of European qualification once more (picking up four points in the following two games against West Bromwich Albion and Birmingham). Against Chelsea, in the 75th minute on the final day of the season at St James' Park, in front of a crowd of 52,309, Titus Bramble smashed in the only and winning goal. Newcastle finished seventh and qualified for the Intertoto Cup.

This time the call came from Shepherd to go and see him in his office.

'He said, "You've done very well, I'd like to offer you a long-term contract,"' added Roeder. 'It is what dreams are made of. I'm an adopted Cockney-Geordie. I had the best days of my life in Newcastle.

'When I signed, Arthur took me to the training ground. You don't turn Newcastle down.

'All these years later, Freddy offered me the manager's job. It was a great moment, one of the most outstanding of my career in football. I was very grateful to Freddy for giving me that opportunity. I will always appreciate that he did that for me.'

I spoke at length with Roeder in his office that summer, about what needed to change. There was a double take when he said there would be an increase in the number of scouts, which stood at two.

'Some managers before me said this club is impossible to manage, it's not impossible, it's a great honour to manage Newcastle United,' he added. 'The hardest bit is getting the right personnel, the right people in the shirt, that's all it is.

'The recruitment is difficult.

'I brought Oba Martins in the summer, he was expensive. The player I wanted before Oba was Dirk Kuyt at Feyenoord. I flew over to see him playing pre-season and came back on the airplane saying to Freddy we should be signing this player but very quickly.

'Very quickly Liverpool showed their hand and once Dirk knew about Liverpool they had the advantage of being a club winning trophies. We couldn't win that fight. Then I remembered a player who played for Inter Milan at Highbury, a year or two earlier and scored two fantastic goals with lightning pace behind the defence.

'That was Oba. I know how the deal was structured. It was five years at £2 million-a-year.

'He probably only played two full seasons. He was one of those who either scored stunning goals or missed from six yards. The ball would go under his studs.

'Whether you liked him or were average about him or didn't like him, not many players at Newcastle bought for good money were then resold to get your money back and he was. He scored one in three for us as well.

'The season before at the club was Alan Shearer, top, top England centre-forward at his best. He retired. Then Michael Owen got injured in the World Cup. When I saw that happen I knew straight away what it was because of how he reacted. If I'd had a bottle in my hand I would have thrown it at the TV. I had a cushion so I threw that instead.

'I knew what that meant.

'Suddenly you now have to replace two wonderful goalscorers, who cost £31 million. That's obviously not easy. We ended up with Oba Martins and last day of the transfer window, a ten to 12 signing, I pushed the button, and I'm still really good friends with him, to get Antoine Sibierski. I explained to Sibi, "You're going to a club that because you're a free transfer they will be very negative towards you."

'He won the fans over quickly. He worked very hard and scored some important goals in Europe and when you know him he is a seriously good human being.

'We had injuries and it was difficult but we had fantastic results in Europe.'

European football would once more offer salvation and a contrast to a disjointed and disappointing league season (Newcastle would actually win the Intertoto Cup, which had begun in July, against Lillestrom).

'We had a fantastic run in Europe,' said Roeder. 'We beat Fenerbahce, managed by Zico, and Sibi scored, we beat Celta Vigo. We got a draw in Germany at Eintracht Frankfurt and it was the noisiest crowd. It was nil-nil and they missed three good chances.

'We beat Palermo one-nil in Palermo and not many British teams went to Italy and won. They were top of Serie A. That was when Andy Carroll got on the pitch as the youngest Newcastle player to play in Europe.

'Tim Krul made his debut and he played like Gordon Banks. I didn't tell him until midday he was playing, I said, 'You okay?' and he said, 'I've been wondering why it's taken so long to tell me.'

'He was very calm, very cool, typical Dutch. He could pass the ball like a midfield player. He made a couple of early saves and nothing was going to get past him.

'Louis van Gaal brought AZ to St James' Park and we beat them 4–2. We were fantastic in the first half hour. We got a couple of goals in front. Oba scored twice and we got to 4–1 at half-time and then it went to 4–2. That should have been enough but we went over there and lost 2–0.

'It was a good run, a fantastic experience but obviously league form suffered because of the amount of injuries and the amount of games that came thick and fast. We were never really in danger of going down but we were never in that top eight that Freddy demanded.'

The start to the 2006/07 league season, a month after the Intertoto Cup, was more mixed, winning two of the first six games and losing three on the trot to Manchester United, Bolton and Middlesbrough during a run of seven games that brought just one goal, a penalty from Shola Ameobi. Scoring goals, without Shearer and Owen, was a huge problem. Newcastle were fighting relegation, in 18th position after a goalless draw at Manchester City.

Then Newcastle won four home league games on the trot that took them to 11th. This was the time to strengthen, but the club had no money.

'Russell Cushing said to me during that second season, "Glenn, the money's gone. When you add up what Michael Owen cost, what Albert Luque cost and what Oba Martins cost, we've gone to the bottom of the well. There isn't any more money to spend."

'I can always remember that January window and the question, who are you going to sign and it was especially important that we bought a defender and I kept saying we will try for this one and try for that one.

'It kept the fans happy to a point because they thought something might happen, but to a degree most of them thought, nothing will happen. Sure enough nothing happened and nothing was going to happen.

'In January we weren't going to sign anyone.

'The next time I saw Freddy, after the window had closed, he came up to me and said thanks, for not hammering him or knocking his door down to get a signing through the door.'

There was also unease at some that he had been left.

'We had Jean-Alain Boumsong and people like that,' he added. 'Boumsong wasn't a bad human being, he was just a limited player.

'Graeme signed him from Rangers. The first couple of times I coached him I just thought, "Christ, you're not seeing the same picture as me. You should be able to. If you don't, we're in trouble."

'It was about positionally as a central defender. I made some coaching points relative to him being a centre-back and he didn't agree with me and I thought, "If he doesn't see it, going forward we will have a problem."

'His view was to let the ball go in behind, because he was quick he could get out of it, but that drags all the other defenders around because they have to get involved in it.

'If you mark on the outside of the striker they won't put the ball in there. As a defender they will play it short and the ball will be in front of you and that's what you want.

'You don't invite people to go in there. Otherwise we all have to turn around and run back. When he couldn't understand that's how I saw it as the manager and the coach you know it's going to be difficult.

'Then he got a move to flaming Juventus, although they were in Serie B.'

Newcastle limped on in the league. There came a punishing third round FA Cup replay exit at St James' Park, losing 5–1 to Birmingham City. They won two, lost one and drew the four following Premier League games. It was that kind of campaign.

Another victory against Sheffield United in April took Newcastle back into the top ten, through goals from Martins and Steven Taylor.

Then came a fateful five game run which yielded just one point and no goals.

There had been 12 serious injuries during the season. In the background a potential manager was quietly questioning the training methods.

'The ironic thing was every single one of those injuries happened in the heat of battle on the pitch,' adds Roeder.

'Some things a manager can't legislate for and one is injury in the heat of battle. On the Sunday morning after we'd lost to Blackburn, Freddy called me into his office. "We will have to call it quits now Glenn," he said. "We can't go any further." It didn't last very long. That was the end of it.

'When the owner or the chairman says that there isn't really a conversation to have.

'There was one more game to go, at Watford.

'There is no point ranting and raving. It is an honour to manage the club. I got us to seventh in the table.

'The win ratio I had, only Bobby and Kevin are higher. There is a lot of names below me, and they are really big names, the Gullits and people like that.

'I actually view my time there as I did as well as I could with what I had. One of the big blows that season was trying to replace Shearer and Owen, who again I've stayed good friends with.

'Michael Owen isn't a greedy so and so who did things for money, he didn't have to. He doesn't have to. Michael has never had to do that since he was 18.

'Michael just had horrendous bad luck with his injuries, that first started with his hamstring injury at 18 and when they looked at a skeletal of his body, there were defects in those injuries that caused it to happen. It was the way he was born and put together.

'If he'd had been fit he had the ability to be a Newcastle legend, if he'd been fit he would have been scoring goals. If he's fit he scores and we finish around that top eight and things could have been different.

'I've come to the conclusion you have to take the good and the bad. I'd not consider my time at Newcastle as a manager as bad.

'It was huge disappointment as I drove away for the last time. It has to be. Who wouldn't be upset? One of the greatest managers they had, Sir Bobby Robson, I bet he was disappointed driving away.

'It's not an impossible club to manage. It's a fantastic club to manage, but I was still devastated when I left.'

ALAN SHEARER
– LOCAL HERO

IT WAS LIKE AN INFESTATION. WHEREVER YOUR HEAD TURNED THERE was what looked like giant black and white bees, there was even a sound as all four sides of St James' Park waved the scarves they had been given around their head.

It was a stunning image, no need for words or song. Just black and white, and it was breathtaking.

There were flames and Ant and Dec and for once you could not hear the Celtic fans tucked away at the top of Level Seven in the Leazes End that now gave you a panoramic view of Tyneside. It had been an eyesore of an end for 15 years but now it looked like a spaceship. It was so huge and powerful. The scarves were being waved for a man in the club's history that matched the imposing development of the stadium.

There was no trophy to show. Ten years, five operations, a smashed ankle, blood, sweat but no tears, at least none that anyone saw, and of course, the 206 goals that made Alan Shearer the greatest goalscorer the club and its support will ever see.

No trophies, a runners-up spot, two FA Cup losers' medals, a UEFA Cup semi-final, 14 Champions League appearances, seven Champions League goals, top scorer 10 seasons running. On paper did not do justice to what Shearer had put down for his club and his city.

He scored on his home debut against Wimbledon, in an evening game from a free-kick and wheeled away in a celebration that would become familiar. He spoke afterwards of relief that he was off and running.

He had scored on his final appearance as a Newcastle United player at the

Stadium of Light in an emphatic victory, that really is the dream for a Newcastle supporter good enough to play for the team.

He limped off and then he limped on at St James' Park. You will never find a more raucous and heartfelt thank you. Generations of supporters have not seen Newcastle win a major piece of silverware. They gave Bob Moncur a replica Cup made of tin foil in 1974 when the ground filled for a defeated FA Cup final team.

They lined the streets twice with more than 100,000 people to welcome the teams of 1998 and 1999 who lost in London. No goals scored, no dreams fulfilled, a Championship (the old Division Two) swagger thrown in and a glorious celebration that felt afterwards like it had lasted weeks, but never a big one, not the major trophies that all crave to win.

That night was as near as most have come. The stadium can fill your eyes with tears and your heart with pride when it roars. That night the people of Tyneside rejoiced. Tumultuous does not do justice to the sound that 206 goals made and if St Mary's Lighthouse, ten miles away at the coast, had wobbled ever so slightly, you would have known why.

Those with black and white hearts do not forget legend easily. When Jackie Milburn died in 1988, the man whose record (of 201 goals) Shearer beat, 20,000 lined the city's streets to pay their respects.

Shearer saw his outpouring first hand. Emotion dripped from the stands like condensation from the ceiling of a perspiring room.

It steered cleverly clear of sentimentality, which was not easy.

Shepherd had called him a Geordie institution before kick-off.

There was a guard of honour from both sets of players as he entered the field for the final time, holding the hand of his son and with his family in tow. To his left the Leazes End became a wonderful mosaic of black and white stripes with a gold number nine in the middle. The East Stand had the same but with gold lettering this time, to spell out Shearer.

Flames burst into the night air and the scarves fizzed and the cry for his name tumbled down with the ferocity of a raging fire and the tenderness with which you hold a young child.

There was not a spare seat anywhere in the stadium, the director's box and the press box both filled to bursting point.

'Here comes arguably the greatest ever player to wear the black and white of Newcastle United,' said Jon Champion in commentary.

Shearer's name filled the ground and the city.

There was even a moment when it looked like he was filling up. It was a night to soften the hardest of men and the coldest of hearts.

The noise grew, Shearer stood next to Shola Ameobi and started the game. Then he limped off.

Albert Luque scored at the Gallowgate End, Shaun Maloney and John Hartson scored for Celtic and then Paul Lawson made it 2–2 when he scored an own goal he was not supposed to.

When the clock struck 92 minutes and 31 seconds, Newcastle were awarded a penalty. His name rang around the stadium once more, and then a roar to stop you in your tracks took hold of the stadium as Shearer made his true, farewell bow.

He looked nervous, fiddling with the captain's arm band he had been given, over the number nine shirt that he had always looked born to fill, the ball tucked under his arm. 'He always had a ball with him, that was the first thing I noticed after he signed,' Keegan had said.

He clipped a right foot penalty past David Marshall, another cheer, and he raised the right arm in salute and in celebration, one more time. Rob Lee was there first, then came the rest of the players, Ferdinand, by now wearing just a vest.

'Shearer finishes with a goal at his beloved Gallowgate,' added Champion.

It had been the end he had stood on when he was 13 and had lost his mates amid the chaos and delirium of Keegan's goal on his debut, back in 1982.

He stood in front of a home made banner.

'You're not just a sheet metal worker's son from Gosforth. You're a legend.'

The goals had never stopped in ten years.

Some unforgettable.

The volley against Villa, a man of power using a Rob Lee cross to deftly redirect the ball past Peter Schmeichel.

There was the blaster against Arsenal, his 300th in English football, which flew through the wall. There was the semi-final against Spurs, outside of the foot, 25 yards, top corner

There was a 30-yarder against Chelsea, at the Gallowgate End, turning Marcel Desailly because he was too strong and smashing a shot so hard that Carlo Cudicini didn't even bother moving.

And of course the volley against Everton, vicious, just vicious; Robert to Ameobi, a head down and then a dipping volley, full of power and accuracy and technique.

Nothing for emotion though, would top Portsmouth, on 4 February, 2006, when he took a back heel from Ameobi, at the Gallowgate End of St James' Park, of course, and held off his old teammate Andy O'Brien and slotted in a goal that was like a cement stamp in history, becoming the club's all-time top goalscorer, beating Jackie Milburn.

He celebrated wildly, and then stepped back, to inhale reverence as it tumbled down from the stands. Overwhelming.

Like Keegan, the man he adored as a child and the man he signed for as a player, he would not lift a major trophy in a black and white shirt, but that moment must have felt like it. Adoration was all around you.

It was the same against Celtic.

His name boomed out throughout the night, scarves twirled.

Glenn Roeder was manager for the evening.

'There can only have been a testimonial like that in somewhere like Newcastle, for someone like Alan Shearer,' he said.

'When they had all the free scarves and people waved them at the same time, the effect was scintillating. It was like a game of football on another planet.

'It was a great honour to be the manager for that game and absolutely stunning. He got the send off he fully deserved.

'I played against him in one of his first games for Southampton at the end of my career. At that time, we did know what he was going to be. I can clearly remember playing against him. For an 18-year-old he'd back into you, he'd be pulling your shorts, he'd pull your shirt. He was fantastic.

'He's up there with the best in Newcastle's history. Everyone will have their favourite, Beardsley, Waddle, Keegan, Milburn, whoever they say, he's alongside them. He has to be in the best Newcastle XI, hypothetically. He's in the team. He was a phenomena.'

It was night time now but everything was black and white, including your soul.

Finally, Ant and Dec walked to a temporary stage in the centre of the pitch. They were mocked, in jest, briefly, but the pair did their time, as youngsters, tucked away in the Scoreboard when the ground was not full and the team was not good and a television programme from Byker was giving them their start.

'Wow, wow, wow,' said Ant. 'What a night! We're all so sorry to say goodbye. How do you feel?'

'I thank you for all the support,' said Shearer. 'As everyone knows I had a chance to join other football clubs before I came here. There was a team in red not far from Manchester but it was always my dream and ambition to come back home to Newcastle.

'Whatever anyone says, I've done it. I did it my way and I lived the dream.'

SAM ALLARDYCE
– REGRET

A GAGGLE OF JOURNALISTS WERE SITTING AROUND SAM ALLARDYCE, the new manager of Newcastle United, in front of the main stage in the media room at St James' Park. The ubiquitous nickname is for a reason, Sam is a big bloke. He can dominate a situation through his presence, and he was not perturbed at all by the allegations that had shaken English football. To the contrary, it was an early indicator that the then 52-year-old had the size of personality to tackle a job that had by now become perceived, contrary to Roeder's thoughts, as impossible.

On 19 September, 2006, the BBC's Panorama programme had made allegations that Allardyce was involved in payments made to his son Craig via other agents in return for deals that took players to Bolton Wanderers, where he was manager. It was alleged that his son Craig received around £50,000 for the transfer that took Tal Ben Haim to the Reebok Stadium in July 2004.

On the night the programme was aired, Allardyce, still the manager of Bolton, was busy leading his team to a 3–1 Carling Cup win at Walsall. At the time he said, 'I'll make a statement at some point, but you have to understand that I am doing my job and tonight has been very difficult. I'm aware of the situation of course, but because I haven't seen anything of the programme, I need to have a look at that and take a view of it before I make any comment whatsoever.'

Five days later he added: 'I am very angry at the lies told about me. The individuals who appeared in the programme making accusations against me have already confirmed in writing to my lawyers they lied to the BBC.

'As a result of their greed, my good name has been tarnished by deceit and innuendo. As a father, of course, it is painful to watch your son talk tall and exaggerate his influence for financial gain.

'If there is any real evidence – and there won't be, as I am utterly innocent of any wrongdoing – I would expect the BBC to give that evidence to both the FA and the [Premier League's] Quest inquiry.'

The following day Newcastle sacked Kevin Bond, who had only joined the club as a coach under Roeder at the start of June after he was implicated in the bungs scandal.

That same night Bolton beat Portsmouth 1–0 at Fratton Park. Jeff Stelling, the Sky presenter, asked Allardyce, 'Have you ever taken a bung?'

'You're out of order asking that question,' Allardyce replied.

To the written media he added: 'Every Premier League game is emotionally exhausting but this one was that little bit more. After what's gone on this week it's bound to mean a bit more.'

He found sympathy from Harry Redknapp, who had also been mentioned in the Panorama programme. 'Sam's had a tough time,' he said. 'He must have been feeling it big time. It must have been a hard week for him. I hope things get sorted out for him.

'Anyone who saw the programme will be wondering why I was on it. It was farcical. I don't think there is anything in it that I need to worry my lawyers about.'

By the start of October Lord Stevens revealed in his findings that 39 transfers involving eight clubs were to be investigated further before he could sign them off.

By the time he delivered his final report, concerns were expressed about a conflict of interest between Allardyce, his son Craig and former club, Bolton Wanderers. Similarly, Stevens' report also stated 'inconsistencies in evidence' provided by Graeme Souness and Kenneth Shepherd, Freddy Shepherd's son, who was working as an agent.

Four transfers at Bolton were mentioned in the report, as were the deals that took Emre, Boumsong, Amady Faye and Albert Luque to St James' Park for a combined £23.5 million.

Souness said of the statement: 'I cannot understand why my name features in this report. I volunteered full information to Quest as a witness and I have heard nothing further from them.'

The Stevens inquiry then said: 'We wish to make it clear that inconsistencies did not exist within the evidence given by Graeme Souness to Quest concerning his role in transfers covered by the inquiry during his time as of Newcastle United.'

Those significant off-field distractions did not impact at all on Allardyce's team. To the contrary, in fact. When he finally brought the curtain down on his seven-and-a-half years at the club, Bolton Wanderers were fifth in the top division of English football. There were two games left in the campaign.

At that point Bolton were set for their highest finish in English football since 1959, when Nat Lofthouse had scored 35 goals in the season. On Boxing Day in 2006 they were joint third. Allardyce had ridden out the storm. No charges were ever brought against him and, to his credit, he ducked nothing on that Tuesday afternoon, just 16 days after he had resigned at the Reebok Stadium.

He had left Bolton for a new challenge. Newcastle were one of the few genuine clubs in England who could challenge the top four. He was unperturbed by the legacy of the bung allegation, he had nothing to hide, he said.

It did not feel like the ideal preparation for the biggest job of his career but Allardyce looked ready.

He spoke of altering the culture of a football club.

'I have been given reassurances,' Allardyce said of the club's commitment to cultural change. 'I want to recreate an atmosphere that is a pleasure to come to, so I will look around the training ground quickly and improve that facility.

'It is a fantastic facility but there is always room for improvement. It might be a picture here, a window there, it might be a personal touch. I am sure if they start working with me they will start enjoying what they do. They will get up in the morning, look forward to training. I don't want a miserable environment. I want a happy environment with smiley faces.'

Freddy Shepherd watched, at the back of the room, with a broken rib.

He wanted a cultural change to the fitness of the footballers he bought.

'I'm sure if Bolton can afford it we can afford it,' he said.

'He [Allardyce] has got my blessing to implement the same sort of system he had at Bolton. That's the whole idea. It would take an idiot not to realise the problems we've had with injuries this season.

'The stats are something like 340 player days lost to injury at Newcastle; at Bolton it was something like 72. We lost five to one to Bolton in terms of injuries. We've got the Premiership record for injuries, which isn't the best one to have, so of course he's going to bring his medical staff in. They're going to look at me first!

'That type of system takes time to bear fruit so we have to be patient. On the medical staff, it's very much a preventative thing rather than trying to cure them afterwards. He's been very successful at that.

'You can't get away from the stats and they tell us that he's had the least amount of injuries with one of the smallest squads in the league. There you go, there it is.'

It had been a long road for Allardyce to get to St James'.

No one was ever really told about the less public life Allardyce had lived. He was born in Dudley, a Wolves fan who made his name at Bolton Wanderers as a player, he had a brief and largely unsuccessful spell with Sunderland and all the while was planning for his future.

At 27 he was doing his coaching badges and shortly after started a building company in Tonge Fold in Bolton. During the season he would buy up old terrace houses, sort out mortgage advisors and solicitors and get his building team together.

In the summer he would land on site.

'Yeah, I would go in and knock down walls and help out,' he told me. 'But you see, in my life, right as a very young kid from when I went to Bolton, I would always work in the summer anyway.

'I went cutting the grass in the parks, I went working in laboratories making aspirins, because you'd get paid more than you were earning as a footballer. Being brought up from a Scottish background [both his parents were Scottish], I was a bit of a tight bastard, which is what I'm not now.

'In the holidays I thought I might as well earn some money. I met my wife Lynn and I thought I'm not going to wait years, I'm going to get married and have kids and I'll have to have my own house. I'll have to graft for it. If I don't make it as a footballer, I've had these experiences in between that might help me.

'There was no money or very little money after the property market crashed. I went into the world of darkness and it was disturbing. My wife caught me staring into fresh air.

'I still had a business with my playing partner, Roy Greaves. We had a couple of businesses between us, licensed pubs and a social and snooker club. I could go and work there for some money. I had a small pension that could keep me going but this was going to be a period of time that, having got on the ladder, I got kicked off it very quickly.

'When I started doing my coaching badges, I thought this might not happen. There are probably a hundred people going for a job every time they become available and if you have no track record, how are you going to break in on the ladder?

'I think by doing your badges early and showing a willingness to learn how to go over to the other side of football, to the FA, and the coaching courses and the management courses, that even though you don't know it at the time, people see you. That gives you an opportunity. It might stay in their mind that they want to give you a job.

'Then I got the daft phone call from Father Joe [Young, the then chairman]. He said, "Come and manage Limerick." He called me because he needed a player-manager. He didn't know me. He said, "I've picked you off the PFA list." He knew about me playing.'

Father Joe had gone down an alphabetical list. Allardyce, an A, was near the top.

'When he first called I thought it was someone taking the piss,' he added. 'I put the phone down, but he called me back.

'West Brom was my first job as reserve-team manager. The second season, Brian Talbot made me his assistant. By January I was sacked with Brian, and you go, "Right, what am I going to do now?"

'Those businesses couldn't afford to keep me. I had a wife and two kids. So Walshy (Mike Walsh) lost Sam Ellis who joined Reidy at Man City and was in charge of Bury. I just rang up and said, "I'll come in." He said, "We've got no money." I said, "It's all right, I'll just come in anyway. I might as well come in and try and help."'

From there he built a managerial career, at Blackpool, at Notts County and then, with his greatest work, at Bolton Wanderers. His backroom staff was not small, he took specialists in all fields.

He was keen on POMO1 and POMO2 [the position of maximum opportunity] in penalty areas. His players were discouraged from shooting from too far out, he used headsets and head doctors, but Bolton had a four year period where they finished eighth, sixth, eighth and seventh and Bolton hadn't had a run like that since the 1950s.

'It rankles with me at times that I have to remind people what I have done,' he added. 'You have to accept it for what it is. If you start talking about it too much, you just get labelled big-headed, people go, "He's blowing his own trumpet again, what's he on about this time?" But if no one else is going to talk about it, you have to talk about it. You have to fight your own corner.

'The lingering long-ball shit, the old style, all that rubbish that's never been me and never been a part of what I am. I'm a purist in football terms. I love football. I hate the politics that are involved in football because it's destructive and not for the good of football. I believe in what I do because it works. People work with me, not for me, they enjoy being in the environment I create.'

He signed World Cup winners, he persuaded Nicolas Anelka to move to the Reebok Stadium, he was creative in the transfer market and used the methodology of metrics, before anyone in the country knew what they were.

'I loved Bolton, where I was allowed to build a football club, it was where I had started my career and then you get the opportunity to manage that football club,' he added. 'We achieved things we were never supposed to do. Then you want to see if you can take it a step further.'

Allardyce lost at the final hurdle to Steve McClaren to become the manager of England in 2006. By then his eyes were wandering and people around him knew Freddy Shepherd and his son Kenneth. The failed move before Souness took the position still lingered.

By the time Newcastle's injury-ravaged season under Roeder was limping to its conclusion, Allardyce was agreeing a three-year deal to become the club's new manager.

The reaction was not outrage by any stretch of the imagination, although there were misgivings that the preferred style of football might not be compatible with what Allardyce would bring. The old argument about winning football was used, but you cannot change the DNA at certain football clubs. Manchester United, West Ham and even Newcastle, with a barren trophy cabinet, had a distinctive way of playing that was more demanded than asked from their supporters.

Keegan's spell at Newcastle as player and manager left an immovable imprint of what was expected. It was a side note to start with, an area to have caution over, but they were not burning effigies when it was confirmed that he would take over. Some felt it was time for a new direction. That was on Tuesday, 15 May.

'My ambition is to win a trophy or qualify for Europe over the next few years,' he said that afternoon, as he sat with reporters.

'A couple of years ago there was an opportunity, which I declined, but now I feel like I'm ready to implement what I did at Bolton for seven years.

'I'm ambitious and I know this club is. It hasn't had the best success but I feel I can turn it round.

'I've left a football club that is very, very healthy so when my time to leave Newcastle does come I hope I have done the same here.

'I hope I can bring the success that the fans are so desperate for. I'm not saying I can get it right at the flick of a switch. If there are some sticky times I hope we can get over them for the best of the supporters and me.

'Everything about it appealed; the resources, the facilities, the fans, the amount of revenue that can be generated by a club of this size.

'No disrespect to Bolton, it's a club I love, but this club is massive in terms of what it can achieve.'

Significantly he added: 'There have been too many injuries. They seem to be forever talking about the everlasting injury list. One of the first things I will have to look at are why those injuries have happened. Far too many players have had too many injuries too often.'

Eight days later, Newcastle had a new owner.

Allardyce never got to work with Shepherd.

He claimed he was looking to buy Luka Modric, Leighton Baines and Phil Jagielka in the summer of 2007. Instead Newcastle signed Jose Enrique, Geremi and David Rozenhal.

It was still another summer of investment. Newcastle spent more than £20 million, with Joey Barton and Alan Smith both moving to St James' Park for £6 million apiece. Cacapa and Mark Viduka also arrived for nothing and Michael Owen stayed.

Things started well enough. Newcastle beat Bolton 3–1 at the Reebok Stadium on an emotional return to his former haunt. It would be the middle of September before Allardyce tasted defeat with his new club, at Derby County. It appeared a blip when a run of three successive home victories at St James' Park followed. Newcastle beat West Ham, Everton and Tottenham and scored nine goals in the process.

After nine games Newcastle had amassed 17 points and sat eighth, two points off fourth-placed Liverpool.

However, then came a rot, a run of six games without a win, and a punishing home defeat to Portsmouth.

After 20 minutes Newcastle had conceded three goals, at the Gallowgate End. Defensively they were a shambles. Cacapa was taken off after 18 minutes. The reaction was hostile. Perhaps there was a greater undercurrent to the appointment of Allardyce than had originally been thought. A punishing afternoon ended with a 4–1 defeat. It could have been more.

'Disappointed is an understatement,' said Allardyce. 'I am devastated by what has happened here today. I am completely gutted inside.

'The players have to be organised, understand how they should play, keep their shape, keep their discipline. Portsmouth did not have to put us to the test because we gifted them the game in those 12 minutes.'

Newcastle drew next at the Stadium of Light, and the mixture of delight and relief that Allardyce and his entire staff showed as they charged out of their technical area following a James Milner equaliser seemed a sign of mounting pressure.

It did not stop the rot. Allardyce's side was well beaten at St James' Park in front of a crowd of 52,307 on 24 November by Liverpool. The manager was jeered. Joey Barton called the support 'vicious'.

The six game winless run was halted by another burst; two wins and a draw. On Christmas Day, Newcastle were in a three way tie for ninth place with West Ham and Blackburn.

There was a loss at Wigan on Boxing Day when Ryan Taylor scored. Newcastle were really poor.

Joey Barton sat in the stands and watched.

JOEY BARTON – LOSE CONTROL

ON THURSDAY, 27 DECEMBER 2007, THE DAY AFTER NEWCASTLE HAD lost at Wigan, at 5.30 in the morning, outside of the McDonalds on Church Street, Liverpool, Joey Barton was caught on camera repeatedly punching a 16-year-old in the face following a row next to a phone box.

He was charged with common assault and affray and kept in jail, where he would spend New Year. Barton, who was 25, wore an All Saints jumper and jeans in court.

When he was told he had been refused bail, he turned to the prison guard and held out his hands to be cuffed.

He was then led back to the cells.

HARRY REDKNAPP
– PANIC

A DEFEAT AT CHELSEA AND AT HOME TO MANCHESTER CITY TOOK
Newcastle to twelfth, on 27 points, just six above the relegation zone. Those close
to the Newcastle board at the time insist senior players had questioned the style of
play. The season was changing, and then a goalless draw in the FA Cup at Stoke
in the pouring rain followed. Allardyce ran across the pitch and he was not jeered
and it was a big away following of 6,000.

By then rumours had started with Harry Redknapp about the possibility of
taking over. Allardyce, aware of the whisper, challenged the Portsmouth manager,
who denied any talks had taken place.

'We all knew that Harry Redknapp was meant to be replacing me,' Allardyce
said in an interview with the *News of the World* in 2010.

On the morning of Wednesday, 9 January, three days after the draw at the
Britannia Stadium, Allardyce was called to attend a meeting at St James' Park
with Ashley by Chris Mort, the then chairmen.

'I was called to the stadium, which was rare,' he added. 'I did think first of all
that Mike and his associates were going to discuss buying new players with me.

'My heart was telling me that they wanted to help me rebuild the squad, but my
head was telling me that they were going to give me the sack, and they did. I felt
very hurt and I was very sad. I didn't deserve to lose my job but I think I learned
from the experience and later became a better manager.

'We had taken 18 points from our first 10 games [this was actually 17 points
from 10 games]. It was our best start in something like a decade but everything

turned on the 4–1 home defeat by Portsmouth on 3 November.

'From then on it was hostile at St James' Park. Up to that point everything had been rosy in the camp, we were moving forward and were in the top half of the table. We all remember the images of the lad standing up in the crowd behind the dugout shouting, "You don't know what you're doing."

'We were 3–0 down very quickly. Benjani still haunts me to this day because he scored for Pompey. He was out of this world. The support I had enjoyed from day one suddenly disappeared and was replaced by hatred in the space of just 90 minutes. I couldn't grasp what was going on.

'The reaction of the supporters to one defeat unhinged the players. Some of the lads stand up in that situation, but others wilt. The Czech defender David Rozehnal was a good player but after the early few games he lost his bottle in that environment.

'As a manager I'm able to take the rough with the smooth, but the players were consumed by a fear factor and became frightened of their own fans.

'The majority of Newcastle fans are terrific. Their club has won very little in its history yet they still turn up every week to watch their team. Having said that, there is a big enough minority of detractors in the stadium to make your life very difficult when they make themselves heard.

'There are 52,000 of them so when even a small percentage of them get on top of you it makes a real difference.

'I didn't feel like a failure because I'd only been there for six months. That's nowhere near enough time to succeed, so to me, it's also not enough time to mess it up.

'We were eleventh in the table and people within the game knew I hadn't failed. Some would call it a failure but I found the whole experience was just sad. That, for me, was meant to represent the next level because I'd gone as far as I could with Bolton.

'My wife really suffered and felt very isolated and trapped in the house we had in Durham. I was so involved in trying to do my best for Newcastle that I ignored how she was feeling.

'I regret that because I didn't realise that this move was different for her. When we moved about as a young family during my playing career she could make friends when she took the kids to school. She would meet other parents, but now the children had left home.

'We had been to the Midlands, the North West, North East, London and even to

America but this time it was almost impossible for her to settle. She felt unwanted. Only when I got sacked did I realise how much she had suffered.

'I have to be careful blowing my own trumpet but I believe I would have stabilised Newcastle United and if you had given me good players I could have made them even better. I was doing that at Bolton.

'If I was given the funds to sign the players that club is able to attract then I believe I could have done what Sir Bobby Robson did and taken them into the Champions League. I could certainly have won them a cup competition.'

The cost to Ashley of sacking Allardyce and his backroom staff would be more than £5 million in compensation. Allardyce picked up £4.25 million.

'I had a three-year plan but I also wanted to rebuild the club from top to bottom,' Allardyce said. 'That plan was in place but in came Mike Ashley and it all fell apart after six months.

'There was disruption with the takeover almost as soon as I arrived. I took the plans I'd agreed with Freddy Shepherd and presented them to Mike but he had no concept of what had been discussed and put in place.

'Frankly, the goalposts moved overnight. The kind of money for players we had talked about with Freddy was simply no longer available when Mike came in. What he was offering me was not enough to make Newcastle great overnight.

'We had to work with what was there and try to find players we could get for the money I had. I got Alan Smith, Joey Barton and Mark Viduka on a free.

'Maybe because Mike had only just taken over he wasn't ready to commit too much cash to the project at such an early stage. It was a bitter experience for me.

'I don't know if Mike himself thought my face didn't fit from day one but I think there were certainly people around him telling him to get rid of me.

'He [Harry Redknapp] was going to be the man but it never happened in the end.

'The Newcastle job is impossible to turn down, but, believe me, it's also an impossible job to do.

'The last 10 years on Tyneside have been so up and down that you start to wonder whether the club will ever actually get things right. The demand for success is so great and needs to be achieved so quickly that the manager comes under threat quicker there than anywhere else.

'The pressure becomes so great that literally all that matters is the next result and, really, a football club cannot live like that. Newcastle United need a strategy in place, some kind of planning. Instead the club simply lives from season to season and nobody wants to listen to a long-term project.'

Newcastle had 26 points from 22 games when Allardyce was sacked.

They thought Harry Redknapp was about to take the position, and the local newspaper, the *Evening Chronicle*, splashed its front page with the story on Saturday, 12 January that he had agreed to come.

Redknapp was getting cold feet by then. It was suggested he had been told by a senior figure at the club that the desire was to buy young, develop and sell. That was not Harry's game.

In the afternoon, Newcastle lost 6–0 at Manchester United. Redknapp decided against the move.

Newcastle and their new owner and their new chairman were now desperately searching for a manager in an industry they had no experience of and one they did not understand.

SEPP BLATTER – MONEY CHANGES EVERYTHING

THE LEAZES END WAS FULL. ABOUT 10,000 NEWCASTLE FANS WERE IN St James' Park to see the unlikely unveiling of Michael Owen. The suspicion was that Owen had nowhere else to go. In the end nobody could live with Newcastle's £16 million offer. From Liverpool to Real Madrid to Newcastle.

Graeme Souness was with Freddy Shepherd, Owen and Tony Stephens, Owen's agent. There was a late call for the entourage to walk out to Amarillo, a song that had been made popular by a sketch from Peter Kay for Children In Need. Owen's people, aghast, said no.

Owen emerged into the bright sunshine of St James' Park, blinked and headed left. A journalist's wife called. 'He doesn't look best pleased with life,' she said.

There were elements of Shearer's first day, it just didn't sound anything like it.

'I want to play football, I love the Premiership, I've missed it while I've been away,' Owen would go on to say.

'It may be unfortunate for Liverpool fans that I am not there, but hopefully it is fortunate for Newcastle fans that I am here.

'I have been honest all along. Just like Alan Shearer said he had a decision to make when he moved here in 1996, I have had a similar decision to make. It was a great decision to have to make, Real Madrid, Newcastle or Liverpool.

'If the Liverpool deal could have been done that would have been a big option, but in the end it came down to Real Madrid or Newcastle and there was no question I wanted to return to the Premiership.

'I spoke to Liverpool and unfortunately that deal couldn't come off. That's life.

Deals sometimes happen, sometimes they don't. All I can do now is look to the future with Newcastle and hope to do well in this black and white shirt.

'I've had a bit of a head-spinning couple of days. There were three great clubs in the frame but the further it got towards the deadline the more it became clear Newcastle was going to be my destination.

'At the end of it all I thought the best for my future was to move to Newcastle.'

Of the reception he was given, he said: 'I've never seen anything like that.'

Souness was more thrilled.

'There are few people capable of filling Alan Shearer's shirt, but Michael is one of them,' he said.

'Our fans will love him because he's an honest lad and a world-class goalscorer, and he will be great in the dressing room.

'We've really done the business with this one.'

'Alan Shearer's been a good friend for a long time,' added Owen. 'It's his last season here and it will be an honour to play with him.

'He shares a lot of the same interests as I do and he was one of a few reasons to join, but so was the chairman's desire to get me here and the manager's desire to get me here.

'I think it's a question of when rather than if Newcastle win a trophy.'

In four seasons at St James' Park Michael Owen would play 79 times and score 30 goals.

'We paid too much money for him,' said Shepherd, the main mover behind the deal.

'Owen was the worst value for money in all of my time at the club, obviously. I'm not talking about his credibility as a footballer, but money wise it was definitely the worst signing. I have to take blame for that. It was the worst signing I did financially.

'When we bought him he was still at the height of his power if you like. Everybody knew Michael Owen. You could see how many came to St James' that day when we signed him. There was thousands there. Everybody agreed with it at the time.

'Was the boat pushed out too far with that transfer? Yeah, I think so. We paid £16 million, plus there were other bits and pieces so it was probably nearer £17 million, at the end of the day he was on good wages. If we'd got our money back off the move, fine, but you know he stayed until Ashley took over. There wasn't a new contract going to be offered, he'd had too many injuries.

'It was too much money for him. When he was sold to Real Madrid from

Liverpool, it was £8 million. He had one year left. You have Shearer up here (raises hand towards ceiling) and you have Owen down there (moves hand towards floor) performance wise. It certainly wasn't a good deal. He was a good player but he got totalled in bloody London, when he did his foot. Then he came back too quick and got done again in the World Cup when he did his knee against Sweden.'

It would lead to a legal battle with FIFA that rumbled on for months.

Owen admitted his eagerness to play for England saw him push for a spot at the World Cup finals in Germany after suffering a metatarsal injury with Newcastle.

In the first two minutes he twisted and did his right knee. Owen, who crawled off the pitch, would miss nine months. FIFA were only insured for players earning less than £50,000-a-week. It had needed double that to tempt Owen to join Newcastle, picking up a salary of around £100,000-a-week.

Newcastle were potentially losing millions in the player's prolonged absence.

Shepherd went to war with FIFA.

'That's when I had the fight with Blatter,' he added. 'Blatter called me, I had instituted legal proceedings against him, and he knew that. Letters were going backwards and forwards. He called me and said, "I'd like to meet you in Manchester."

'I said, "I'll bring the lawyers with me," and he went, "No, just bring yourself."

'I said, "Who else will be there?" He said, "Just Mr Blatter."

'I went to the Lowry Hotel in Manchester and there were 12 other people with him. The English FA were there, with Dave Richards, Blatter and his number two and number three and all the rest were there. They were all sitting at the table. I said, "Well, if there's a fight I'm outnumbered."

'He said, "We don't want you to do this because it will set a precedent."

'I said, "If you don't want me to do it, just pay the money."

'"What if a country like Gambia has a problem."

'"I'm not interested in that. Just give me the money for Newcastle."

'"This money you're asking for, you're part of the football family."

'"Yeah, and I'm not going to be the poor relation."

'I said, "If I don't get the money I will institute proceedings tomorrow as soon as I get back to Newcastle."

'It was the second meeting I'd had. I'd been across to Zurich to see him. His offices in Zurich were unbelievable. The FA took me over in a private plane with their lawyer.

'I didn't make any progress. It's a glass box but it's huge. They had 600 people working there in the middle of Zurich with its own park around it. It must have cost a fortune.

'I couldn't make any headway at all there. I stepped up the legal side. He'd only insured players for £50,000-a-week. Owen was on more than that, picking up a salary of £103,000-a-week plus £18,000-a-week in image rights.

'What they should have done was phone every club with players in the tournament and asked if £50,000-a-week was enough. It wasn't. It was their problem. FIFA had underinsured their product.

'They were liable for the players. It was their competition. They were liable for it. When he came to Manchester he knew I was being serious. We were ready to issue them with a writ. He didn't want any of that. All the other players going back years could have been challenging him.

'He knew I had him. He knew he had a choice to make, of whether he wanted problems or do a deal.

'Anyway, I got a phone call the next day, saying, "Yeah, we'll pay you the money, just back off."

'I said, "Yeah, I'll back off the minute we get that cheque."

'The next day we got six and a half million pounds.'

FREDDY SHEPHERD
– THIS IS THE END

HEAD OUT OF NEWCASTLE'S TRAINING GROUND TOWARDS THE CITY centre, take a sharp left about two miles later at the roundabout before the Brandling Pub, and drive for another 400 metres and you will come to the Freeman Hospital, one of the main organ transplant hospitals in the UK.

It is set back from the trees that line Melville Grove and opposite the popular Paddy Freeman's Park. In 1922 John W. Freeman had donated his family home as the site for a new hospital, in honour of his late son Orley. It grew over the following decades until in 1975 it extended on land donated by Myron Macintosh and in 1986 came a further £12.5 million expansion.

In 1987 the first paediatric heart transplant was carried out there. A hospital that started with five doctors had around 250 by 2007.

Just off Ward 25 at the start of May of that year lay the chairman and second largest shareholder of Newcastle United. Freddy Shepherd was lying in a bed on that ward when he took a phone from a nurse.

He was seriously ill. His lung had collapsed and he was suffering from severe pneumonia.

He picked up the phone.

'You what?'

Freddy Shepherd's father and his two brothers had been heavily involved in the scrap business on the banks of the River Tyne in the late 1940s. Shepherd's father, Charlie, went into the transport business. In 1952, he sold his business to the government when it was nationalised.

'As soon as he sold out we went to Australia to avoid the tax man,' revealed Shepherd.

Freddy Shepherd was 12 when he first went to Sydney. He lived there for three years.

'We came back to Newcastle and he bought the same company back off the government. Labour nationalised it, the Conservatives got in and started selling it off again. Things never change. We went into transport and they decided to build the Byker Wall. Our property was in the middle, off the Byker Wall, they had to pay us off. That was when we first came down to the Tyne.

'We bought Whitbread Brewery's premises and it just went from there. It was as simple as that. My dad insisted I had a profession and I worked for BP for eight years as a marine engineer. I went to South Shields Marine Tech and I moved up to Swan Hunters for BP for three years and then I went to sea, I've still got my uniform, I can't get it on now mind!'

At the age of 22, Shepherd came home and joined the family business. 'It was transport warehousing and the scrapyard was still gong then but we developed the offshore business from there, servicing vessels for oil rigs etc. Storage of offshore equipment, that kind of thing.'

He went to watch Newcastle United play with his dad, who had two season tickets in the West Stand.

'I used to go to the match with my family when I was young,' he added. 'My old man had a couple of seats in the main stand. John Hall and my old man were pals. That's where the family connections came together. I worked with John for 15 years. Come October 1991, we went in.

'I didn't have a problem with it at all. I think we bought 10 per cent at the time. John wanted as much support as he could get. Do you blame him? It was a huge task he was taking on. Oh yeah, nobody stepped in, we had to put £250,000 in then, in '91. The club needed the money, £250,000 was a big ask. Luckily we could afford it. We went from there.'

Shepherd would become central to the transformation that took place at St James' Park. He was at the heart of transfers, the ground redevelopment, he was party to every major call and then, when Sir John Hall left office in October 1997, he became chairman.

By then the club had become a public limited company, the move that had led to Keegan's departure.

'It had got too big for the Halls to justify the money they were guaranteeing,' he explained. 'It was John's money. Business is business. It just exploded from £500,000. He said, "I'll lend the club £500,000 for theses shares," and then the whole thing just went whoof.

'Kevin has to be given credit for what he did, both him and John. It was a shame when Kevin went.

'The club was going to become a PLC regardless of Kevin's position. It had to happen. It had to be floated. [Mark] Corbidge, who was joint chief executive with Freddie [Fletcher] at the time, was a bit too blunt for Kevin. I think Kevin, as he was, could get a bit annoyed with people who didn't agree with him. Kevin is Kevin, at the time it had to be done to give us the financial power to compete.

'The money went into the club didn't it? For shares and one thing or another. We were riding high then, second in the table. To get the securitisation for the new stand all that stuff had to be done. We had to be a public company, we would never have got it as a private individual.

'It was hard work keeping up with the growth of the club. At the end of the day it was me, Douglas and Freddie [Fletcher], who can't be dismissed, he was a big, big, part of the club. I always stick up for him, he was in at the beginning, he was there from 1992.

'He came in after me. Russell [Cushing] was running it then. I joined and Freddie came in after that. He came down from Scotland, he was with Rangers. He took it over. He was there until 2000. Bobby was the manager when he left. He was really important to the club.

'When he left it was like a different thing. There was only two main shareholders. It wasn't really a public company. Really the Halls and the Shepherds, with their percentage, could force anything through or stop anything.'

By the start of May, in 2007, Sir John Hall had begun talks with representatives of Mike Ashley. Incredibly he did not meet the would-be buyer during protracted talks, that was left to Ashley's lawyers.

Shepherd was completely oblivious to all of this. Of more concern right then was his health.

'I had a collapsed lung,' he said. 'I was really unwell. I was in hospital for a fortnight. How did I catch pneumonia? God knows. I was all over the place in those days. I thought I had a broken rib. I was playing golf and I thought, "Ooh that's sore." It wasn't. It was bloody pneumonia. I was in the Freeman for two weeks. I had a tube going into me. I was carrying the thing around with me with all the fluid coming off it.

'Douglas phoned me up and told me.

'I went, "You what?"'

John had done the deal when I was in hospital so I was never informed about it.

'Douglas said, "As chairman they need your permission to sell the shares." He could have went to court and got it. To do it legally you need the chairman's permission.

'Russell Cushing phoned and said, "Are you giving permission?" I said, "What's the fucking point? He's already sold it. Permission is a load of bollocks. He's already sold them."

'What Ashley didn't do, he didn't know anything about the fifty odd million [to redevelop the stadium], so he said. He said John never told him about that.

'To be fair to John, Ashley didn't do DD [due diligence]. Who's fault was it? He thought it was a *fait accompli* with me and I'd have to sell them.

'He sent Chris Mort, the lawyer from Freshfields to see me. Mort said, "You have to sell your shares."

'I said, "I haven't got to sell them."

'He went, "John said you would."

'John never asked me. He did the deal when I was in hospital so I was never informed about it.

'I said, "I'm not selling my shares for the same as John got." He said, "If we pay you any more we have to pay the rest more." I had 30 per cent, John had 40 odd. We had 75 per cent between us. There was still 25 per cent out there.

'I had bought NTL's shares [ten per cent]. I think there was 23 per cent left. He said, "No, no! You can't have anymore."

'I said, "I'm not selling. I tell you what, I'm off to Barbados for three years, give me a ring when I get back!"

'I put the phone down on Chris Mort. Then they came up to see me. I said, "I'm not selling." They said, "You have to sell."

'I said, "I don't need the money, I'm not selling, I don't have to do anything."

'They came back and said, "We'll pay you more than John, one pence more than John." It must have cost Ashley, I had 38 million one ps. Work that one out! [Ashley would have to pay an additional £380,000 to buy the Shepherd shareholding].

'Ashley got the hump because I wouldn't do what I was told. He got the hump, simple as that. He fell out with me. I never met the guy. It was all done through Chris Mort.

'I think that's how Ashley ran his businesses. He never got involved personally. Middle men to do the deals.'

I tell Freddy that Sir John Hall never met Ashley too.

'John never met him either?' he said. 'I thought he had.

'You can imagine. It was the worst time possible for it to be done. If I'd been there I would have put a fight up.

'Was there anything I could have done? Oh, yeah. Of course. He only had forty-odd per cent. I could have put a counter bid in. It would have been a bit of a war. It wouldn't have done the club any good. At the same time I didn't like being told what I had to do. I never met the guy. I didn't really know who the guy was. That's how it started.

'He got a surprise when he had to pay the securitisation of the stand. If the Halls sold their majority shareholding, it had to be repaid or renegotiated.'

It had been included in the club accounts that the £57 million loaned to the club to build the imposing structure that wrapped around from the Milburn Stand to the Leazes End, covering half the ground, would have to be repaid to Barclays Bank within 60 days if the Halls sold their shareholding.

Not finding it would be a huge oversight from Ashley and his team.

He would admit later to finding that debt, amongst others, when he took control.

'When I floated Sports Direct on the stock market earlier this year I realised it wasn't just my company going public so why not do things I've always wanted to do, like buying a football club?' he said in a *News of the World* interview.

Ashley's team had moved quickly to open talks with Sir John Hall, who had been involved in discussions with a Malaysian group who were in the middle of due diligence.

'There was no time to do the usual due diligence,' added Ashley. 'I paid £140 million for the club with the expectation that there was a debt of £70 million. Actually it was around £100 million so there was suddenly an extra £30 million to find. I just thought, "I'm a big boy and I didn't cry."

'Was the debt bigger than I thought? Yes. Would it have changed my decision if I'd known the full extent of the debt? Not one iota.'

The suggestion later came that a number of financial institutions had been in talks about refinancing Newcastle's debt. Restrictions would have followed.

Newcastle had signed a four-year deal with Northern Rock and had a contract with kit suppliers Adidas. It was said that the money from both deals had been spent on the Michael Owen deal.

Shepherd is adamant there was not a debt left on the prohibitive Owen deal.

'No,' he added. 'There was no outstanding debt on the Owen deal. The Michael Owen transfer was paid cash. The only debt was what every club had, transfers, and then if you took the assets of what was on the pitch.

'It was just the securitisation, which was the fifty-odd million, on top of the £136 million I think he [Ashley] paid. At the end of the day everybody who was interested in the club at the time would do DD. If you were buying a sweet shop you wouldn't just walk in and say, "I'm buying your sweet shop. How much do you want for it?"

'It's as simple as that. He decided to take it and obviously if he'd done DD it might have been a different outcome. Who knows?

'How much would it cost to build that ground now? £200 million? Probably. It cost £50 million just to do the bit that we'd done. It would be £200 million now. You're talking about a lot of money. The biggest thing is when we floated, when we went to London to do the deal, they said, "When you go to the well, always take the biggest bucket."

'I think it was overvalued at the time, when we did the share issue. I think it was £1.35 a share. It was a lot of money then. It was £200 million. Bearing in mind the improvements had to be done. The stand had to be built. We couldn't compete at 36,000 (the ground's capacity). It went up to 52,000 and we needed that. He got the completed ground, he got the players. In my opinion he got a good deal.'

There can be no question that the Shepherd and Hall family got good deals as well.

According to the club accounts for the year to June 2008, the Halls, who owned a larger stake than Freddy Shepherd and his brother Bruce, made £95,748,570 in total from selling their shares, salaries and dividends from their first involvement 1992. Freddy Shepherd and his family made £50,099,604 doing the same period.

'We just wanted the club to succeed,' said Shepherd. 'In our time the club played 110 games in Europe, reached Wembley and played in the Champions League. We built a new ground and a new training centre. I didn't want to sell and I did not need the money.'

Shepherd woke in a hospital bed to discover that Mike Ashley was on his way to owning the city's football club. It was the same for Newcastle fans.

Nobody knew anything about Mike Ashley.

MIKE ASHLEY – LONDON CALLING

THE COLOURING ON THE SCHOOL TIE WAS BLACK, RED AND YELLOW. The blazer was black. A youngster was holding court.

'One day I'll own my own shop,' he said.

It was Burnham Grammar School and it was 1979 and the child was Mike Ashley.

'Most kids are fairly malleable,' said Margaret Fleet, a teacher at the school at the time. 'You can kind of subtly change their views about things. Mike was different. I remember him having quite strong views about things and being quite determined. It doesn't surprise me that he has gone on to be successful.

'I remember him talking to his friends about his Saturday job in a sportswear shop, and talking about how one day he would own the shop.'

At that stage Mike Ashley, a keen squash player, was restringing squash rackets. A school friend, Martin Blackmun told the *Sunday Mirror* in 2007 that he was not into football.

'Mike didn't show any particular interest in football at school,' said Blackmun. 'I don't remember him supporting a team as a boy, he never wore a football shirt or anything like that. You would never see him on a bike or a skateboard or playing football like most of the boys.'

Ashley would claim years later that he was an England fan. Those closest to him insist the link to Tottenham was wrong and that he favoured Chelsea.

He was born in Walsall, in the West Midlands, in 1964. His father, Keith, was manager at a food distribution depot. The whole family – his mother, Barbara, a secretary and his elder brother John – moved to Burnham.

He left school, aged 16, with one O-Level, a C grade, in economics and, two years later, he is said to have borrowed money from his parents, who lived in a bungalow in Burnham, and moved to open his first store, at 3 High Street, in Maidenhead, a kilometre from the A4094. He called the three story terraced property with a single doorway Mike Ashley Sports. It was 1982. (Many years later, the same store would be a haberdashers called Sew Crafty).

It has been said that both his parents assisted him in the store, his father with the books and his mother in the store.

Two years after Mike Ashley Sports, he opened a second store, Preston Sports Shop, in London. Ashley had started to sell lots of discounted socks in packs to his customers. He was on his way.

He married Linda Jerlmyr, a Swedish property developer five years later and by 1992, when Newcastle United were kicking off a season that would see them win the first 11 league games in a row and go on to become the champions of the second tier in English football, Ashley had 12 shops. The chain was called Sports and Ski.

In 1995, when The Entertainers would come within touching distance of landing Newcastle's first top flight league title since 1927, Ashley's chain was rebranded Sports Soccer and he opened more than 100 stores across the UK.

Head office and warehouse facilities at that point were moved to Dunstable in Bedfordshire. By 1999 Ashley's firm became a limited liability company and at that point he began buying brands – like Dunlop Slazenger – and existing stores – like Lillywhites.

He had come to the attention of Dave Whelan, the JJB Sports founder. 'There is a club in the north, son, and you're not part of it,' was the much used line from Whelan with regards to Ashley. The club he referred to was a close knit bunch of Manchester businessmen who dominated the thriving sports retail sector during the 1990s.

'The club in the north referred to JJB, founded in Wigan, while David Makin and John Wardle founded JD Sports in Heywood, near Manchester,' said a piece in the Guardian's business section in 2009. 'The now defunct Allsports was based in Stockport, while brands such as Umbro, Nike and Reebok all had bases there.

'By 2000, Ashley was the upstart southerner snapping at their heels. His revenge was to report their plan to fix the price of England and Manchester United shirts to the Office of Fair Trading, prompting an investigation that landed the protagonists with multimillion-pound fines.'

By 2003 Ashley had 150 stores.

Four years later, Ashley's Sports Direct chain, as it had become, overtook JJB Sports as the United Kingdom's biggest sports fashion retailer.

On 27 February 2007, in a move missed by the vast, vast majority of Newcastle United supporters, Ashley floated 43 per cent of Sports Direct at 300 pence per share. Applications outnumbered shares on offer by 2.7 times, and the share price initially fell by 19 pence. What mattered, if you were a Newcastle fan, was how much Mike Ashley suddenly had in his pocket.

It was £929 million.

By April, the shares had dropped to 222.5 pence and there was disquiet in the city at the low profile taken by the newly floated company.

At this point Sir John Hall had stepped up his desire to sell the majority shareholding that his family still held in Newcastle United. He flew to London to meet a Malaysian Consortium.

'On the Monday of that week, I arranged to meet them at a London hotel to do a deal to sell Newcastle United,' Hall recounted to Michael Walker in his social history of north east football, Up There. 'On the Thursday I got a call from an agent on behalf of an Icelandic bank. He said: "We have someone interested and we'll give you your pound per share. Can we meet?"

'I said, "Well, I'm meeting these Malaysian businessmen at 11."

'He said, "Don't go. We'll come and see you."

'I said, "I'm honour bound to go and see them."

'I was met off the train at 10 and I was taken around to see Ashley's people and lawyers at Freshfields. The Malaysians wanted to do due diligence – six to eight weeks – and I knew Freddy didn't want to sell. I said, "I'm sorry I can't give you that time."

'I brought in my lawyers and said I'd do a deal.'

By the time the deal was concluded, the absent Ashley had spent £55.3 million of his newly acquired wealth on the Hall family's 55,342,223 shares through a company called St James' Holding Limited (SJHL).

'I am delighted to have this opportunity to invest in Newcastle United,' said Ashley in a statement. 'The club has a fantastic infrastructure, for which Sir John and the board must take much of the credit.

'I am pleased that Sir John has agreed to remain as life president of the club. Newcastle United has a wonderful heritage and the passion of its fans is legendary.

'I am sure that, like me, they are already excited about the prospects for next season under the new manager's stewardship.'

Hall added: 'I have enjoyed my years at the club and I will always continue to be involved.

'The club has moved forward massively and I don't think Freddy Shepherd and Douglas have been given full recognition for the work they have put in. I would like to thank them personally.

'When you look at where we are now compared with where we were before it is a very different place.

'I have been associated with the direction of Newcastle United for nearly 20 years.

'In that time, I have led the club and, before I retired, led the team responsible for the modernisation of the club we all see today.'

In total, it cost Ashley £133 million to purchase Newcastle United. It was 7 June, 2007.

The Halls and the Shepherds, after almost two decades at the club, were gone.

Just about nothing was know about Ashley at the time. He was labelled a recluse. The quote often used then was that he liked to park his tanks on other peoples' lawns. He started wearing the black and white shirt in the director's box. When he was told he wouldn't be allowed in the boardroom at the Stadium of Light, he had a mini bus organised (with security) to take him in the away end.

He was turned away from Blu Bamboo, a club in the Bigg Market because he was wearing a Newcastle strip following a 2–0 win against Barnsley in the Carling Cup and that was not allowed. Chris Mort, who he was with, explained who it was.

Ashley was let in and bought everyone in the bar a drink (thought to cost around £2,500), a £500 tip was left and Mort started singing Newcastle songs with a microphone. They were there until 3am.

Ashley was 42 and determined to have fun.

A rocky patch under Allardyce came. The support was unhappy. Talks had started with Harry Redknapp.

Finally, on 9 January Ashley pulled the plug on Sam Allardyce. Newcastle were eleventh in the Premier League and set for an FA Cup replay against Stoke City at St James' Park. The draw pitted the winners with a tie at Arsenal.

Allardyce would be gone before the game and Ashley, unrepentant, claimed in an interview in the *News of the World*, printed on 13 January, 2008, that there was no chance of success if he had remained in charge.

Ashley claimed then that he wanted a return to The Entertainers, to the free flowing style of football that Kevin Keegan had created.

'I want a team that will go all out to try to give Chelsea a walloping, that'll try to stuff Tottenham and that will be brave and bold enough to attack Man Utd,' he said.

'To date I have invested £250m to try and make it happen and I'm not the only one who could see it wasn't working with things as they were, so when my chairman told me it was time for a change I knew it had to happen. I just knew it was time for me to become involved.

'After all I bought this club to make it a success and the harsh truth is there wasn't much prospect of that. I bought this club to have some fun and I wasn't having much fun at all so I did what I should have done in the first place and decided it was time to run the club the way I wanted.

'I had to act and now I'll do it my way!'

Ashley said his gut instinct had been to bring in his own team straight away. He wanted to sack Allardyce.

'That's no reflection on Sam, that's just the way I have always done things but for once in my life I ignored my intuition and, looking back, that was a mistake.

'My instinct had never let me down in the past, in fact it's been one of my biggest strengths, one of the major reasons behind my success yet I went against that better judgement after buying Newcastle.'

Then he made reference to the desire to replicate the football of the early and mid-1990s.

'I want a team that is going to be admired up and down the country because of our brilliant, attacking football, like they did when Kevin Keegan was in charge here,' he added.

'In those days everyone in the land loved to watch Newcastle in action. I certainly did and I'm determined it will be like that again.

'People might mock me for that and reckon that's all pie in the sky but this is a football club, remember, it's about passion, about dreams, about glory. If it's not, then why bother?

'Make no mistake I bother, I care and so I will try my hardest to make this club successful and I know I don't stand alone, I stand at the head of the Toon Army.'

Ashley then revealed the financial outlay buying Newcastle United had cost him.

'Let's get this straight, I paid £140 million to buy this club,' he added. 'I've also paid off £100 million worth of debt so today this club doesn't owe a buck to anyone and I also gave Sam funds for new players. Yet I've been hammered by certain people and for what? Yes, wearing my Newcastle shirt and sitting with the fans.

'Do you know something? I don't regret those days with our supporters at all. I might own the club but they are the heartbeat and I had a lovely time with them and I guarantee that you haven't seen the last of me out there with the lads and lasses.

'I will do it again from time to time.

'It's a game of drama and emotion, of highs and lows, of highlights and heartbreaks and I want to live it so from now on it's all down to me.

'I am here because I want to be here and because I want to win trophies. That's it, period, to get trophies in the cabinet and have a ball doing it. I can't see anything wrong with that at all.

'Buying a football club is something I've always wanted to do so it's living a dream. I always said I bought this club to become part of its passion.

'I'd like to think I've done that. Now I want to channel that passion into bringing success and I just can't wait until it happens.'

KEVIN KEEGAN
– PAINT A VULGAR
PICTURE

'KING KEV! WHAT CAN I DO YOU FOR?'

That was how Mike Ashley greeted Kevin Keegan on the phone.

Keegan had hoped the Newcastle he had rejoined seven months later was about to become major players in the transfer market.

He had waited and waited and finally, on 30 August, the phone had gone.

It was Dennis Wise.

'We're going to sign Ignacio Gonzalez,' said Wise. 'He's Uruguayan, 29. Have a look on YouTube.'

Keegan went to his computer. He wasn't impressed.

A second player was put to him, Xisco, a young Spanish forward.

He called Ashley.

Ashley told Keegan he was aware of the moves to sign Gonzalez and Xisco.

The conversation ended.

Derek Llambias, by then the managing director, called Keegan and wanted to know why Keegan had broken the chain of command.

It was already at breaking point by then.

Keegan had already been summoned to a meeting in London, at the law firm, Freshfields. His wife picked him up in a black 4x4 after training. You watched him get in the car. It didn't looked like Kevin Keegan. He looked beaten by it all. The pair drove down to London.

Chris Mort, the lawyer was there, as were Tony Jimenez, Dennis Wise and Ashley.

It was one of the most important meetings in the history of Newcastle United.

205

Wise was said to have been hostile towards Keegan. Jimenez and Wise on one side. Keegan on the other. Ashley and Mort found themselves in the middle. Keegan wanted immediate investment because the team was weak and because he wanted to galvanise the club, as he had done so successfully during his first spell as manager. Jimenez and Wise argued against that idea. They would sign young players and develop them, increase their value. The club needed to be pointed in one direction or the other. It got neither.

Keegan had famously made reference to his position at Newcastle not being like it was portrayed in the brochure, when he believed promises made to lure him out of retirement were being reneged on. That was in 1992. By 2008, the football club had changed. The clock was ticking too fast. It was about to end, you knew that, it was just how bitter and acrimonious it would become that mattered.

It had been a long fall.

Ashley is still said, by those close to him, to have been thrilled by the team Keegan put together at Newcastle in the mid-1990s. When Redknapp, who Jimenez had told the Newcastle board he could land as manager, at the eleventh hour and beyond, decided he didn't fancy life in the north, and was filmed by Sky at the Portsmouth training ground signing a new deal to stay in charge at Fratton Park, Ashley's men had to find a manager.

With few options, they turned to Keegan, who had left the game following a successful spell with Fulham, a tough time with England that ended in resignation, and then a swansong with Manchester City. By 2008 he was busy with a venture called Soccer Circus in Glasgow.

There was a phone call from Mort to arrange a provisional meeting. Keegan met Ashley, Mort and Jimenez in London. Those from the Ashley camp insist Keegan was told then that Wise would be joining as director of football. There were assurances over ambition and Keegan agreed to sign a three-and-a-half year deal on Wednesday, 16 January. It was a whirlwind. By tea-time he was heading to St James' for the FA Cup replay against Stoke City.

'It's nice to be home,' he said. 'I'm delighted to be back.'

Mort, who sat to the left of Keegan during the Stoke game in the directors' box (Ashley was to his right), added: 'We didn't think we'd be able to get Kevin back to the club but he's the right man and we're absolutely delighted.'

Newcastle won 4–1. Michael Owen, James Milner, Damien Duff and even the hapless Cacapa scored.

It was all smiles.

The dash of realism came from Nigel Pearson, who had been given temporary control following Allardyce's sacking. 'It won't be easy,' he said. 'We haven't got a huge squad.'

He was right.

Newcastle drew the next game with Bolton, and lost 3–0 to Arsenal. The FA Cup was gone. Two days later came another bombshell. Dennis Wise, who had never enjoyed a good relationship with Newcastle fans, was appointed as Newcastle United's executive director [football]. It was announced just before Keegan held his press conference ahead of a league game with Arsenal.

It was one of his least convincing performances.

'I'm reluctant to tell all I know because I really do not know everything,' he said on Wise's appointment. He said he was happy, but he didn't look it.

Keegan himself had been touted for a similar position at St James' Park when Sam Allardyce was in charge. Then he had said: 'It's absolutely impossible to give Sam a job at Newcastle and then go and fetch someone who is going to be some sort of threat, it doesn't work.

'Sam would be a fool to let it happen and the guy who goes in would be a fool to accept it.'

The executive structure at the club changed dramatically. Tony Jimenez became vice president [player recruitment] and Jeff Vetere was named technical co-ordinator.

Both men knew Paul Kemsley, and Paul Kemsley had been Mike Ashley's friend since the pair were young. In 1992 Kemsley, who had trained as a junior surveyor, went to work with Ashley.

Three years later, along with Joe Lewis and Daniel Levy, he started Rock Joint Ventures, an investment company. In 2001 Kemsley became a director at Tottenham and then vice chairman.

Kemsley knew Jimenez, a season ticket holder at Chelsea who in 2008 in a article in the *Guardian* was described as, 'essentially a businessman and an agent'. He had been director of Casa Sports Holdings. He spoke Spanish and was said to have a network of contacts.

Those in the Keegan camp would come to refer to Jimenez as 'a former doorman at Stamford Bridge.'

Jeff Vetere had been a former apprentice at Luton, moved to Rushden and Diamonds as a coach in 1997, before he worked with the youth team at Charlton. He was a part-time scout at West Ham and worked briefly at Real Madrid before moving to Newcastle.

The policy that lay behind the series of appointments was to scout young talent from around the world and develop it and possibly then sell for a profit. It bore similarities to the model undertaken at Tottenham, under the guidance of Daniel Levy and Kemsley.

Newcastle had to pay compensation to land Wise from his role as manager at Leeds.

Mort's tone differed hugely from Keegan's.

'Two of the conclusions of our strategic review were that the club would benefit from having a football person involved at board level, which it has not had historically,' said Mort.

'Also, that further senior resources are needed for recruiting players of the highest quality from this country and further afield.

'Dennis would like to move away from day-to-day football management to a board role and, with his considerable energy and intelligence, we believe he will do very well.

'With Kevin able to devote his efforts to developing and running the first-team squad, Dennis, Tony and Jeff will each help us to secure success for Newcastle at all levels for the long-term.

'This is all part of the vision that recently helped us to secure Kevin Keegan's return to the club as manager.'

You needed only the slightest grasp of the club's modern history to realise that Ashley and Mort had left a trail of gunpowder between the St James' Park boardroom and the manager's office.

It seemed unfeasible that the dilution of Keegan's role, despite the brave talk, could work.

The clock ticked for that first spark to light the explosion.

Meanwhile, the team, in desperate need of investment, struggled.

There was a 4–1 defeat at home to Aston Villa and then a 5–1 loss to Manchester United in the following game, a loss to Blackburn and then another 3–0 defeat, this time Liverpool.

The squad was short in many areas.

Keegan sat down in the media suite at the training ground. He was about to call out the owner.

'Mr Ashley said he wanted to win something in three-and-a-half years,' he said. 'When we sit down in the next few weeks we will see how desperate he is to win something in that time.

'That will become clear when we see the players this club will go after in the summer. We haven't had that conversation yet.

'It's a different world now compared to when I first came here as a manager. Without showing any disrespect to my players I think you could take any one of the players on the benches of the top four and they would be five of the first six names on the team sheet at most other clubs.

'You look at Manchester United and their bench is £60-70million worth of players. You've got a Nani or a Hargreaves on the bench.

'It's not practical or feasible for a manager of Newcastle United to say what I said before, "Watch out Sir Alex, we are after your title."

'They have gone on and in many respects we have gone backwards. You hope you could appeal to some of the players who go to the top four clubs and don't play every week. We need four or five players but if you are clever that doesn't need to cost a lot of money. You can get Bosmans worth £10m so we will see what we can do there too.

'We can go for the top players but we can't offer them European football – and we can't offer them a top-four finish next season.'

Nothing said more about the changing face of Newcastle United than what he said next.

'We've got a group of teams such as Spurs, Villa and Everton we can challenge but not the top four,' he added.

'If you forget ability and look at the size of the club, the turnover, the fan base and take everything into consideration we should finish fifth to eighth. Outside of the top eight would be unacceptable.'

Newcastle rallied. A draw with Birmingham was followed by three successive victories, against Fulham, Spurs and Reading. Michael Owen, deployed in the hole, behind Oba Martins and Mark Viduka, scored three times. After a goalless draw at Portsmouth, Newcastle swatted Roy Keane and Sunderland aside. They went joint eleventh, with Spurs.

It would be the last victory of the season. Three games later Newcastle finished the season twelfth, six points off the top ten.

It was clear to everyone that the team needed a lot doing to it.

JOEY BARTON –
GOING DOWN

AT THREE O'CLOCK ON TUESDAY, 20 MAY 2008, AT LIVERPOOL
Crown Court, Joey Barton was jailed for six months for assault and affray.

'It was a violent and cowardly act,' said Judge Henry Globe QC.

The court had heard that Barton had been caught on CCTV punching one
man 20 times before an attack which left a teenage boy with a broken tooth.

The court heard that the Newcastle player had been on a Boxing Day night
out with his brother, his cousin and other friends in Liverpool city centre. He had
drunk 10 pints of lager and five bottles of lager during the night before going to
a McDonald's on Church Street.

The group became involved in a heated discussion with youths outside the
restaurant. Barton was captured on CCTV knocking an unidentified man to the
ground. According to the court he then straddled him and punched him four or
five times as his cousin threw food at the victim. Barton then punched him up to
15 times more. Then he attacked a 16-year-old, punching him and leaving him
with broken teeth.

The court heard that Barton was remorseful about the incident and had
admitted he had an alcohol problem.

Two references were read out in court. The first was from Kevin Keegan.

'There were a number of issues in his life and events, some of which have been
well documented,' his statement read.

'Had I been asked to give a character evidence for him then, I probably wouldn't
have been able to do so.

'There has been a massive change. He is a far more responsible individual now.'

The second reference given came from Peter Kay, the co-founder of the Sporting Chance clinic.

'Joey recognises he has an addiction to alcohol and the only way forward is total abstinence,' he said. 'Joey despises the man he becomes after consuming alcohol.'

Barton, who admitted the charge against him, was ordered to pay £2,500 to the youth whose teeth were broken.

'You were restrained by others but ignored them and acted in an extremely violent and aggressive manner,' said Judge Globe on sentencing.

'You have a high profile as a footballer and you know that draws attention to you. Yet you drank to excess and behaved in an aggressive, disgraceful manager.'

A statement from Newcastle United read: 'The club is considering the verdict and will be making no further comment at this moment.'

KEVIN KEEGAN –
I KNOW IT'S OVER

IT WAS FALLING APART BEFORE ARSENAL, BEFORE MIKE ASHLEY WAS pictured downing a pint in the away end at the Emirates Stadium. It was suggested – you are not allowed to drink in your seat at football – that it was non-alcoholic.

The blurring of lines was becoming a theme.

Newcastle did have new faces, but it was not the overhaul that Keegan had called for. Fabricio Coloccini had been the major signing of the summer. A centre-half. Newcastle had paid Deportivo la Coruna £10.5 million for the Argentinian, who was 26. It was Friday, 15 August when a man with curly hair, jeans and a denim shirt, sneaked almost unnoticed into the back of the media room at the Benton training ground to be unveiled.

He would make his debut two days later, at Old Trafford. Jonas Gutierrez, another Argentinian started the game. Gutierrez was signed at the start of July from Real Mallorca, also on a five-year deal.

Newcastle, under the transfer dealings of Wise and Jimenez, thought they would be able to sign the player for nothing because they had invoked FIFA's controversial Article 17. That ruling at the time enabled any player between the ages of 23 and 28 to buy out their contract if they had been at the same club for three years or more.

Mallorca, however, claimed they were owed compensation and valued the player at £12 million. (The two clubs reached an agreement in April the following year. Newcastle paid £5.2 million and 20 per cent of any future sale of the player would go to the Spanish side).

The only other new player was Danny Guthrie, a central midfielder signed on Keegan's recommendation. It was not quite the revolution Keegan had in mind.

He would admit at the end of the month, following the defeat at Arsenal, that he had wanted to sign Samir Nasri. 'He's a player we tried to bring in this summer,' said Keegan. There had been other names on his list. Bastian Schweinsteiger, who was 23, was one. His name was mentioned in conference calls between Newcastle's decision makers. When the call went in, Bayern Munich said it was too late, too near to the start of the season, to do business.

Luka Modric flew into Tyneside and was shown around the city. A £17 million offer was lined up. Newcastle's salary package was not great but they were still stunned when the player instead moved to Tottenham. There was even talk of Frank Lampard.

This was not what Mike Ashley or Derek Llambias wanted to hear.

Llambias had joined the club's board on 6 May, three months earlier. He was a friend of Ashley and had been managing director of the Fifty Club in London, where membership cost £650-a-year and Ashley gambled.

Llambias had taken the position of managing director and when he joined Mort said: 'Derek's experience in the hospitality industry will certainly complement the work already being done by the club to realise its full potential.'

Ashley had said he would bring in his own team after sacking Allardyce, and he had done just that.

Keegan was isolated.

What Keegan did want, was a guarantee that no player would be sold. James Milner, signed from Leeds for just £3.5 million under Shepherd and Robson, was attracting interest.

The team, without the investment Keegan wanted, did well on their opening day, drawing at Old Trafford. Obafemi Martins scored and Darren Fletcher equalised.

'That was a good, good performance from us and we thoroughly deserved a point,' said Keegan.

'Newcastle fans will go away saying how they witnessed a team playing for the supporters, playing for the badge, playing for the club – and that's what they deserve.

'There were lots of good things for us to build on but we mustn't get carried away as there are a lot of tough games to come.'

Newcastle beat Bolton 1–0 in their next game. There were still no new players. Sebastien Bassong, the other player signed in July, was on the bench. Obafemi Martins went off injured in the second half. Mark Viduka was already injured.

Alan Smith was not fully fit. Owen scored with 19 minutes remaining.

'We battled and scrapped,' Keegan said. 'I'm very pleased with that and the togetherness. We can play better. Shay's save from the penalty spot got us and the crowd going. We could have got more.

'Is there a wow signing in the offing? I don't know. We've got nine days left till a week Monday. We definitely need a midfielder and a defender in. If at the end the owner gets us this wow signing I'll be delighted, not just me but the fans, who deserve it.'

Newcastle were joint second in the Premier League table. They went to Coventry on a Tuesday night in the Coca Cola Cup, surrendered a 2–0 lead and eventually went through after Owen scored in extra-time.

By then, all talk was of an offer of £12 million being tabled by Aston Villa for Milner.

'The last player we will want to sell is James Milner, and I am talking about the owner and myself, and I am sure he will not be leaving St James' Park,' said Keegan.

'We have Shola Ameobi talking to Ipswich. After that there will be nobody else going out, and we want one or two more coming in.

'What we have to do is to make sure we get better players coming in than those who are going out, and this will take some doing because they are quality players who are going out. As far as our signings have been concerned, the quantity is low but the quality is very high.'

Three days later, James Milner signed for Aston Villa.

Keegan looked crestfallen when he attempted to justify it.

'He's a player, in an ideal world, you would not want to lose, but I just want to make it absolutely clear that at the end of the day, it was my decision to sell him,' Keegan said.

'We got an offer that I feel was his value. We are all aware James has had a difficult time, he almost signed for them once before and was dragged back.

'He has always behaved impeccably. He's a fantastic professional, and there's no doubt about it, they've got an outstanding player and we have got to move on.

'I'm convinced that to our fans it won't look like a positive move but what will happen in the next two or three days and the future, will be positive.

'In the short term it isn't ideal.

'We had a great meeting [with the owner]. The owner is committed to the club. It's a case of us trying to get the quality we want in. The secret is to pick the right players.

'Mike Ashley is 100 per cent behind me.

'I would think there is a very good chance of getting three or four players in. Mike can only give us the ammunition. That is the finance we have to get the right players.

'We're looking for three or four to come in and I believe we will get them.'

Newcastle moved onto Arsenal. There were still no new players.

They lost 3–0 and it was comfortable for the home side. Robin van Persie scored twice in the first half. Denilson added a third.

'Arsenal played well,' said Keegan. 'They're a very good side. No one in England would deny that. They have quality players. We're three players short of a very good side here. We have good characters. There were some good performances.

'We're short of personnel. We'll spend the next two days doing our very best to bring quality players in. I stress quality players, not just bodies. We have to do it right.'

They would be the last words Kevin Keegan said in an official capacity as the manager of Newcastle United.

Wise told him who the two players would be that night. It was not Modric or Schweinsteiger. They were unheard ofs. Keegan had been pushed to breaking point. On Monday, 1 September, Newcastle confirmed the signings of Gonzalez [on loan] and Xisco [for £5.7million].

Keegan had clashed with Llambias on Sunday and Monday about transfers. Ashley is thought to have intervened to stop a possible resignation. There became a futile attempt at reconciliation.

By then, the anger of supporters had reached the board of directors. Keegan felt compromised by Wise in a role above him for the recruitment of players. The club had still not signed the left-back he asked for in May.

Newcastle released a statement.

'Newcastle United can confirm that meetings between members of the board and manager Kevin Keegan were held both yesterday and today,' it read. 'Kevin has raised a number of issues and those have been discussed with him.

'The club wants to keep progressing with its long-term strategy and would like to stress that Kevin is extremely important, both now and in the future. Newcastle United values the effort and commitment shown by Kevin since his return to St James' Park and wants him to continue to play an instrumental role as manager of the club. For the avoidance of doubt the club has not sacked Kevin Keegan as manager.'

By then, however, an exit looked inevitable, and the bitter legal fight and compensation claim that would follow. Keegan had missed training on Monday as talks about club policy continued.

The impasse continued. By then the situation had become irreversible. More talks took place but Ashley and Newcastle United had a structure in place that they would not reconsider and it was one Keegan was incapable of working in.

On Thursday, 4 September 2008, just before 10pm, it was confirmed that Kevin Keegan had left his position as manager at Newcastle United.

The mood of the city darkened. Around 200 supporters gathered at St James' Park to protest.

'I've been working desperately hard to find a way forward with the directors, but sadly that has not proved possible,' Keegan said in a statement.

'It's my opinion that a manager must have the right to manage and that clubs should not impose upon any manager any player that he does not want.'

Three more days of turmoil were over, but the two sides were still miles apart. Another fight was looming, in front of an independent arbitration panel.

'I have been left with no choice other than to leave,' he added. 'It remains my fervent wish to see Newcastle United do well in the future and I feel incredibly sorry for the players, staff and most importantly the supporters.'

The League Managers' Association, who were by now heavily involved in discussions, said: 'The letter which Kevin received today from managing director Derek Llambias has failed to resolve the matters in issue between him and the club and accordingly he feels he has no alternative other than to resign.'

Those at Newcastle insisted Keegan had been made aware of the structure the club would be operating under, with a director of football and a desire to sign young players. They insisted there had been efforts to bridge a gap that always seemed unlikely to find resolution.

'Over the last few days, the club has devoted itself to the discussions it has held with Kevin and as a result of those discussions had put together a set of practical suggestions for how to move forward,' the club statement read.

'The club made it clear to Kevin that if he had any outstanding concerns on its proposals, he should raise them with the club. The club regrets that Kevin has, instead of taking up that offer, chosen to resign.'

Once more there was not even agreement in the use of that word. Keegan was ready to fight Newcastle for constructive dismissal.

Less than two weeks later, when Llambias and Ashley were in Dubai, the accusation came that the managing director had expressed a desire to 'slap' Keegan, whilst Ashley, who was then 45, had said a potential offer of less than £200 million for the club was insulting.

Peter Cadman, a solicitor representing the pair, said in a statement that was a reaction to a story in the *Daily Mirror*, 'Mr Ashley may well have expressed his views that the discussed valuation for the club was too low.

'Mr Llambias does recall saying he was very frustrated by Mr Keegan during a negotiations meeting that he could have slapped him.'

Before then, and as Tyneside reacted to the news that Keegan had gone, the anger was heading in the direction of Ashley and Llambias. The city prepared to march to show its feelings.

Newcastle were playing Hull in the Premier League and it was no place for the faint hearted. Chris Hughton took a call from the Newcastle board. He was to take charge of the first team.

CHRIS HUGHTON – QUIET MEN

THE WIND BLEW AND A STORM RAGED. CHRIS HUGHTON STOOD outside of Jesmond Dene House and waited for the lift that would take him to the first day in his new job.

A car arrived and the window dropped, 'Jump in Chris,' said the driver.

Hughton gripped the door, braced himself for the wind and got in.

'Morning Kevin,' he said.

The call from Kevin Keegan had come the previous week.

'It's an absolute fact that Kevin called me and it was out of the blue,' said Hughton. 'I knew Kevin, but I didn't know him so well. I knew him through football circles having played against him and met him before.

'Out of the blue I got the phone call. Nigel [Pearson] had left. "Would you be interested in coming Chris?" Kevin asked me.

"Absolutely yes."

"I'll call you in a couple of days to give you more details."

'That was it. From the moment the call came I was very, very interested.'

Newcastle lost 5–1 at Manchester United and two days later Hughton made the drive north.

'I had played at Spurs and West Ham, I'd played at Brentford and I'd coached at Tottenham for 14 years,' he added. 'But I'd never been out of London, not literally. I'd never worked outside of London so I drove up that first time.

'It was a long drive but I remember approaching up the A1, I'd been to Newcastle but I'd never driven up, I remember approaching 10 minutes outside of Newcastle, and I remember the view I had at the lights, and thinking, "How fabulous does that look?"

'The stadium dominates the skyline. That stuck in my mind. I went to find the hotel, and had a problem finding Jesmond Dene House, which was lovely, and then Kevin picked me up the next morning from the hotel for my first day.

'It's the normal one when you arrive at a new work place for the first time. There was apprehension and excitement. There are familiar faces and of course you walk in and speak to the people you know and I knew Kevin and Terry McDermott and Paul Barron. Probably Paul was the one I knew the most from his time in London at Crystal Palace. It was great to be welcomed by everyone, but the large majority of people I didn't know.

'I was impressed by the training facility, and then there was the storm. The weather was that windy we had to train indoors.'

Hughton had come from Spurs, where he had been for 23 years, first as a player, then a coach, and twice as caretaker manager.

He had left school at 16, started a four-year apprenticeship as a lift engineer and he combined that with playing for Tottenham's youth team. He fought to prove he was worth a contract. There were brief spells at West Ham and then Brentford after playing almost 300 games for Spurs. He was capped 53 times by the Republic of Ireland, who he qualified to play for because of his Irish mother.

He was a respected figure in the game, and he was put alongside Steve Round, who had stayed after the Allardyce reign.

Newcastle lost their next two games, but then the season did a U-turn. Of the next seven games they won four and drew three, scoring 14 goals and comfortably beating Sunderland at St James' Park. It felt like the stirrings of a Keegan team. Newcastle entered the top ten.

'From a tactical point of view and I remember that well, we changed shape. Kevin had changed the shape from what had been a predominantly 4-4-2, into a diamond and that was very much instrumental in the upturn in performances and of course results. He played Michael Owen at the head of the diamond.

'It would have been Viduka, Obafemi Martins and Michael Owen behind which was a tremendous decision by Kevin. Kevin is the one who makes the decisions and I could only feel that when you had somebody like Michael Owen who was the player he was and the presence he was, he was somebody Kevin wanted in the team. I think it was for Kevin about getting a formation that could get the best out of Michael and of the team and it very much worked.

'I'd found an apartment I was living in and I was enjoying living there.

'All the time I enjoyed living in Newcastle. Summer was fine. I was very much looking forward to coming back to pre-season training, as you always do.

'The end of the season we had which was a good end to the season. I was brought in to do what was to very much be first team coach, work with the other coaches, who were Steve Round and Terry McDermott.

'Most people know Kevin's big strength was his management, his man management and management of the team. Strong personality, he determined the team the tactics and what we did as coaches was work off what he wants.

'Myself and Steve Round would work together, we would do most of the coaching. I think most people know Kevin wasn't one who took a lot of coaching sessions. That was our role and responsibility and it was always around what Kevin wanted.

'What Kevin wants is a good high tempo in the sessions. There would be specific tactical sessions, there would be because there always has to be. Kevin is one that likes players to have a lot of touches of the ball, likes a high tempo and that would include a lot of small sided games where players are getting a lot of touches.

'There would be tactical work in there. I knew before I came what the football club meant to Geordies. Part of the excitement for me to come up was what I knew, the stadium, how massive it was, I knew the support base and I knew how football mad the region was. That was a big pull for me. I was never disappointed.'

Keegan's fight with the board and the growing resentment was kept from staff.

'A lot of the difficulties Kevin might have had, Kevin dealt with himself,' added Hughton. 'It wasn't one where he was pulling us in and making us aware of difficulties he had, and I think that's the character of Kevin.

'He did what managers do. He tried to manage it the best way he could. He took that responsibility himself.

'Kevin was a very big personality. He had brought me in to be a coach and my role as a coach, along with the relationship you had with the players, was putting on the sessions to support the manager.

'A lot of the difficulties Kevin might have been having I wouldn't have been aware of them.'

That had changed by the time Newcastle travelled to Coventry on 26 August. By then the row about the possible sale of James Milner to Aston Villa had become public. Events would move quickly. By the time of Newcastle's next home game, against Hull City, when supporters marched and sang against Ashley underneath the Milburn Stand, Hughton was the caretaker manager of Newcastle United.

'Yes, it was difficult,' said Hughton. 'I don't mind saying that. It was difficult because I'd been brought in by Kevin and it became obvious to me before that Kevin wasn't going to get the support he wanted.

'It was difficult. Kevin had brought me in and was somebody I was very, very fond of. Yes, it was hard. Anything like that is always a difficult time at the club, always.

'I think the phone call would have come from Lee Charnley to tell me that Kevin had resigned and could I take over until something was resolved.'

Nothing would prepare Hughton for Hull and an afternoon of vitriol towards the club's board.

'I'd been in that position before, when a manager leaves or loses his job. I'd been in the position before when I'd been the caretaker for a short period of time at Tottenham.

'I'd been at Tottenham through a lot of managers. It's always a bit surreal. The atmosphere is always different because you know that everybody's minds are on what has happened. What happens to players in my experience, players always get on with it the best they can, that is what they are paid to do. It's always difficulty circumstances when managers lose their jobs.

'Kevin was a very popular manager with the players.

'I think it was a difficult time. What you can have is a manager who loses his job or a manager who resigns somewhere else and I wouldn't say it's glossed over fairly quickly, I would never say that, because every place is different, but in particular Newcastle, and probably if I didn't know before, or I hadn't learnt already in the period of time I was there, how big a club Newcastle was, I soon found out.

'At somewhere else it might not get the coverage that Newcastle did. This is probably the time when I found out how big a club it was and what it meant to people. The coverage was massive and of course the area is Newcastle United FC first and almost everything afterwards.

'Yes, it was a hard time. It was getting so much coverage. Certainly locally, local press but also nationally and if I was ever to find out how big a club it was and how it dominated the area, it was then.'

On Saturday, 13 September, Newcastle fans marched on their own stadium. Ashley and Wise did not attend the game, but that did not stop the vitriol. It was everywhere. In the fans who surrounded the exit outside the old Milburn entrance, having started their march at 2pm, in the fury of the songs that echoed outside the ground and in a stadium that had become toxic.

Keith Barrett's flags in the early days of Kevin Keegan's return to Newcastle as a manager in 1992 were expressions of joy. They travelled around Europe. Huge, black and white, statements of passion. He was stopped by stewards on his walk around the stadium against Hull, a simple message on a white sheet, 'Cockney Mafia out.'

There were placards, 'No more Geordie cash for Ashley'. Police on horseback split up the crowds outside the ground. 'Sack the Board,' as it had been before Keegan arrived as manager, was the song of choice. His name reverberated around St James' Park as well.

It seemed inevitable that Newcastle would lose. Marlon King scored twice and then Xisco would score the only goal in his entire Newcastle career with eight minutes left. It was not enough. Guthrie was sent off. Newcastle lost. The marches started again.

By Sunday 14 September, even Ashley had had enough.

Just after lunchtime he released a 1644 word statement.

'I am putting the club up for sale,' he said. 'I hope that the fans get what they want and that the next owner is someone who can lavish the amount of money on the club that the fans want.

'I have the interests of Newcastle United at heart. I have listened to you. You want me out. That is what I am now trying to do, but it won't happen overnight and it may not happen at all if a buyer does not come in.

'You don't need to demonstrate against me again because I have got the message. Any further action will only have an adverse effect on the team. As fans of Newcastle United you need to spend your energy getting behind, not me, but the players who need your support.

'I don't want anyone to read my words and think that any of this is an attack on Kevin Keegan. It is not. Kevin and I always got on. Everyone at the club, and I mean everyone, thinks that he has few equals in getting the best out of the players. He is a legend at the club and rightly so. Clearly there are disagreements between Kevin and the board and we have both put that in the hands of our lawyers.

'I bought Newcastle United in May 2007. Newcastle attracted me because everyone in England knows that it has the best fans in football. When the fans are behind the club at St James' Park it makes the hairs on the back of your neck stand up. It is magic. Newcastle's best asset has been, is and always will be the fans.

'But like any business with assets the club has debts. I paid £134 million out of my own pocket for the club. I then poured another £110 million into the club not to pay off the debt, but just to reduce it. The club is still in debt. Even worse than that, the club still owes millions of pounds in transfer fees. I shall be paying out many more millions over the coming year to pay for players bought by the club before I arrived.

'But there was a double whammy. Commercial deals such as sponsorships and advertising had been front loaded. The money had been paid upfront and spent. I was left with a club that owed millions and part of whose future had been mortgaged. Unless I had come into the club then it might not have survived. It could have shared the fate of other clubs who have borrowed too heavily against their future. Before I had spent a penny on wages or buying players Newcastle United had cost me more than a quarter of a billion pounds.

'Don't get me wrong. I did not buy Newcastle to make money. I bought Newcastle because I love football. Newcastle does not generate the income of a Manchester United or a Real Madrid. I am Mike Ashley, not Mike Ashley a multi-billionaire with unlimited resources. Newcastle United and I can't do what other clubs can. We can't afford it.

'I knew that the club would cost me money every year after I had bought it. I have backed the club with money. You can see that from the fact that Newcastle has the fifth highest wage bill in the Premier League. I was always prepared to bank roll Newcastle up to the tune of £20 million per year but no more. That was my bargain. I would make the club solvent. I would make it a going concern. I would pour up to £20 million a year into the club and not expect anything back.

'It has to be realised that if I put £100 million into the club year in year out then it would not be too long before I was cleaned out and a debt ridden Newcastle United would find itself in the position that faced Leeds United.

'That is the nightmare for every fan. To love a club that over-extends itself, that tries to spend what it can't afford.

'That will never happen to Newcastle when I am in charge. The truth is that Newcastle could not sustain buying the Shevchenko's, Robinho's or the Berbatov's.

'My plan and my strategy for Newcastle is different. It has to be. Arsenal is the shining example in England of a sustainable business model. It takes time. It can't be done overnight. Newcastle has therefore set up an extensive scouting system. We look for young players, for players in foreign leagues who everyone does not know about. We try and stay ahead of the competition.

'We search high and low looking for value, for potential that we can bring on and for players who will allow Newcastle to compete at the very highest level but who don't cost the earth.

'I am prepared to back large signings for millions of pounds but for a player who is young and has their career in front of them and not for established players at the other end of their careers. There is no other workable way forward for Newcastle.

'It is in this regard that Dennis and his team have done a first class job in scouting for talent to secure the future of the club.

'You only need to look at some of our signings to see that it is working, slowly working. Look at Jonas Gutierrez and Fabricio Coloccini. These are world class players. The plan is showing dividends with the signing of exceptional young talent such as Sebastien Bassong, Danny Guthrie and Xisco.

'I have set out, clearly, my plan. If I can't sell the club to someone who will give the fans what they want then I shall continue to ensure that Newcastle is run on a business and football model that is sustainable. I care too much about the club merely to abandon it.'

It was another bombshell.

The backdrop became almost impossible. Newcastle lost the next three games, to West Ham, Tottenham and Blackburn. They were 19th.

THE MEDIA ROOM, BENTON, OCTOBER 2008

JOE KINNEAR – BIGMOUTH STRIKES AGAIN

'WHICH ONE?'

That was how the circus opened on Thursday, 2 October, 2008. That was how Joe Kinnear made sure he would never be forgotten as a Newcastle United manager, no matter how good or bad a job he did.

Back then the media room at the Benton training ground was a media room in name only. In truth, it was three leather settees positioned haphazardly, the whirring of a snack machine a reminder that journalists weren't originally supposed to be there.

Kinnear was unhappy with the coverage of his first day as Newcastle manager, a stunning appointment.

He had had a heart problem and had worked once in football, at Nottingham Forest, in the previous five years, and he had resigned from his post with the club 22nd in the Championship. Journalists were bemused that he had not cancelled the players' day off to meet his squad on his first day in the post. Television cameras were for once not allowed into that small room, tucked away on the very end of the training facility.

Kinnear kept the journalists waiting two hours. Two hours is a long time in the company of other football writers, but it was worth it. Oh, it was worth it all right. No one will forget Joe Kinnear. How could you?

Kinnear, with his greying, curly hair slicked back at the sides, bowled up – and he really did bowl up – and stood in the middle of that room. He could have been Danny Dyer's old man. More *Football Factory* than Tyneside shop floor.

His words have gone down in football folklore.

The first words he spoke to the local press as Newcastle manager – 'Which one?' – was to discover which person had been the most 'out of order.' The first response he made was, 'You're a cunt.'

Kinnear swore 52 times. It was theatrical gold. He gave and he got.

He was 61 years old then. He had the hands of a man who has spent a life working with heavy machinery and the gnarled right finger pointed at those who had provoked the most ire. The left index finger and thumb held a bit of paper with names on it and the rage was such that the paper shook in his hand. Occasionally his voice trembled.

Kinnear produced a press conference the likes of which I do not expect to witness for the rest of my career. How could you forget that?

Joe Kinnear: Which one is Simon Bird [*Daily Mirror* journalist]?

Simon Bird: Me.

JK: You're a cunt.

Bird: Thank you.

JK: Which one is [Niall] Hickman [*Daily Express*]? You are out of order. Absolutely fucking out of order. If you do it again, I am telling you, you can fuck off and go to another ground. I will not come and stand for that fucking crap. No fucking way, lies.

Fuck, you're saying I turned up and they fucked off.

Bird: No Joe, have you read it, it doesn't actually say that. Have you read it?

JK: I've fucking read it, I've read it.

Bird: It doesn't say that. Have you read it?

JK: You are trying to fucking undermine my position already.

Bird: Have you read it, it doesn't say that. I knew you knew they were having a day off.

JK: Fuck off. Fuck off. It's your last fucking chance.

Bird: You read the copy? It doesn't say that you didn't know.

JK: What about the headline, you think that's a good headline?

Bird: I didn't write the headline, you read the copy.

JK: You are negative bastards, the pair of you.

Bird: So if I get a new job next week would I take the first day off? No I wouldn't. If I get a new job should I call my boss and say I am taking the first day off?

JK: It is none of your fucking business. What the fuck are you going to do?

You ain't got the balls to be a fucking manager. Fucking day off. Do I want your opinion? Do I have to listen to you?

Bird: No, you can listen to who you want.

JK: I had a 24-hour meeting with the entire staff.

Bird: Joe you are only here six weeks, you could have done that on Sunday, or Saturday night.

JK: No, no, no. I didn't want to do it. I had some other things to do.

Bird: What? More important things?

JK: What are you? My personal secretary? Fuck off.

Bird: You could have done the meeting Saturday night or Sunday? You could have had them watching videos, you could have organised them?

JK: I was meeting the fucking chairman the owner, everyone else. Talking about things.

Bird: It is a valid point that was made in there. A valid point.

JK: I can't trust any of you.

Hickman: Joe, no one could believe that on your first day at your new club, the first team players were not in. No one could believe it in town. Your first day in the office.

JK: My first day was with the coaches. I made the decision that I wanted to get as much information out of them.

Hickman: But why Monday, no one could believe it?

JK: I'm not going to tell you anything. I don't understand where you are coming from. You are delighted that Newcastle are getting beat and are in the state they are? Delighted are you?

Hickman: Certainly not. No one wants to see them get beaten, why would we?

JK: I have done it before. It is going to my fucking lawyers. So are about three others. If they can find something in it that is a court case it's going to court. I am not fucking about. I don't talk to fucking anybody. Everything I fucking say or do. It is raking up stories. You are fucking so fucking slimy: you are raking up players that I got rid of; players that I had fallen out with. You are not asking Robbie Earle, because he is sensible. You are not asking Warren Barton? No. Because he is fucking sensible. Anyone who had played for me for ten years at any level you will find some cunt that ...

Journalist: How long is your contract for Joe?

JK: None of your business

The contract, it would later be revealed, was rolling, as was Joe.

When it finished, when the squabbling and the swearing, when a man who should have been nowhere near Newcastle United had finished his finger pointing, the circus rolled out.

Then he had to sit in the more intimate surrounds of a Sunday briefing.

Less journalists, less hostility, less antagonism.

'You're right about one thing Joe,' said a voice. 'The daily's are a bunch of cunts!'

There was huge laughter.

It was all a big joke.

Kinnear started his reign with two 2–2 draws, against Everton and then Manchester City, then went to Sunderland and lost, the first Newcastle manager to do so since Bill McGarry in 1980. Nineteen different managers had been in charge between the two defeats. That run was over.

Kinnear's first win came in game four, against West Brom. There were three draws in a row, two wins and then another defeat, at Wigan. Newcastle were 12th, but they were just two points off a relegation place. By then it had also emerged that papers from Kevin Keegan's legal representatives had been submitted to the three-man Premier League tribunal that would rule on his claim for constructive dismissal. The sum claimed was thought to be around £8million. No buyer had emerged for the club at that point.

SHAY GIVEN – THE DYING OF THE LIGHT

TAKE A WALK ALONG THE CORRIDOR BETWEEN THE CHANGING rooms at St James' Park and the media suite, deep within the bowels of the stadium, and the walls are adorned with players who have made a difference to a football club. They are all there; Gallacher, Milburn, Ferdinand, pictures and records and stats that made the people of Tyneside fall in love with a man in black and white stripes.

Turn a right through the double doors and the visual past does not end. There are great teams and not so great teams scattered on walls, and two immaculately presented lists, set in black and written in gold. These are perhaps two of the most significant group of players to have played for Newcastle United since its formation in 1892.

On one list is the top ten goalscorers of all time, with Alan Shearer at its summit, and then followed, closely by Jackie Milburn. They are the names you expect to see, Macdonald, Cole, Beardsley, Robson, all huge crowd favourites, revered for putting the ball into the back of the net.

On the other list is those more unsung, full of defenders and goalkeepers and players to whom longevity mattered more than headlines.

At number four is Frank Clark, who went to Nottingham Forest in 1975 on a free transfer and proceeded to win the Division One title and the European Cup. Beneath him is Bill McCracken, a player so steeped in success his name should role off the tongue of every Newcastle fan. It won't. McCracken was born in Belfast in 1883 and moved to St James' Park in 1904.

Along with the incomparable Colin Veitch, he sat in cafes and devised a way of playing the offside trap so well that the FA had to change the rules, bringing the number of defenders between the foremost attacker and the goal line down to two, from its previous number of three.

McCracken won three League titles with Newcastle United and picked up an FA Cup winners' medal as well, making him one of the most decorated players in the club's entire history. He also played 432 times for the club, the fifth most of any player. Clark was fourth on 457, both men failing to catch the 496 appearances Jimmy Lawrence made during an 18-year association with the club, similarly to McCracken at the start of the 20th century.

Lawrence moved to Tyneside from Scotland. He too won three League titles, one FA Cup and was a loser in four more finals during the richest period in the club's history.

Shay Given had quietly, during a 12-year period also between the posts, moved up to third position in the list of those to have played for the Newcastle United. Given was at 462, and the topic of beating Lawrence's record came up many times in private conversation. He knew what it was and he knew what he would have to do to beat it.

Given had been in the house in Harwood when eight of Graham Fenton's friends had descended from Whitley Bay, the night before Blackburn played Newcastle. They had got drunk, made a racket and nobody had slept. That was his first real taste of the club.

He had been born in Lifford, a small town with a population of around 1,600 in the north of the Republic of Ireland. Hard work probably helped forge relationships when he finally did move to Tyneside.

'I had to work hard with my dad when I was a kid in the fields,' he told me. 'We used to have a market garden sort of trade. We used to be weeding vegetables for nine hours, a full day on your hands and knees.

'I did it for as long as I can remember. I grew up with four brothers and three sisters.

'My mum died of cancer when I was five so it is something that is very close to me.

'Cancer hits so many people. My dad had to make a lot of sacrifices to keep us all together and put food on the table. We didn't have an easy time of it. He made a lot of sacrifices when we were younger and you don't really appreciate it at the time.

'I know I'm very privileged with the job I have now. I left Lifford to go to Celtic when I was 16. I don't think I've changed. All my brothers were digging as well and it stood me in good stead.

'We use to grow potatotes first and then at the weekends we would have to go out and pick them.

'We had Dad to drive the tractor and we had to get all the spuds and things.

'I still enjoy the same things I always have done. I like a Guinness with my friends, playing with my kids. I know what a hard day's work is and maybe some of the kids now have it a bit too easy. It's the way of the world and maybe I'm just getting old!

'You sort of reminisce. Your upbringing has a lot to do with it. I don't think I've changed too much. I'm pretty much the same person as when I left Lifford in Donegal all those years ago.

'I still like to think I would speak to anyone on the street. I respect anybody no matter what they're doing with their lives.

'I don't think you should ever change, no matter what you've done or how good you think you are or whatever.

'Nothing has changed me, nothing ever will and I don't think it should. If you do well for the club and put in performances and people know you're giving your all, the supporters will back you and support you.

'There are some tricky characters in football but just because you kick a football around a pitch doesn't make you any more special than the man on the street. You play football, it's something you enjoy doing, but it doesn't make you better than anyone.

'It's important you respect everyone in every walk of life, it's just the way I am and I don't think that will ever alter. I still do the shopping every week and nothing's going to change that.'

He had done exceptionally well at Sunderland on loan, setting a record of 12 clean sheets from 17 games as the side, led by Peter Reid, won what was the First Division Championship in 1996. A year later he signed for Newcastle for £1.5 million. It was fine business from Kenny Dalglish, who had worked with Given when he was in charge at Ewood Park.

One by one, his family followed him to Tyneside. His brother still lives in Tynemouth, his sister is in Gosforth. His Auntie was in Fenham.

'Kenny Dalglish was a big influence on me coming to the club. I'd been with him at Blackburn as well. Newcastle had almost won the league so joining was a no brainer.

'I was buzzing to get there. Kenny signed me at Blackburn as well. He brought me there from Celtic. I built a relationship with him over a few years when he was the manager. He must have seen enough, I was still young to be taken to a Premier League team at 21. He put me straight in the team as well.

'I can't speak highly enough of the guy, just as a player and a manager he was brilliant, he would always stick by his players no matter what. The players respected him not just for that. He had your corner.

'Obviously an unbelievable player in his day as well. We just wish he had of stayed longer at Newcastle. There wasn't much time for Kenny to get his ideas across after Kevin left.

'He wanted to bring more players in. He wasn't given enough time at that time, I felt. From a players point of view he had huge respect. The players really liked playing for him as well.'

Robson impacted hugely on Given as well.

'Bobby Robson was very special,' he added. 'He had an affiliation with the North East. It hit home with the fans. He had a huge personality of course and he got the best out of people. He was probably the best man-manager I ever worked with.

'I know he played Alan Shearer and Craig Bellamy up front together and they didn't see eye to eye.

'He would put his arm around Craig and say whatever he said, about Al probably, and then he would put his arm around Al and say whatever he said, about Craig probably, and when they both played together they were fantastic. That was down to the manager. He got the best out of them. He was fantastic.'

It was a brief spell of working with Keegan, turmoil rumbling on in the background.

'I was excited when he came,' he added. 'There was a big hoo-ha with the fans and rightly so after what had happened previously.

'Of course, you were disappointed that he left. Again I felt he left too soon, but similar to myself, I don't think he felt the ambition was there that Kevin had.

'He was a guy who wanted to lift Newcastle back to the top of the league really and I don't know if the owner matched that ambition.

'It was unbelievable to work with Kevin, unbelievable, a great guy. His enthusiasm rubbed off on everyone, not just for football but for life in general.

'He was a bubbly character. He had huge respect in the North East for what he'd done before and even now if you talk to most Newcastle fans they'd love to see Kevin Keegan back. It shows the job he done before and what he meant to the fans.'

Given lost a Cup final to Manchester United, handed in and retracted a transfer request he regretted, lost his place in another Cup final against Arsenal to Steve Harper. He lost a semi-final at Wembley, saw a UEFA Cup dream die against Sporting Lisbon at the quarter-final stage, his lowest point (another went down in the semis) and played in three Champions League campaigns.

'When it goes bad at Newcastle it is horrific, but when it goes well it really takes off,' he added. 'You get the whole place rocking.

'We've been in the Champions League before and finished third, fourth and fifth in the Premier League. There is definitely the potential to get us back up there.

'There's been very good moments. It's a huge part of my life and it always will be, whatever happens in the future. There were lots of highs and lots of lows.

'Getting to the FA Cup final twice were real highs. Losing them were two huge lows. We had a good run in the UEFA Cup and got to the quarter-final and I saw the teams left and thought we had a real chance of winning it.

'But we lost to Sporting Lisbon, that was the hardest.'

Then came Kinnear.

'Joe was a bolt out of the blue. Everyone was in shock he got the job. He hadn't been a manager for such a long time. He had health fears. We didn't even know he was a manager in a sense.

'It was a bit of a shock when he came in. He was all right. He wasn't a big hit with the fans. When you're offered the Newcastle job you don't turn it down. Most people would take it, a little bit old school I suppose.

'We once reckoned there had been 44 defenders who had played in front of Given. Some defenders are better than others. At least it kept him busy.'

He went on a run between 2000 and 2006 when he became one of the best goalkeepers in the country. There was a run of 139 successive Premier League appearances, and there were some outstanding displays, perhaps his best saved for the derby victory at the Stadium of Light when Dabizas had scored in 2002. He made three flying stops in the second half.

There was serious injury in September 2006 when a collision with West Ham's Marlon Harewood left him with a one centimetre tear in his bowel that was likened to a car crash.

In a five season run he missed two Premier League games.

By 2009, the best part of 12 years after joining, things were coming to a head.

After 462 games, unflinching service, Given raced from the pitch at St James' Park after a crushing 5-1 defeat at home to Liverpool – he was man of the match

– unable to speak to anyone. Clearly in tears he ran straight down the tunnel to the solace of the changing room.

He'd had enough.

Four days later a statement followed that he was considering his future. There were few dissenting voices, little blame.

'If you lose 5–1 and the 'keeper gets man of the match it's not a good day at the office,' he said.

'Personally I was frustrated to concede five goals. It could have been more. We were totally outclassed on the day. The gulf was massive between the two clubs. We were in the same division but it didn't look it. It was a frustrating day.

'I was upset. Very much so. I went straight down the tunnel. You feel let down.

'It's not just about me. You're in the team. It was disappointing for the team as well and the performance was poor. The gap between both clubs was massive on the day. It felt like a shooting in game for them.

'It was frustrating. I had eleven-and-a-half years and I felt the club was selling the best players. I didn't feel there was any ambition there anymore. I had been there so long. When I signed for the club we were pushing for the title.

'There was a new owner involved and it didn't feel as if he was going to put the club back into the top four or five in the country. It felt like we were just getting by, staying in the division, not showing ambition, just getting by.

'I met him once briefly before I left. I didn't get the helicopter treatment, no! That was it really. We had a brief conversation and that was about it. He wanted me to stay, but I don't think he went about it the right way, I don't want to get into other stuff. We didn't talk for long to be honest.

'Then Manchester City came in and there was the opportunity to go a club with huge ambitions.

'I felt it was too good to turn down, but it wasn't an easy decision. I have such an affiliation with the club and the fans and everything. It wasn't easy.

'My brother still lives in Tynemouth and my sister lives in Gosforth. I still get up there to see them. I have nephews and nieces and they are Geordies.

'My two eldest were born in Newcastle as well. You ask them where they're from and they say Newcastle as well. They're Newcastle born and bred. It will always have a special place in my life.

'I thought I would never leave Newcastle. I was there that long.

'I had some great times at Newcastle. It was nearly 12 years of my life, you are going to have strong feelings for the area and the people.

'Newcastle was my home, 95 per cent of the fans in years to come will hopefully thank me for what I did. I gave my all to Newcastle when I was there, in every training session and every game.

'I would love to have beaten that record of Jimmy Lawrence but it wasn't to be.

'It's amazing. It's an amazing place when it's going in the right direction. You've got to be a certain kind of player to play at Newcastle, with that crowd and that atmosphere and when it's going well you feel ten foot tall.'

HOSPITAL, THE MIDLANDS, FEBRUARY 2009

JOE KINNEAR – I'LL BE BACK

AFTER THE 5–1 DEFEAT TO LIVERPOOL AT HOME A ROT SET IN THAT Kinnear could not stop. Two draws followed with Hull and West Ham and then came defeats to Hull (in the FA Cup replay), and Blackburn. Joey Barton and Jose Enrique argued with each other on the pitch at the end of the game. The Newcastle fans sang for Keegan. In training three days later, two players fought for real.

Andy Carroll was emerging as a raw, powerful centre-forward. He had scored his first Premier League goal, against West Ham before clashing with Charles N'Zogbia in training.

Carroll wiped out the French winger with a late tackle.

As Carroll walked away, N'Zogbia got to his feet and floored the 6ft 4in forward with a sucker punch. Carroll got up and the pair went for each other. Training was cancelled. The row raged on. There was a scuffle in the dressing room and then another row in the car park.

Kinnear, who by this point said he was on a monthly rolling contract, dismissed it as handbags. He did, however, struggle to pronounce the player's name so much N'Zogbia wanted to leave.

Another defeat followed at Manchester City, when Carroll scored again and there was a draw with Sunderland at St James' Park, Shola Ameobi scoring with a 69th minute penalty.

It would be the last game Kinnear ever took charge as a manager.

It was half past six on the morning of 7 February, 2009. Chris Hughton was in his hotel room when the telephone rang. It was the Newcastle doctor.

'Joe's had a heart attack,' the doctor said.

'It was massive shock,' said Hughton. 'I think particularly because Joe had had a scare before.

'At that moment everything football wise goes out the window.

'It did do during the game. We played the game, but of course right the way through it you're conscious there is a medical situation that is more important than anything.

'It was a shock.

'We won 3–2 but the first thing I did was check how he was.

'Testament to the players. There are also the times, irrespective of what anybody thought, whether they were in the team or out the team or aggrieved or not, that's the time when everybody pulls in the right direction and the players did.'

Hughton had known Kinnear from his days at Tottenham, where Kinnear, like Hughton an Ireland international, had played 196 times for the club.

'No, I didn't see the appointment coming, but probably I would have to say there isn't anything in the game that surprises me,' added Hughton.

'One thing that will never change in the game is that people have to make decisions.

'Yes, it was a surprise, but it wasn't one that lasted too long. It's not one where two or three days later I still can't believe it. It was a surprise but these things happen in the game.

'I knew Joe. I'd met him over the years. He was obviously an ex-Tottenham player, also an ex-Republic of Ireland player. I got on well with Joe. Joe worked in a different way and I had good responsibility. At that stage when he came in I think Steve Round had left to go to Everton. I had fair responsibility once Joe came.

'Over Joe's period he did steady the ship as regards results and I can't remember too much changing in the way Joe worked. It was just the course of the season.

'Yes, Joe was very old school. As regards the training Joe was very much one who would orchestrate the training but didn't take too much of the actual training, but he was manager in the way where he would expect to do the team talk before the game.

'He would get into players at half-time, Joe was the type of manager, his record at Wimbledon had been good, he'd been used to managing a group at Wimbledon, he was more of a manager than a coach.'

From 7 February Chris Hughton was once again the acting Newcastle United manager.

'It was very much game by game for me after his heart attack,' he added.

'It certainly wasn't one where I was told you've got it through to the end of the season. It was very much game by game.

'We lost against Manchester United and Arsenal and whenever you're a caretaker manager, if anything you almost want to win more because you know. You know you're caretaker for a manager, because that's what the job is.

'There isn't a permanent manager at the time and it's difficult. Your head thinks more about the club and what's the best way forward. You want to win a game. You're even more desperate.

'The performances in those two games, I remember the players, not being able to fault what the players gave. What we were up against in a difficult season was two big, big teams.

'Certainly the results weren't a reflection of what the players were prepared to give.'

There was a free weekend before Newcastle's next fixture. Derek Llambias met executive box holders. He spoke of the desire to replicate the magic and connection that Sunderland were enjoying with Niall Quinn, who returned to the club to launch a takeover, having enjoyed a successful spell as a player at the club.

Still, no one could guess quite what Llambias and Ashley would do next.

ALAN SHEARER –
THERE IS A LIGHT THAT
NEVER GOES OUT

'EXCUSE ME PLEASE, CAN I JUST GET PAST TO GET TO THE SEAT NEXT to you?'

'No.'

'What?'

'No. The show's about to start?'

'The show?'

'Yes, I've been here for half an hour and the show's about to start. I'm not moving'

'What do you mean the show? It's a press conference, and I don't want your seat, I want the one past you.'

'I'm not moving.'

And she didn't.

I still have no idea who she was, or who some of the people in the media room at St James' Park on 2 April, 2009 actually were, but it was full.

Mostly it was full of journalists, the usual select from the region, but this time it was bursting with television cameras and the number ones from national newspapers.

That told you something special was happening.

But a show? Maybe she was right.

Shearer was back centre stage, at the heart of Newcastle.

He only smiled once in 23 minutes, for a quick joke at Iain Dowie's expense, who was sat to his right.

Both men were besuited. The bruise brothers.

Shearer didn't go for a black and white tie. It was still striped, and the shirt was light blue, the suit grey, which reflected the club, the situation and the severity of what he had been persuaded to walk into, with eight games remaining and with Newcastle now nineteenth and two points from safety.

'I got a call on Saturday morning from Derek asking one or two things,' Shearer revealed. 'Then I got a call the following day to ask if they (Derek and Mike Ashley) could come and see me the following day, on Sunday.

'We had a good chat for over an hour on Sunday. It was put to me they would like me to take charge of eight games. I asked for a night to think about it. They agreed to me bringing Iain in, which I think was very important, a fresh look, if not so much a pretty one.

'I went back on Monday morning and said I would do it. Everything was right. I spoke to Mike and it was from then onwards. It was a matter of getting contracts drawn up. I had one or two issues I had to sort out with my employers at the BBC who have given me an eight-week sabbatical. It was all agreed late last night.

'I love this football club and they're in a very bad position, I've been given an opportunity to do something about it. I believe I can. If I didn't think there was enough quality in that squad I wouldn't have come. Having seen it this morning there is quality there but they're not playing with much confidence. It's my job to get that.

'I haven't taken this job for me. I could have been sat on the sofas on a Saturday evening and been analytical and critical. I love that job. The opportunity is right. I believe I can help this football club get out of the position they are in.

'I have to say the response has been fantastic, not surprising. I've come in this morning and spoke to all the players and all the staff and the training was superb. They have set a standard now this morning that we want them to keep to. I said to them after training, if you keep the standard up then we will be okay, I really believe that.

'We have a massive a massive fight on our hands, a massive job to be done in difficult circumstances.'

He had headed down the tunnel at St James' Park as a hero, feted and adored, 50,000 supporters singing his name. There were fireworks, Ant and Dec, the acclaim that scoring 206 goals for a team brings.

Was he concerned, came the question, of how eight games could affect his relationship with the supporters who had serenaded his arrival and departure as a player?

'They know me as well as anyone does,' he added. 'They will get 100 per cent, 24 hours a day for the next eight weeks. I hope that will be good enough, I really do. It would sadden me and the thousands of people who support this club if it was in the Championship. They don't deserve that, they deserved better, the powers that be have admitted mistakes have been made this season. We would all agree with that.

'It's important whatever mistakes have been made they have gone. We are third bottom of the league. It's gone. It's history.

'It's definitely only eight weeks. That [the following season] hasn't been discussed.

'Joe Kinnear is recovering at home. We all wish him well. What part Joe has to say, you will have to speak to the necessary people. It has nothing to do with me. It's eight games only.

'If I keep Newcastle up there will be a huge push for me to stay? Good. I want that.

'I was asked to try and keep Newcastle in the Premier League. That's my job. I have eight games to do that.

'I'd be daft to say I don't understand the clamour, why the fans are outside, why the press is here. It's myself and Newcastle United. We have to get away from this Alan Shearer thing. It's not about me. It's about keeping this club in the Premier League. I will be trying as hard to get away from that. I will go out and see the fans and sign the autographs, but we have a job to do.

'There's a big bonus at the end of it, and it's keeping this club in the Premier League. That is the bonus.

'The players are the important ones. They've had a tough time. I'm holding nothing against them. I enjoyed my football and I've watched over the past few months and it doesn't seem like they're enjoying it. They had a buzz this morning. That's very important. You have to enjoy what your doing.

'The be all and end all is staying in the Premier League. We have to get over the line and keep us up.

'I looked at the squad. I looked at the players who are likely to be fit for the remaining games and I believe there is enough quality in there.'

Will you really only stay for eight games?

'That's the plan,' added Shearer. 'I want this football club to stay up and then the powers that be will decide in what direction they go in. The important thing is, "Let's keep the club up."'

Shearer revealed he would not have to work under a director of football.

'They thanked Dennis for his services and he's gone his own way,' added Shearer.

'That was happening irrespective of whether I came in. I wish him well. I made my feelings known earlier in the year about directors of football. That was my opinion. Whether it upset people or not I don't know. That was my opinion.

'I envisage sitting in the stand next season watching Newcastle as a Premier league club.

'I'm really excited to get out there, but I don't think we could have asked for a tougher start.'

The show was over.

Shearer stood outside the entrance to the Milburn Stand and those supporters sang his name. It felt like fresh optimism. Newcastle had won one of their previous 12 Premier League games. They were in free fall.

Shearer was the final throw of a dice from a former casino manager and someone who enjoyed spending his time in one.

They both knew the odds, and by the end of Shearer's first game, at home to title-chasing Chelsea, they had worsened.

Shearer looked like a manager but his players still did not resemble a team. It was a comfortable afternoon for Guus Hiddink's men. Newcastle lost 2–0, Frank Lampard and Florent Malouda scoring, the gap to safety, now with just seven games left, was three points.

'I'm still confident and my players are still confident that we can avoid the drop,' he said. 'I am optimistic. We have to get some confidence into the players. I'm trying to get as many positives into them as I can. They don't want to hear negatives. They want to hear positives.

'I want the team to be the story. I will try to do everything to deflect everything away from the result.

'It was always a very hard task. It still is. We have seven games instead of eight. We have a few more days to prepare and work with the players. That will benefit everyone.

'We have conceded two soft goals. We made a mistake in the second half and we know at this level you will be punished. You are reluctant to open up against a team like Chelsea because of the quality they possess.

'It was tough from then on. Effort wise from the players, there are no complaints, but quality wise, we can get better.

'We did well in the first half and we have to look at that and take it from there but we have to stop conceding silly goals. We all make mistakes.

'We know what has to be done but knowing and doing are two different things. I wish we could rewind this and start all over again. I'm pleased it's over with. We will come in on Sunday morning and prepare for Stoke on Monday.'

Seven days later, Newcastle were at Stoke. You could almost hear the clock ticking. There was so little time. Newcastle's back four was Habib Beye, Sebastien Basssong, David Edgar and Ryan Taylor. They had played less than 50 times in the Premier League between them.

By half-time, Abdoulaye Faye, signed by Sam Allardyce in the summer of 2007, sold to Stoke exactly 12 months later, on the ground where Allardyce took charge of his final game for Newcastle, from a corner that should have been a goal-kick (the final touch had come off Ricardo Fuller) headed past Steve Harper. At that point news came through that second bottom Middlesbrough were beating Hull. Stoke themselves were not completely out of it, but they were if they won.

With 20 minutes to go Shearer took off Ameobi and put on Carroll, who by now had scored twice in the Premier League. It was a bold move. Carroll was still raw, but in the 81st minute Damien Duff sent over a cross, the 20-year-old centre-forward stretched his neck and sent a looping header over Thomas Sorensen and into the Stoke goal, right in front of 3,000 Newcastle supporters. It was an explosion. Carroll was mobbed by teammates, Shearer punched the air.

'It was well deserved, particularly for the way we played in the second half,' he said.

'For the majority of the match, for what they threw at us, we handled it very well. We showed great character in going one-nil down to then go on and get the equaliser and take the game to Stoke.

'I said to Andy after his two goals for the reserves in mid-week, you've got a big part to play. You've got to show me the hunger and desire you want to play a part. He came on and got us a point. It was a fantastic header from Andy and thoroughly deserved.

'It has been a real team effort. It could prove to be a real valuable point. We have to have more confidence and belief to get on the ball.

'There are six games left and without a doubt there is enough. The players have shown that. I have seen it in training. They've shown they can play at a very difficult place. I'm disappointed it's not more than a point but it could be a valuable one.

'It's going to be tight. It's going to right down to the wire. There will be nerves jangling, but I believe in my players and they believe in themselves.'

Finally, there was hope.

Shearer was relentless. Behind the scenes, at the training ground, a mini-revolution was taking place. It was a big ask, to attempt a change of culture with so few games left to play with.

Shearer was the fourth different voice the players had been instructed by that season. The instability, the disruption had propelled Newcastle to the brink of their first relegation since 1989.

Shearer tightened discipline, training sessions were harder, injured players were told they would get seven hours of treatment a day and days off for anyone were cancelled.

Ice baths became mandatory after games, there were more severe punishments for being late, heart monitors were worn during training and there were team bonding sessions, to bring the players closer together.

'I've seen the psychological mood of the dressing room improve,' Shearer said two days before Newcastle travelled to White Hart Lane.

'It was pretty despondent when we came in and understandably so.

'Morale wasn't great but I think particularly with last week's result there has been a belief and a little bit of confidence that we can get out of the mess we are in.

'We will approach the Spurs game the same way we approached Stoke and try to win it.

'I'm under huge pressure. It's hard work but I'm enjoying it. I'm definitely getting a buzz out of it, without a doubt, but it's been manic and it's been crazy with the amount of work we have had to do.'

Then Newcastle went to Tottenham and lost one-nil. Darren Bent scored in the first half. Carroll started the game but Newcastle were poor. Sunderland had won against Hull, Blackburn had lost but Middlesbrough had drawn.

Second bottom, four points from safety. It was mountainous.

Next up were Portsmouth at St James' Park.

Shearer played Mark Viduka, Michael Owen and Obafemi Martins.

Martins and Owen spurned one on ones with David James. Portsmouth hit a post late on. There were jeers when Mike Riley blew the final whistle.

'We're disappointed not to get three points,' said Shearer. 'We went for it tonight with the big hitters and they had a chance each and on another night they could have put them away. We had enough chances to bury them.

'There will be more twists and turns. We have to make sure we're still in there fighting. I'm sure we will be and I'm sure it will go to the wire.'

He was smiling as he spoke.

At the training ground, Shearer addressed his players as he sought to bring through his cultural change, of professionalism and raising standards.

'You are not going to take the piss out of this football club and you are not going to take the piss out of this city,' he told them.

Then Newcastle went to Liverpool for a Sunday game, on 3 May, and there, once again, all hell broke loose.

JOEY BARTON –
DON'T LET ME DOWN

IN THE 11 PREMIER LEAGUE GAMES AT ANFIELD SINCE THE SECOND OF the dramatic 4–3s, Newcastle had managed two draws. It did not fill anyone with hope. Liverpool's merciless display at St James' Park had persuaded Shay Given it was time to leave.

When Newcastle headed back on a Sunday afternoon it felt like the old days of trips to Merseyside. Liverpool were second in the table, in a rich seam of form, the country's top goalscorers under Rafa Benitez. They had turned Manchester United over 4–1 at Old Trafford in March, when Fernando Torres had shone and they had won seven and drawn one of the eight games before they faced Newcastle.

Parallels were now being drawn between Newcastle and Leeds, who had reached a Champions League semi-final before financially imploding on the back of bad decisions at boardroom level.

Alan Smith had been at Elland Road.

'It's a bit different to Leeds,' he said on the eve of the game. 'On a personal note I've only been involved in a few games. It has been more frustrating this time having to watch.

'I have not been able to help them. Hopefully we can get our heads down and we are determined to stay in this division.

'I just hope we stay up and the manager who is in charge now decides to stay for a long period of time. We have a squad of players who are determined.

'Survival in this league is key for any football club.'

The result was a formality.

There were chances for Steven Gerrard and Dirk Kuyt, before Yossi Benayoun scored after just 22 minutes. Harper denied the same player a second with a great save but before the half hour mark Kuyt headed in number two.

Xabi Alonso struck another shot off the crossbar after 39 minutes, Newcastle could not breathe. A Gerrard shot went narrowly wide after the break before Alonso struck a shot off the crossbar. Then, in the 77th minute, as a cleared ball bounced aimlessly towards the corner flag in front of the Kop, ushered by Alonso, Joey Barton, an Everton fan in his ninth appearance of the season, slid in with both feet off the ground and wiped Alonso out. The Spaniard's left leg buckled. Phil Dowd produced a straight red.

With three minutes remaining Lucas Leiva headed in number three.

In the visiting dressing room Shearer seethed.

'I made a mistake putting you back in,' he told Barton.

Barton told Shearer he was the best player at the club.

'You're not. You're shit,' replied Shearer.

'You're a shit manager with shit tactics,' said Barton.

Mark Viduka stepped in-between the pair.

'You're out of order,' Viduka told Barton.

Shearer had not calmed down by the time he faced the cameras.

'I'm not the only one hurting,' he said. 'There are thousands back in Newcastle, we brought 3,500 here today. They don't see it as a losing battle. We are all hurting.

'I am bitterly disappointed to lose the game, but I have no complaints.

'They were the better side. They deserved to beat us. We will regroup. That game wasn't going to save our season but the next two will.

'The third goal was disappointing. We made subs determined not to let any more in, the goal difference could be important come the end of the season. It's bitterly disappointing.

'Yeah, I've seen enough in training to suggest we can stay up. I haven't seen enough out there [today]. I saw enough against Portsmouth at home. If we play in a similar way that might be enough to keep us up. We know how important the Middlesbrough game is for both teams.

'It's the next two home games. If we win our next two that might be enough to survive, I don't know.'

Then Shearer was asked about Barton.

'I wasn't happy at that and the way it happened,' he said.

'We all don't need those headlines. I put him in to do a specific job and I asked him to keep calm in the heat of the battle, it's a stupid tackle and he got sent off and he now misses the rest of the season and we'll take it from there.

'It's about keeping calm for 90 minutes, not 75 or 80. I'm not very happy as you can see.

'Barton wasn't unlucky to be sent off, it was the right decision.

'We will be without him for the rest of the season and I'm not happy at all.

'He has let me down, definitely, and the same goes for the whole club and himself. From a disciplinary point of view, I will do whatever I can.'

Two days later the club released a statement.

'Newcastle United can confirm that Joey Barton has been suspended from the club until further notice,' it read.

'The club will be making no further comment on the matter at this time.'

Barton was fined two weeks' wages, around £120,000.

He was not allowed into Newcastle's training ground for the rest of the season.

STEVEN TAYLOR –
STAND AND DELIVER

THERE WERE THREE GAMES TO GO WHEN I SPOKE TO STEVEN TAYLOR.
His career felt like it was going somewhere, even if everything else seemed to be
falling to bits. He had played 116 games in the previous three seasons for Newcastle,
captained the England Under-21s and even been called up to the full squad for a
friendly against Germany.

Born in Greenwich he had moved to North Tyneside within weeks of his birth.
His dad, Alf, a former police officer, was certainly a Geordie, and Taylor never felt or
sounded like he was anything but from the region. Whitley Bay Boys Club, Cramlington
Juniors and then into the Newcastle Academy. It was a path similar to Graham Fenton.

Taylor was 16 when Newcastle took a punt on him. He had been a centre-forward
until he was 12. As soon as he left school, John Carver pushed Sir Bobby Robson to
play him in the reserves. GCSEs one day, training with Alan Shearer, Craig Bellamy
and Laurent Robert the next.

'It was huge,' he told me. 'I wasn't used to that. I had to grow up quick. Having
them around me made me realise how much I wanted to make it.'

Robson sent him to spend some time with his hero, Tony Adams, then in charge
at Wycombe. He grew up a bit more and came on as a substitute at Real Mallorca in
the UEFA Cup in March 2004. He was 18. Four days later, at the Reebok Stadium,
he became a Premier League player, but eight months followed without another start
and doubts crept in about whether he would make it. Graeme Souness was manager
by that time. In training he would throw asides at Taylor, asking him if he really
wanted it enough.

'In that year, I just thought, "Will I ever get a chance again?" After the Bolton game all the big names came back and that didn't help. Then Souness took over and a week before the Everton game I was training with the reserves and he was saying to me, "You look like a player but are you really one?" He just questioned me over and over again about whether I wanted it or not.

'I got that chance. We didn't lose. I think we drew 1–1 and I was delighted and from then on I've never looked back.'

He was there in both the semi-final defeat at the Millennium Stadium and the UEFA Cup quarter-final loss in Lisbon. Twice he dislocated his shoulder and each time he returned too early. When Taylor finally scored at St James' Park, they had to lock the gates to curb his celebration.

'Has it been difficult to keep my feet on the ground? Not when I have a dad like mine. He's a Newcastle supporter himself but he's been the guy who's always kept my feet on the ground. I've got a family very passionate about Newcastle and they've been unbelievable towards me. My mam and dad are always there for me but they've always been prepared to knock me down to size whenever I've needed it.

'I can still remember the first time I went into the ground with my dad when I was a little boy. I had one of those little Newcastle hats on, it had pin badges on and I had Philippe Albert. That is why I wore No 27. He was massive to me. I always remember the boots he used to wear and the green Fila sign on the bottom. I remember being a ball boy a bit later on and taking some of the grass off the pitch and putting it in my back pocket. I was a massive fan. I never thought I would get the chance to play at St James' Park.'

By 2009, he was on his eighth manager.

Much later I would talk to him, again, about each man.

On Sir Bobby Robson (1999–2004): 'He was a legend. He gave me my chance. I had massive respect for him for doing that. I will always be grateful for getting the chance to play for Newcastle United. He was the man who did that for me.'

On Graeme Souness (2004–06): 'He was a very hard man. I got on with him really well. I had to prove to him that I wanted to be a player. I wanted it.'

On Glenn Roeder (2006–07): 'Glenn came in and I was training well. The team was doing well. He criticised me a lot and he got on at me a lot but it was for the right reasons. At the time I was getting mad, I thought he was picking on me but at the end he was really good and I enjoyed playing for him.'

Sam Allardyce (2007–08): 'He was big on his team spirit as well. He had a massive staff and he wanted the best for the players. His philosophy was about percentages and at a later date I think he would have worked for us but we were unlucky in some games when he was in charge.'

Kevin Keegan (2008): 'He was what the fans wanted. The atmosphere was really upbeat when he arrived. When he took over, even if we got beat there wouldn't be loads of criticism because it was Keegan. He was very good with the players, always having a laugh and banter with us and they were good training sessions. He would put an arm around you and make you feel like a million dollars.'

Chris Hughton (2008): 'He was a coach at first and I had been doing some defensive work with him. People were saying, "Can he handle it?" when he took over because the club had had big names but I think he is underestimated.'

Joe Kinnear (2008–09): 'The first media interview Joe gave didn't help. The players at the time respected him because he had something different about him that the players had not experienced before. I definitely had not experienced anything like him before. He would give you kisses if you did well! I can understand why Wimbledon did well.'

Alan Shearer (2009): 'When Big Al came in, for me, playing under him it was a massive thing. He had been my club captain beforehand at Newcastle. Everyone had been waiting for him to be manager. The games he was left with were difficult and it was a bad situation for him to come into.'

By the time Newcastle faced north east rivals Middlesbrough at St James' Park on 11 May, with three games of the season remaining, they were third bottom, level on 31 points with Middlesbrough and West Bromwich Albion beneath them. Hull were three points ahead on 34, Sunderland a further two points north on 36. Of the teams fighting for their lives, Newcastle and Middlesbrough had played 35 times and the rest 36.

Newcastle had taken two points from the previous 18. Middlesbrough had mustered four, as had Sunderland. Hull had managed only one. These were football clubs flapping around like dying fish out of water.

Only West Brom had shown any kind of form, winning two and drawing one to muster seven points in that same period.

Even amid that bleak picture it still felt that some people weren't listening.

'I keep saying it time and time again, you have to show much you want to play for Newcastle United and the black and white jersey,' Taylor said to me on the eve of the game.

'It has hurt me. It has choked me seeing Newcastle United in the bottom three. There is no worse feeling than that. It has been so disappointing but we have to put it to bed and we have to change it and get on with it.

'If we don't think we can turn this situation around, we might as well pack our bags and go home now. Of course it is a night for men. We need 11 leaders out on the pitch.

'Everybody has to put a shift in. We have to give all we can for the club, we have to play out of our skin. It is as simple as that. We have players as well on the bench who can come on and make a difference.

'The players who are starting have to go out there and give it their all. We need players coming off the pitch with their black and white shirts absolutely drenched in sweat for the cause.

'You have to show how much you want it and how much you want to play for this football club. It is a massive football club.'

It was a very late rallying call.

'When I go shopping, the people on the tills tell you what it means to them and how important the football club is,' he added.

'Everyone knows what it means. When I'm out it's all anyone talks about.

'It reminds you of how important the football club is here.

'If you get a bad result at Newcastle people talk about it for a week.

'In London, or anywhere in the country, they will talk about it for a day.

'It is massively important we win the match. It's the biggest game of our careers.'

Taylor was by now the last Geordie standing in the team, one with the understanding of what was going on and what it would mean if the club was relegated, to the second tier of English football, and from the Premier League for the first time.

He was still rash with his words, he sometimes inflamed situations and there was a guilt, not on his behalf, of being over interviewed because he was prepared to talk. The fall against Aston Villa had not looked great and he had almost ran out of the ground when he scored his first goal at St James' Park, against Celta Vigo.

But inside there was a very young man, with the backing of his father, who did care about the club, and the black and white shirt.

'It is so important to this city that we do and we are good enough,' he said. 'I can't ever remember a game as big as this. This is the most important game in Newcastle's history for my liking.

'As players we have to perform and get the result we need. Alan Shearer demands the best from the players and that is what he is going to get. He is a very strict guy and everyone knows not to cross him.

'He has strict routines and that is how it should be at this football club. He doesn't want slackers. You have to be on time for everything.

'If you are late for anything you get a fine. There are no favourites at the football club. That's how it should be, but it hasn't been at this football club since I've been here.

It was a big ask to change the culture of a football club in eight games.

As can happen in these occasions, it is what you cannot use that is often the biggest sensation.

He warned teammates with a lack of desire to ship out, he demanded they man up. There was another call to arms that didn't get printed, about the players who weren't up for it going off home, but it went off record.

That didn't sound quite so encouraging.

Nor did it look so encouraging when Habib Beye put into his own net, in the third minute, the ball bouncing back off his feet from Steve Harper, into the Newcastle goal, at the Gallowgate End.

Right then there was panic.

But just six minutes later, Taylor was good to his word, brilliantly heading in a Danny Guthrie corner, on the angle past Brad Jones.

That added an element of calm to the crowd, but it was raucous and at times desperate. It was such a huge game.

Shearer the manager made his call, and took Owen off, and it got better, really quickly.

Obafemi Martins, his replacement, had been on the field for less than a minute when a Kevin Nolan knock down came to him and he went left and then right and crashed his shot into the Middlesbrough goal.

There was joy and relief and Martins ran half the length of the pitch to jump into the besuited Shearer's arms.

Shearer for once looked flustered, he called for calm, but how was that possible, with Newcastle ahead in a Premier League game for the first time in two months?

That would only come with five minutes remaining, when Nolan crossed this time, from the right, and Peter Lovenkrands, another Shearer substitute, ran in unmarked and struck the third.

The commentator Jon Champion called it perfectly. 'The Gallowgate End, one of the most famous areas in English football, lets forth a collective sigh and roar of utter relief,' he said.

When Mike Dean blew the final whistle, Shearer joined the players, 'his' players, on the pitch at full time. There was celebration. Newcastle moved out of the bottom three, above Hull on goal difference. There were two games to come, at home to Fulham, who had won twice away all season and then at Aston Villa. Fulham were seventh and Aston Villa were fifth, but that was forgotten at full time.

There was euphoria, but more so relief.

'It's a magnificent feeling, it really is,' said Shearer. 'I thought the players were brilliant tonight. I asked them to show courage, determination and the ability that I know they've got. They've done all of that.

'It would have been easy for them to feel sorry for themselves after going 1–0 down but they didn't let it affect them. They went on and still had the belief and the ability that they could go and get something.

'There were some big, big performances from big men and I couldn't ask any more from them.

'We asked them to go out and get three points – they've done that and I thought they were magnificent under difficult circumstances.

'They've got to now go and do all that again on Saturday and enjoy that winning feeling. Hopefully there's another one there on Saturday, but it'll be just as tough, because Fulham are flying themselves.

'I don't want to sound negative but it was one win, we've got to get another two and make it safe. I really don't know what's going to be enough – another performance like that on Saturday will make us confident of getting three points.

'What a great arena to play football in, what a great arena to get a result like that in. I thought the fans were brilliant, they stuck with us when we went 1–0 down. It would have been easy for them to turn against us as well, but they kept with us and kept cheering us. We gave them something to smile about, it's been a long time.

'We've been in a rut for a little while but I've said before about the importance of confidence. I've just said to them in the dressing room: "Enjoy the winning feeling, enjoy being out of the bottom three and make sure we don't go back in it."'

The winning feeling lasted less than five days.

Then you could not see Michael Owen doing his hamstring in training, or of Newcastle retreating back into their shell against Fulham, or of Diomansy Kamara scoring before half-time.

You could not see Sebastien Bassong being sent off pulling back Kamara, or a goal from Mark Viduka being disallowed, probably because the same move in front of the goalkeeper by Kevin Nolan in Newcastle's first goal against Middlesbrough had been highlighted on *Match of the Day*.

You did not know that a player called Craig Fagan would score at Bolton in the second half and Hull would grab a point that moved them back out of the relegation zone and Newcastle back into it.

But all that happened. Newcastle at home to Fulham was the antithesis of Newcastle at home to Middlesbrough.

After the party came the hangover, another stinking hangover.

Beaten and back heading for the drop.

Aaron Hughes was born in County Tyrone. He came through the ranks at Newcastle and made his debut at the Nou Camp when he was just 18. He didn't shout about a lot of things but he was dependable and played more than 200 games before he was sold by Graeme Souness.

His affection for his adopted city did not go with his transfer, to Fulham.

'It's just a huge club that's embedded in the city and dominates it,' he said after Fulham's victory. 'Alan Shearer understands that. Everyone can see there's been no stability and it's not always about what's happening on the pitch.

'I can't imagine the club in the Championship, the size of the stadium, those amazing fans.'

By that point they, however, could.

ALAN SHEARER – PLEASE, PLEASE, PLEASE, LET ME GET WHAT I WANT

ALAN SHEARER WAS SMILING, AND HE WAS RELAXED. THAT FELT fairly significant.

He was back in the room where Kinnear had ranted and raved just eight months earlier. Eight months? It felt like a life time.

It did not show on Shearer, sat back in his chair, laughing but not underplaying the significance of what would happen, in 48-hours' time.

'Staying up on Sunday would be greater than anything I've achieved in the game,' he said. 'Definitely, 100 per cent!

'It would be everything. It would be bigger than anything. Bigger than winning the title. Even bigger than captaining England, which was the biggest thing in my playing career.

'I remember everything about winning the title with Blackburn at Anfield in 1995, but avoiding relegation on Sunday would top that. It would be because of the season that we have had. It has only gone on for me for eight weeks but it has been an incredible eight weeks.'

Would it be your lowest moment if Newcastle go down, he was asked.

'Yes.'

He was told he looked confident.

'Do you think I'm mad?' he laughed.

'I'm not contemplating going down. I'm contemplating how I will feel if I keep the club in the Premier League. I believe we will do that.

'You can ask me the other part of it on Sunday if it goes wrong, but it isn't entering my head. I think it will be a fantastic occasion. I'm a betting man. I do like a bet now and again. I would say if we win the game it might be enough. I say might, it might not, but I would have a guess it would be.

'We know the stakes. Villa are beatable, we have already done that this season. Hopefully, I have a game plan that can be successful. Whatever team I put out will be a team to try and stop them and, more importantly, win the game.

'I am enjoying it. I will enjoy it a hell of a lot more on Sunday night if we stay up. I enjoy the emotions. The emotions you go through are incredible, you have your ups, your downs, you have your challenges.

'It's a fantastic football club. Yes, huge mistakes have been made but we have one last chance to rectify that and, hopefully, those mistakes will never be made again. Sunday's result will not affect my decision of whether I stay.

'Whoever is in charge of this club starting from next season has to get the best youngsters to this football club. There is no doubt about it, not Sunderland, not Middlesbrough, they must come here. They have to come here, but the football club has to make it attractive for them to want to come here. That is massive.

'I will have a meeting with Mike next week and we'll see what is best for the club.'

There was no concern about what other teams might do. Chelsea and Manchester United had nothing to play for.

'Alex Ferguson will never, ever put a team out that he doesn't think can win a game.' he added. 'He will do what is best for his football club.

'He has earned the right to put whatever side out he wants by winning the league early and being in the Champions League final.

'You are talking about Manchester United, the biggest football club in the world. They will want to win the game. Would I do the same? Of course.

'I have had a million encounters with Alex over the years and we have both said our stuff. We get on fine, there is no problem between us at all. We have laughed and joked about it.'

In buses, on trains, by road and by air Newcastle fans headed to Villa Park.

It was hot and the mood was good. It had to be.

There was tension, but there was belief.

Newcastle were actually the form team of the four teams fighting for their future. Sunderland, Hull and Middlesbrough had all taken just one point from their previous four games. That alone told you the likelihood of any of the three winning was slim. Middlesbrough were at West Ham and had won twice away from home all season. Sunderland were playing Chelsea, who were third, and had won their last four games on the trot and free falling Hull, who were playing an admittedly weakened Manchester United with the title already secured and a Champions League final on the horizon, had drawn three and lost seven of their previous 10 games.

Given those failings, it felt like it was in Newcastle's hands, that a result of any description might be enough.

That spirit filled the A section of the top and bottom tiers of the Doug Ellis Stand. It was boiling hot so people drank and sang and it did not feel like a relegation wake. It felt like a last stand, a valiant one at Villa.

'Oh when the Mags go march in,' was sang. It didn't sound ironic.

All Newcastle had to do was get a better result than Hull (their goal difference was much better than Middlesbrough) and there would be a chink of light.

Sunderland 36 points (-19), Hull 35 (-24), Newcastle 34 (-18) and Middlesbrough 32 (-28), West Brom 31 (-31).

It wasn't a great team that walked from the tunnel at Villa Park, they hadn't made anyone proud, but they received unequivocal backing as they emerged. All they had to find was one performance.

Shearer's options were limited. Carroll, who had started the previous two games, had been injured in training. Michael Owen was still not confident enough in his hamstring to start. Oba Martins and Mark Viduka started. Shola Ameobi, with Owen, was on the substitutes' bench. In Newcastle's previous 13 games the quartet had managed one goal. Iain Dowie had spent the week working with Viduka. Any straw was worth clutching.

Viduka had a shot cleared off the line early, Martins shot wide, Duff saw a deflected shot saved by Brad Freidel.

At 24 minutes past three news came from Hull. Darron Gibson had scored for Manchester United. The league table changed. The point being won at Villa Park moved Newcastle above Hull on goal difference. Newcastle moved out of the relegation zone. The away end could barely contain itself.

Carlton Cole scored for West Ham. Middlesbrough were going, but then it all went wrong.

Gareth Barry shot, in the 38th minute from about 25 yards out, when a corner had not been cleared properly. It wasn't even on target, the ball was going wide, but it struck Damien Duff and he succeeded only in redirecting the ball towards his own goal. It was like slow motion, the ball gently tiptoeing its way into the far corner of the goal, far enough away from the desperate, outstretched right hand of Steve Harper.

Harper got back to his feet slowly. It was a hammer blow.

Owen came on with half an hour to go. He touched the ball five times.

Newcastle still did not fight back.

Barry curled one wide of the far post with his right foot.

Shearer had his hands on his hips, Carew had a chance.

The clock ticked.

Sunderland were losing, then drawing, then losing.

But it was down to Hull and Newcastle now. Both were trailing by a single goal.

The rallying cries were from the away end, desperate appeals for more.

Somehow the team looked lifeless. Spineless. Gutless.

Minutes remained.

Mike Ashley and Llambias sat in their white shirts as Rome burned.

'Absentee landlords,' Sir John Hall had called them the day before.

David Edgar was sent off in injury-time for a second bookable offence.

And then Chris Foy blew his whistle. The piercing shrill of reality, and relegation.
Your soul wept.

It was all over.

What Keegan had started, in 1992, against Bristol City, Ashley had finished
in 2009.

Shearer was ashen faced, the top button of his shirt undone. He didn't know
what to do or what to say.

He walked over to the travelling support, the mad dogs of Tyneside, sunburnt
and shell-shocked.

There were tears this time, and it was not an emotion of choice. This was not
Anfield, and the first four-three and what felt like the long wait of some to get on
television, a tear here, a look of anguish there.

This was pain, gut wrenching pain, there was anger, but when the whistle
went, just devastation. Dejection. Humiliation. Hurt, and as much as anything,
no more words. They had all been said, everything had been said and nothing
had been done.

There were metaphorical towels that had been thrown in all over the pitch. A
captain courageous in the dugout led a team who hid.

When the call came for a hero, no one answered.

In 90 minutes of football to save a city, four shots were all they could muster.
Four paltry shots on target. Three measly corners. Villa were just as bad, if not
worse. They managed two shots of meaning, but one had been enough, misdirected

and misguided, just like the club it sank.

There was delight amongst the home support, genuine, mystifying delight. They even took the time to make banners.

The one that mattered had been made on Tyneside.

'Proud to be a Geordie,' it read. 'We'll support you ever more.'

The songs came. The final act of defiance.

The players trudged back up the tunnel, to sanctuary. There was a suggestion some had gone straight on their phones. Not according to Chris Hughton.

'The dressing room was devastated,' he said.

'That's one thing I won't forget.

'There are things that stay with you and I've been in lots of changing rooms when the result has gone against you, a big result, or you've been knocked out of the semi-final of a cup.

'Them times there isn't too much you can say. This time there was nothing.

'"The changing room was devastated. That I knew.'

Shearer, a rare sense of failure still coursing through his veins, stood in the middle of the players.

'We can make all the excuses you like,' he told them. 'I wasn't good enough, Mike Ashley wasn't good enough, Kevin Keegan wasn't good enough, Chris Hughton wasn't good enough, Joe Kinnear wasn't good enough.

'Forget that. It's what's been in the dressing room that hasn't been good enough. All of us. We're all in it together.'

Then he spoke to the media.

'I've said to them I'm not sure everyone has played to their maximum this season,' he said.

'The simple fact is what's been inside the dressing room hasn't been good enough, and I include everyone in that. I'm not sure everyone has played to their maximum. People can have their opinions on who has played well and who hasn't. As a group, you get what you deserve. There's no hiding from that. You can blame referees, decisions, chances. The simple fact is we deserve to go down.

'I have a tremendous relationship with the fans. The city centre was packed with black and white shirts. They love their football, they love their football club and they have been badly let down. I'm hurting. I love the football club. It's a great club.

'But it needs rebuilding.'

EPILOGUE

'RIGHT, THAT'S IT. ENOUGH. WE CANNOT GO ANY LOWER. YOU ARE either with us or you are not.'

The visiting dressing room at Brisbane Road remained silent.

Newcastle, fresh from relegation, had just lost 6–1 to Leyton Orient, then of League One, in a pre-season friendly.

This was a new low.

Kevin Nolan started talking again.

'Look, if you want to go you must say so now,' he said.

'There won't be a problem. Let us know and we will help get you to a different team.

'We have to sort this club out.

'It has to start here.'

One by one hands, from those who wanted out, started going in the air...

ACKNOWLEDGEMENTS

'WHO PASSED THE BALL TO ALAN SHEARER WHEN HE BROKE HIS FIBULA at Everton in the friendly? I think it was Philippe Albert but the Observer says it's David Batty.'

'How many major operations did Shearer have?'

They were relentless texts, at all hours, with the expectation of an immediate reply.

Michael Bolam, from the excellent nufc.com, fielded them all. It was perhaps as if he was sitting an exam, and he passed. I'm extremely grateful to the endless texts and conversations and days and weeks of research that writing Tunnel of Love entailed.

The same goes for Michael Walker, the author of Up There. You spend hours and hours and hours dissecting the minutia to make sure everything ties together and you need the help of good people to do it.

Mark Hannen in the Newcastle United press office proved invaluable in his help as we sought needles in the haystacks of old photographs. Nothing was too much trouble. I'm extremely grateful.

I would like to thank Ian Horrocks, the photographer whose work is used in this book for capturing the period so well.

Tunnel of Love covers a 13 year period in Newcastle United's history, and my previous work, Touching Distance, covered 14 years. In that time the role has changed from fan to journalist and alongside that is now author.

There were many interviews and experiences over that period of time. To that end I would like to thank Alan Shearer, Freddy Shepherd, Graeme Souness, Chris Hughton, Chris Mort, Sir John Hall, Sam Allardyce, Rob Lee, Glenn Roeder, Shay Given, Keith

Gillespie, Steve Harper, John Carver, Philippe Albert, Kevin Keegan, Steven Taylor, Kevin Nolan, Terry McDermott, Nikos Dabizas, Lee Clark, Peter Beardsley, Sir Bobby Robson, Douglas Hall, Martin Tyler, Faustino Asprilla and Steve Fairs.

Research really is endless. I would like to thank Marc Corby for archives, Dave Morton (the nostalgia editor) at the Newcastle Evening Chronicle, Andy Bowman for additional information, Rob Beasley and also Wendy Taylor from Newcastle United. I'd also like to thank Leslie Priestley for setting Tunnel of Love and for Paul Dalling for editing the work (similar thanks go to Ian Allen for his work with Touching Distance). Similar thanks on production go to Sabahat Muhammad.

To James Corbett, the founder and principle of deCoubertin Books, I would like to offer my thanks for seeing the potential in a follow up to Touching Distance and for all his help along the way. It is most definitely a marathon and not a sprint and you need guidance and patience which he offered. Thanks also go to Simon Hughes and Jack Gordon-Brown from deCoubertin books for their help with the final read through.

To my family, for my dad's endless ideas and energy, to my mam and sister, Alyson, and to Jane, thank you for the support and for putting up with me again. The same goes for my friends, although hopefully it hasn't been quite as draining an experience as the first book.

To Newcastle supporters who play such a pivotal role in this work, and in Touching Distance (which was short listed for an award), I would like to thank you for the memories and for the support, both for the club and for my first book. At times the fondness for Touching Distance has been genuinely overwhelming.

And to Matthew, who has taken such great pride in my switch to working as an author, this book is for you son.

BIBLIOGRAPHY

Walker, Michael, *Up There: The North East, Football, Boom & Bust*
    (deCoubertin Books, 2014)
Bolam, Mike: *The Newcastle Miscellany* (Vision Sports Publishing, 2007)
Gillespie, Keith: *How Not to be a Millionaire* (Sports Media, 2014)
Ginola, David: *From St Tropez to St James'* (Headline Book Publishing, 1996)
Lee, Rob: *Come in Number 37* (CollinsWillow, 2000)
Joannou, Paul: *Newcastle United, A Complete Record 1982-1986* (Breedon Books, 1986)
Keegan, Kevin: *My Autobiography* (Little, Brown and Company 1998)
Hardisty, Tony: *Peter Beardsley, Proud to be a Geordie* (Knight Fletcher print, 1986)
Ferdinand, Les: *Sir Les: The Autobiography of Les Ferdinand*
    (Headline Book Publishing, 1997)
Milburn, Jackie: *Jackie Milburn's Newcastle United Scrapbook* (Souvenir Press, 1981)
Joannou, Paul: *Newcastle United: the Ultimate Who's Who 1881-2014:*
    An Official Publication (N Publishing 2014)
Beardsley, Peter: *My Life Story* (HarperCollinsWillow, 1996)
Morgan, Piers: *The Insider, the Private Diaries of a Scandalous Decade* (Ebury Press, 2005)
Shearer, Alan: *My Story so Far* (Hodder and Stoughton 1998)
Cassidy, Denis: *The Day the Promises had to Stop* (Amberley Publishing 2010)
Shearer, Alan: *My Illustrated Career* (Octopus Publishing 2007)
Dalglish, Kenny: *Dalglish, My Autobiography* (Hodder and Stoughton 1996)
Robson, Bobby: *Farewell but not Goodbye* (Hodder and Stoughton 2005)
    – *An Englishman Abroad* (Macmillan 1998)

Gullit, Ruud: *My Autobiography* (Century 1998)
Keane, Roy: *The Autobiography* (Penguin Books 2003)

Articles

Evening Chronicle
New York Times
Sky Sports website
SportsMole
Sunday Times
Coventry Telegraph
Daily Mail
Independent
BBC website
Shields Gazette
The Guardian
Retail Week
4-4-2
Dutch Soccer Site
Property Week
Daily Record
Sunday Sun
News of the World
Newcastle Journal
The People

Others

nufc.com – Archives and various material
statto.com – Numerous historic league tables

INDEX

269